Peter L. Brill, M.D., is Director of the Center for the Study of Adult Development at the University of Pennsylvania in Philadelphia.

John P. Hayes is Assistant Professor of Communications at Temple University in Philadelphia and an established freelance writer.

PRENTICE-HALL INTERNATIONAL, INC., *London*
PRENTICE-HALL OF AUSTRALIA PTY. LIMITED, *Sydney*
PRENTICE-HALL OF CANADA, LTD., *Toronto*
PRENTICE-HALL OF INDIA PRIVATE LIMITED, *New Delhi*
PRENTICE-HALL OF JAPAN, INC., *Tokyo*
PRENTICE-HALL OF SOUTHEAST ASIA PTE. LTD., *Singapore*
WHITEHALL BOOKS LIMITED, *Wellington, New Zealand*

Taming Your Turmoil

MANAGING THE TRANSITIONS OF ADULT LIFE

Peter L. Brill, M.D., and John P. Hayes

PRENTICE-HALL, INC., *Englewood Cliffs, New Jersey 07632*

Library of Congress Cataloging in Publication Data

BRILL, PETER L.
Taming your turmoil.

(A Spectrum Book)
Bibliography: p.
Includes index.
1. Adulthood—Psychological aspects. I. Hayes, John Phillip, (date) II. Title.
BF724.5.B74 155.6 81-5127
ISBN 0-13-884445-3 AACR2
ISBN 0-13-884437-2 (pbk.)

For those who have taught us the how;
for those who have shown us the why

This Spectrum Book can be made available to businesses and organizations at a special discount when ordered in large quantities. For more information, contact: Prentice-Hall, Inc., General Book Marketing, Special Sales Division, Englewood Cliffs, New Jersey 07632.

Editorial/production supervision and
interior design by Carol Smith
Cover art and design by Al Pisano
Manufacturing buyer: Cathie Lenard

A SPECTRUM BOOK

10 9 8 7 6 5 4 3 2 1

Printed in the United States of America

Contents

Preface

This book is about adult development and the transitions and crises of adult life. It is intended as a guidebook for individuals, executives, and therapists who want to know more about adult development and what they, and organizations, can do to prevent many of life's crises and to improve the overall quality of life in America.

The point of the book is that adapting organisms progress only when their environments support them. We know there are age-related unstable stages (midlife, for example) that we call transitions, and there are environmentally triggered transitions (a promotion, for example) as well. A person's capability for coping and adapting through any transition depends on psychological maturity and a sensitive environment. When people are not prepared to meet these everyday ups and downs of life, they often become unhappy, lonely, and depressed. They then risk the chance of being labeled mentally ill, when in fact they are normal people in need of guidance, some enlightenment, and personal care.

This book is an outgrowth of our personal experiences. For Peter Brill, who has supplied the concepts and technology, the book was made possible by an eclectic psychological education and numerous experiments and explorations at the Center for the Study of Adult Development (CSAD), which he founded in Philadelphia in 1976. For John Hayes, who heads the magazine-writing sequence at Temple University, the book germinated while he was researching an in-depth article about adult development for the Associated Press and after he experienced the CSAD's Transition Planning Workshop.

At times this book questions some of the assumptions and methods of psychiatry, but there is no intention on the part of either of us to lessen the importance or value of individuals in this field or the field in general. Rather, this self-examination should result only in improvements in the ability of psychiatrists and other therapists to help people.

Helping people is really what it's all about, and through the developmental models and adaptive strategies suggested in this book, all of which have been tested through various services at the Center for the Study of Adult Development in Philadelphia, we believe that people, and organizations, can learn how to do more for themselves.

Acknowledgments

Numerous people helped us during the course of writing this book, and we wish to thank these staff members of CSAD: Ann Rosen Spector, M.S., for help with the section on mentoring and for being there to provide moral support; John Eldred, M.D.A., for endless help and a discussion about the quality of working life; Matilde Salganicoff, Ed.D., for help with the section on death and dying; Margaret Baker, Ph.D., for information about two-career marriages; Mary Davenport, M.S., for help with the section on marriage; Marc Lipschutz, M.D., for keeping Peter Brill humble; Lucille Pack, for library and personal assistance; K.C. Baldadian, M.S., for help with the sections on career counseling and employee assistance programs.

Thanks to the following people who have assisted Peter Brill: Carol Pierskalla, Ph.D., for information about retirement; John Paul Brady, M.D., chairman of the Department of Psychiatry at the University of Pennsylvania, without whose support the CSAD would not exist and this book could not have been written; Joseph DiGiacomo, M.D., who taught Peter about therapy; Rodney Napier, Ph.D., who taught him about behavioral science; and Eric Trist, Ph.D., who taught him about organizations.

Thanks to the following people who have helped John Hayes: Philip Goldberg and Ralph Keyes for their encouragement; various students at Temple University for their criticism; and Jo Ann Hayes, his wife, for her patience, wit, and specialness.

And thanks to four women who helped us both: Susan Sherman, secretary at CSAD, for endless hours of typing; Mona Greenberg, for typing the final manuscript; Ray Lincoln, our agent; and Mary Kennan, of Prentice-Hall, for guiding us along the way.

Finally, we wish to extend grateful acknowledgment for permission to use the following material:

The quote on page 1 is from *Culture and Commitment* by Margaret Mead (New York: Doubleday & Company, Inc., Anchor Books, 1978). Used by permission of Columbia University Press.

The paraphrased excerpts describing stages of adult growth on pages 17-18 and 23-26 are from *Seasons of a Man's Life* by Daniel J. Levinson, et al. Courtesy of Alfred A. Knopf, Inc.

The quote on page 21 is from *The Shadows of the Gods* by Arthur Miller. Reprinted by permission of International Creative Management. Copyright © 1958 by Arthur Miller.

Figure 4 on page 33 is from "Marital Satisfaction Over the Family Life Cycle" by Boyd C. Rollins and Harold Feldman, *Journal of Marriage and the Family,* February 1970. Copyrighted 1970 by the National Council on Family Relations. Reprinted by permission.

The quote on p. 41 is from *Adaptation to Life* by George E. Vaillant. Copyright © 1977 by George E. Vaillant. By permission of Little, Brown and Company.

The quote on p. 65 is © 1949 by Erich Fromm. Excerpt from *Psychoanalytic Characterology and Its Application to the Understanding of Culture,* published in "Culture and Personality" edited by S.S. Sargent and M.W. Smith.

The quote on page 85 is used by permission of Herbert A. Shepard.

The material on pages 89-94 is based on the Conflict Management Survey authored by Jay Hall and published by Teleometrics International, 2203 Timberloch Place, Suite 104, The Woodlands, Texas 77380. Copyright 1969, 1973.

The material on pages 115-116 is from *What Color Is Your Parachute? A Practical Manual for Job-Hunters & Career-Changers*, 1980 Revised Edition, by Richard N. Bolles, © copyright 1972, 1975, 1976, 1977, 1978, 1979, 1980 by Richard Nelson Bolles. Used by special permission. Those desiring a copy of the complete book for further reading, may procure it from the publisher, Ten Speed Press, P.O. Box 7123, Berkeley CA 94707.

The material on pages 120-121 is adapted from John L. Holland, *Making Vocational Choices: A Theory of Careers*, © 1973. Adapted by permission of Prentice-Hall, Inc., Englewood Cliffs, N.J.

The "Social Readjustment Rating Scale" on pages 128-129 is reprinted with permission from *Journal of Psychosomatic Research, 11*, T.H. Holmes and R.H. Rahe, "The Social Readjustment Scale," Copyright 1967, Pergamon Press, Ltd.

The excerpt from "Interview with Erdman Palmore, Ph.D." on pages 133-134 is reprinted from the July 1, 1980 issue of Family Circle Magazine. © 1980 The Family Circle, Inc. All rights reserved.

The first quote on page 137 is used by permission of Hans Selye.

The second quote on page 137 from *Stress* by Walter McQuade and Ann Aikman is used by permission of Walter McQuade.

Figure 25 on page 144 is adapted from "The Ills of Man" by John H. Dingle, *Scientific American*, September 1973.

The material on pages 148, 161, and 162-163 from *Coping and Adaptation* by G. V. Coelho et al. is used by permission of Basic Books, Inc.

The "Work Environment Scale Subscale Dimensions" chart on pages 163-164 and Figure 31 on page 164 are reproduced by special permission of the publisher, Consulting Psychologists Press, Inc., 577 College Ave., Palo Alto, CA 94306 from *The Family, Work and Group Environment Scales Manual* by Rudolf H. Moos, Paul Inset and Barrie Humphrey © 1974.

The material on pages 166-167 is from *Ego Development* by Jane Loevinger, reprinted by permission of Jossey-Bass Publishers with approval from Jane Loevinger, Washington University, St. Louis.

"Some Principles of QWL" on page 209 is from *Work and the Quality of Life: Resource Papers for Work in America* by James O'Toole. Reprinted by permission of MIT Press.

"Properties of Jobs" on page 212 and "Old Paradigm/New Paradigm" on page 220 are from "Adapting to a Changing World" by E. Trist in *A New Role for Labour: Industrial Democracy Today,* edited by George Sanderson and Frederick Stapenhurst. Used by permission of E. Trist.

"Some Generalizations about QWL in North American Workplaces" on page 217 is from "Making Work More Human" by Roy LaBerge in *Adapting to a Changing World* edited by George F. Sanderson and published by Labour Canada.

Philadelphia, 1980

CHAPTER ONE

Are Unhappy Adults Sick Adults?

"There is a pattern in our lives,
a pattern of adult development stages
which, once recognized, can be managed."

MARGARET MEAD

Teetering on top of a picnic table in his brother's back yard, prominent criminal attorney Theodore Banks said he was going to kill himself because "no one understands me anymore, not even me."

Suddenly, someone at his family reunion knocked him off the table, and half an hour later Ted Banks woke up in the psychiatric ward of an established university hospital in the Midwest. He stayed there for a couple of weeks, and then, upon his release, he came to me for psychotherapy.*

At the time, Ted was 41 years old and enormously successful. He was well educated and very entertaining. He had dozens of friends, all around the country, and his lifestyle of travel and excitement was envied by most of the people who knew him. What they didn't see, however, was his loneliness and his confusion about himself, his career, and his marriage. Somehow life had collapsed on Ted Banks and he didn't know why or how. It was the unknowing that ate at him as much as it was his perpetual state of depression.

In our first session Ted told me his life story. When he was about 18 years old his father, who was a stockbroker, kicked him out of the house for no specific reason. They just couldn't live together, so Ted moved in with some neighbors. His mother had passed away several years earlier and he had been very close to her, but his father always seemed to resent him.

After Ted graduated from a parochial high school he enlisted in

*All first-person references in this book apply only to Peter L. Brill. Also, for the sake of convenience the masculine personal pronoun has been used throughout most of the book, but unless we are specifically talking about a man, as here, all discussions pertain to women and men alike.

the Marines and following a short tour he worked his way through college with the assistance of the GI bill. He struggled. He worked nights and weekends at odd jobs, went to school during the day, hated his father for refusing to help him, and felt sorry for himself much of the time. But he graduated at the top of his class. He had decided on a career in law and he was accepted by one of the more prestigious law schools in the country. He had to borrow money to put himself through but he was a manipulative sort of guy, successfully so, and he managed very well.

While he was in law school he met a woman who he later married and after he was graduated they settled in a major metropolitan area and Ted developed a challenging private practice as an attorney. He was satisfied, comfortable, and generally happy. His family was healthy, they lived in a big home with an enclosed swimming pool, they belonged to the country club and ascribed to all the values that seemed important.

For many years Ted felt good about himself. He thought his role in life was important and that he was a man of achievement. Then at about the age of 40, for no obvious reason, he seemed to lose interest in life. There was something about life that bored him.

He had always had a fairly satisfying relationship with his wife, but now married life, or family life, was pleasureless. He got involved with several other women, but not emotionally. He was in it purely for the sex. Cheating was a form of entertainment to Ted, and it didn't actually make him feel emotionally secure or vital.

Professionally, Ted was bored as well. His law firm continued to expand and he was handling some of the most interesting cases of his career, but the sense of achievement he had once derived from law just wasn't there anymore, or it wasn't as intense. For some reason, work didn't excite him.

Eventually, Ted became anxious and depressed and he started worrying about his health, but he was in phenomenally good condition. He had a lot of energy. He played squash a couple of times a week and jogged three miles every day. He drank a lot—two or three drinks a day—but he wasn't an alcoholic. He *was* drunk, though, in his brother's back yard. Otherwise, he told me, "I would never have climbed on top of that picnic table. I just had had enough of feeling like I should be dead. The booze and depression got to me, and it made it easier for me to do something about it."

Thinking back, Ted couldn't recall what had happened after he stood up on the table. He didn't remember what he said. He didn't remember being knocked down; he had blanked it out. But when he awoke in the hospital and realized he was in a psychiatric unit, it made sense to him—not how he had ended up there, but that he belonged there. In his opinion, he was mentally ill. It was then that Ted decided to follow his doctor's advice and consult a psychiatrist for therapy.

THE HISTORICAL SEARCH

As I studied Ted's case I searched continuously and thoroughly for a historical explanation—something in his background that would explain his crisis—but I could never find it. I kept interpreting his relationship with his father. That was a dreadful period of life for Ted, but none of it explained his condition. He had eventually enjoyed a good relationship with his father. He had been furious for years but then he worked that out and accepted his father. And his father was conciliatory. Ted used to buy him presents and visit him every week and when his father became terminally ill, Ted saw him almost every day until he died.

I also suspected that Ted had been psychologically affected by his mother's death. Possibly he needed to mourn his loss. But no matter how I interpreted his background, I could never arrive at a satisfactory historical explanation for his crisis.

During the time I was treating Ted Banks it never occurred to me that my approach was wrong or misguided. I searched historically because that was the way I had been taught. My job as a psychiatrist was to ferret out Ted's illness and return him to a state of normality. The problem, I later discovered, was that Ted was not abnormal! My training prevented me from knowing that, however, or seeing the adult developmental process that was occurring in Ted's life. At the time, no one was talking about adult development. Adults, psychiatrists understood, were already developed, so I never considered the possibility that change was occurring anew in Ted's life, or that change was normal.

Since the time of Freud, psychiatrists have thought that personality is fixed by the age of 5. After age 5 there's a period of latency that is abruptly interrupted by adolescence and the eruption of sexual interest and conflict. This rocky age of adjustment is followed by adulthood, a period of life that Freud and others said should be smooth, balanced, calm, and relatively satisfying. Thus, adults should be happy people, and when they are not, many psychiatrists believe they are sick. That is, they are mentally ill and may require some psychological therapy to adapt.*

In recent years, however, a few psychiatrists have begun to realize that adult life isn't entirely dependent on psychological history, and that adult development isn't completed by age 21, or age 30, or even age 55.

There is psychological growth after adolescence, and it's normal! Therefore, adults can't always be happy in life, but neither can all unhappy adults be labeled ill. Freud's reductionistic theory is incomplete. Adult development is another stage of emotional growth, like adolescence, and it requires intense exploration and understanding.

This means Ted Banks wasn't any more mentally ill than he was physically ill. I couldn't see it at the time, but I later realized that Ted simply needed to do something different with his life, and not because of the past. There *was* no historical explanation! Ted was tired of the way it had been. He was tired of being a lawyer. That's not what he said exactly, but that's what he implied. He did not need his personality rearranged, as I was attempting to do; he needed time to look at his life reflectively and thoughtfully. He needed help to change his environment, and to adapt, and then once through a difficult period, he would be on his way again.

It is a mistake for individuals or therapists to assume that nothing completely new occurs in adult life. This has been one of the most startling and reassuring discoveries for adults, particularly middle-aged men and women. They have assumed, because it's what they've been taught by society—the schools, the media, the fields of psychology and psychiatry—that they have to be happy, relatively happy and satisfied, or they are abnormal people. It just isn't so.

I'm not saying that mental illness doesn't exist, or that, as psychiatrists R. D. Laing and Thomas Szasz claim, it is in the mind of the beholder whence it breeds sickness. Some people do develop

*In this book *adaptation* means that people change both self and environment, whereas *coping* assumes the constancy of the environment and changes only self. Adaptation provides a better person/environment fit.

psychological disorders that affect their ability to cope and adapt, and they are mentally ill.

NORMAL VERSUS ABNORMAL

But who is mentally ill? That is the dilemma of modern psychology. How do psychiatrists determine normals from abnormals?

Until very recently there was no psychological theory to explain adult development, and one has still not been fully developed so that it can be accepted by the majority of therapists. This is a serious shortcoming of psychiatry. Without a comprehensive theory for adult life therapists cannot determine when their patients are experiencing normal, developmental growth and when in fact they are mentally ill. Therapists instinctively know to search historically for an explanation of unhappiness, just as I did with Ted Banks, but they won't search developmentally, and in many cases that's the only way they'll discover the root of a problem.

This dilemma of normal versus abnormal, which has reerupted most forcefully in the fields of psychology and psychiatry, may seem fundamental to the layman, and he may be surprised to know that therapists can't always identify normality in many adult patients.* After all, why go to a psychiatrist? Regardless of how basic the dilemma may be, however, it is deeply rooted in the tradition of the profession and in the nature and style of the therapy that is commonly practiced. My own experience is a good example of what I mean.

WHAT IS THERAPY?

An eclectic residency left me with three distinct conclusions about psychiatry. First, there are a number of completely different methods for arriving at a satisfactory outcome with a patient.

Second, there are a wide variety of theories to support each method, and the same method might be suggested by two different theories.

*The theoretical issue of normal versus abnormal has existed since the inception of psychiatry. However, the most prevalent assumption has been that people who come to therapy are sick.

And third, in most cases there is no satisfactory method to determine which of two or more theories will be most effective. Each theory is eternally consistent and has a ring of scientific truth about it, and if it fails, each theory has a solid internal justification to explain why it failed. As the comedian Flip Wilson used to say, "What you see is what you get," and in the case of therapy, if a patient fails to get "well," it is never the therapist's fault, nor the fault of the theory.

These conclusions left me with one glaring question that eventually attracted me to the study of adult development: What *is* therapy? If the same method produces different outcomes, and different theories support the same methods, then what is therapy?

CONVERSION TO A BELIEF SYSTEM

In pursuit of an answer to that question, I read Jerome Frank's *Persuasion and Healing*, an absolutely fascinating book that considers therapy a process of conversion to a belief system. As Frank explains, conversion to a belief system helps people feel less anxious by providing an explanation for reality. When a person finds a belief system that explains his problem, the trauma of the problem is reduced significantly. The belief system may be philosophical, such as "Everything happens for the best in life." Or it may have some religious connotation, such as "God created the world, and the world is controlled by God." The belief system may be less grandiose as well, and specifically tailored to an individual problem: "A penny saved is a penny earned." Or "The way to a man's heart is through his stomach." Folklore has provided thousands of these bits of wisdom, and to some extent they determine peoples' behavior and attitudes, and they control lives beginning not long after birth.

A baby in a crib discovers very early in life that when he's hungry and he cries, mother comes. Then, as a toddler, he learns that by flipping a switch, a light comes on or goes off. By simple trial and error a child builds a system of cause and effect that is efficacious. Later, as he learns language, his family will delight him with a variety of additional beliefs. Some of them will be contradictory, but all of them will imply a consequence and to some extent control his life. The power of belief systems is so great that it shapes what a child perceives and in many ways limits his behavior. For example, if he's taught that all men are competitive, then in any situation with another man he will either avoid or produce competition. For the remainder of his life, unless he reexamines his belief system, male competition will be an issue for him.

Or, if he's taught that the people of another race are inferior (or superior), then in any situation with people of that race he'll act accordingly.

In this way, a human being assumes various roles and learns when to act out those roles. All of the behaviors of any one role are never explicitly stated, but no role can be underestimated because the individual realizes that if he doesn't behave according to others' expectations, he will suffer some consequence or social sanction.

This system of beliefs constitutes an important component of the human psyche. For many people it is a prison, a confining, restrictive model that inhibits or retards normal adult development. For others it is an open-ended system that welcomes learning and growth.

APPLYING THEORIES

If therapy is conversion to a belief system, then psychiatrists and other therapists are actually helping patients undergo a social learning process. Once I arrived at that conclusion, it left me with a second question: Is there an ultimate belief system which accurately teaches human beings about how the world operates? If so, then there's likely to be a more efficient means for transferring the benefits of therapy. Instead of going through the mumbo jumbo of theories, therapists could teach directly to this belief system! Few therapists, unfortunately, have considered these possibilities or have fully understood their implications.

Psychiatrists and other therapists aren't solely treating personalities, they are also experimenting with theories, and many aren't aware of it—or if they are, they're reluctant to admit it. When a patient visits a therapist, he selects a theory for the patient's problem, and to the extent the patient improves the therapist believes the theory is validated. He minimizes the process of the therapy and emphasizes the applicability of the theory even though the theory could have been one of several. In many instances he could have taught the patient anything from alpha meditation to transactional analysis and it might not have made much difference.

The effect of the therapy was the conversion to a belief system. The patient either needed to clarify his own belief system, which may have become distorted, or needed to adopt a new belief system.

By assuming that the theory was successful, and ignoring the process of application, therapists build theories of personality upon office population—patients—and thus cannot separate who is normal from who is abnormal. To the therapist, every patient who comes to his office is sick.

This was a shocking realization for me because it meant that I was as sick as some of my patients. Many times a man would visit me with a problem that I had personally confronted a month or two earlier. At other times patients complained to me about problems that I had also faced, but hadn't resolved. So I either had to assume that I was sick, or that I, and my patients, were experiencing normal issues of life. If we were normal, then why didn't we know it? Thus, a third question.

We didn't know we were normal primarily because psychiatry cannot measure normality. Even the most sophisticated tests of psychological health cannot entirely separate normals from abnormals. In a little-known study in the 1950s, a student population was administered the Minnesota Multi-Phasic Personality Inventory (MMPI), one of the best-documented tests for separating categories of psychological pathology. Following the test psychiatrists interviewed those students who had scored normal in every category and concluded that a third of them needed therapy and another 20 percent of them could probably have benefitted from therapy! Apparently many psychiatrists are either not aware of this discrepancy or they don't think it's very serious because the MMPI is one of the most widely administered tests for measuring personality.

Many psychiatrists insist they can separate normals from abnormals on the basis of symptomatology: People with psychiatric complaints are sick. In view of their extensive medical backgrounds, which focus on illness, this is a natural assumption, but it is not necessarily accurate.

A DEEPER UNDERSTANDING

Prior to asking these questions, I consistently adopted the theory that unhappy adults are sick adults, but as I dug into what little research existed about adult development, I began to change my mind. A few studies of adult development had been conducted prior to the 1970s, and in my typical psychiatric education, the studies were mentioned but their implications were left unexplored.

A most insightful study was Robert White's *Lives in Progress* in which he chose twenty Harvard students and followed them for more than twenty years, a luxury not possible for the therapist, except in cases of extreme psychiatric disability. White struggled with the same issues that are being discussed now. He spoke of "a gap at the center of our knowledge about personality. The neglected area can be identified as continuous development over periods of time amid natural circumstances." In several of his case studies, White discovered it was possible for lives to change without one hour of psychotherapy. And yet, if personality was fixed by the age of 5, how could that be? There was no psychological model to explain it.

Then there was Erik Erikson's significant book *Childhood and Society,* which presented eight stages of man, three of which occurred in adult life. While his thesis was interesting, it lacked specific therapeutic utility. No methodology was suggested to help people determine what stage of life they were at, or what skills were necessary to reach different levels of growth. Furthermore, Erikson did not completely explain how his stages were influenced by the environment, or how they differed for men and women. In time, somewhat conveniently, his findings were shelved and largely unutilized.

There were several other studies as well, but prior to the mid-1970s I never seriously considered them because I had no application for their theories. In spite of this, I had been puzzled by what I saw happening during my education and training.

Before my psychiatric training I had interned in a county hospital to which one of every ten medical students in the country applied; about thirty of several thousand were accepted. This had to be a highly skilled group of people in one of the nation's best hospitals, and yet the quality of care in this institution was surprisingly poor. After a while it was obvious what was happening. The nurses, for example, were hired right out of nursing schools and they were always idealistic, excited, interested in human care, and eager to work, but then, in about six months time, they turned indifferent and angry. This radical exchange of attitudes baffled me. What had happened to these nurses? In a sense they had experienced a change of personality, but again, how could that be? There were no theories to explain it, and yet, something did happen to these nurses.

Later, as a resident of the University of Pennsylvania Hospital, the split in my belief system was widened even further. One day a political rabble rouser and counterculturalist complained to me about certain familial and social issues in his life. He was terrified of being socialized into a value system that would bury his revolutionary attitudes. In the midst of our discussion he cited two poignant examples that eventually helped to clarify my own thoughts. The first was the story of the Buddhist nuns in Southeast Asia who had set fire to themselves in protest of the attacks there on human rights and dignity. The second was the story of the Japanese who had become so disturbed by the thought of his country losing its military that he committed hara-kiri. Were these people mentally ill? Or were they simply using dramatic forms of protest against the ills of their societies? At the time I had no answer, and I remained confused by the dilemma of who was normal and who was abnormal.

ORGANIZATIONAL ISSUES

Then, in studying at the Wharton School with Eric Trist, one of the founders of organizational development, and concurrently managing the psychiatric consultant service at the Veterans Administration Hospital which was staffed by the University of Pennsylvania, I began to sense that the environment had some impact upon society and personalities. At the VA Hospital I discovered that about half the patients were in desperate need of psychiatric counseling. In spite of their medical diagnoses, about half the patients were not there for medical reasons—they were there waging war against social adversity in their lives. They would become discouraged and frightened and then enter the hospital. They did have medical problems, but few were sufficiently severe to warrant hospitalization. So why were they there? I didn't know, but I wondered if chronic, enduring environmental problems could cause physiological or psychiatric distress.

As my experiences led me into other kinds of organizational consulting I eventually understood that certain phenomena were best understood as organizational issues, and others were individual psychological issues. For example, I counseled one man in an organization who had always tried to please his boss, and he was good at it. For eighteen years he had been considered one of the company's best employees, and all of that time he had worked for one man. But then his boss died and his new boss wanted him to take charge of certain responsibilities in the division. Almost immediately this man fell apart. He became frustrated, scared, and terribly confused. No matter what he did, or how hard he tried, he could not please his boss, and no one understood what had happened.

Looking historically at this client's life, I discovered that he had experienced a compliant relationship with his father. He had walked in his father's footsteps and never questioned any of his father's values or beliefs. It had worked for him then, and it worked for many years of his adult life as well. But when his environment demanded something else from him, he could not deliver, and he failed. In this case, unknown to me at the time, there were both organizational and psychological issues involved. My client had not experienced any adolescent rebellion or individuation from his father, that much I knew, but I just didn't realize that the organizational issues—his boss requesting different demands without a gradual developmental process—could be that complicating.

THE EFFECT OF THE EXTERNAL ENVIRONMENT

Finally, on one consulting mission, I began to see that the external environment—the world that surrounds us—is more important than psychiatrists are taught.

I went out with a team to diagnose the operation of a major oil refinery on the East Coast and my role was not so much that of psychiatrist as it was quasi-business consultant. Our job was to design a training program for the management of the refinery's Maintenance Department, which was one of the two major divisions of the refinery.

Maintenance was responsible for routine upkeep as well as the efficiency of the refinery's machinery in the Operations Department where crude oil was processed into gasoline, grease, heating oil, and various by-products. The refinery made money only by selling its products, so every hour that Operations was shut down, the company lost revenue. For economic reasons the Operations Department dominated the Maintenance Department.

The Maintenance Department wanted to begin an autonomos managerial program to allow employees greater control over their work and greater interdependence with fellow workers. Since the program was innovative and rarely tried in industry, managers in the Maintenance Department required some additional training. That's why my team was involved.

Before we could design a training program, however, we needed to know more about how the refinery functioned and what forces influenced its day-to-day operation. In the process of this routine investigation, we discovered an amazing phenomenon. The four zone engineers who managed Maintenance were all clinically depressed! They made comments such as "I feel overwhelmed," "I can't do my job," "I don't know what's wrong with me," "I feel unhappy." And not one of them was able to accurately pinpoint the organizational cause of his problem.

We didn't know the cause either until we completed our investigation. Whenever there was a breakdown in the Operations Department, any and every Maintenance employee on duty, by a directive of top management, could be called to the scene of the breakdown to help make a speedy repair. The objective was to return the refinery to its full level of production as quickly as possible. Since breakdowns were occurring about once a week and becoming more frequent, the routine maintenance of the plant was suffering, which in turn resulted in even more breakdowns and created a crisis atmosphere within the company.

The four zone engineers were caught in a cycle that precluded the efficient supervision of their department and frustrated them in their jobs. Neither they nor top management would discover the cycle unless they stopped to analyze the functions of the refinery.

Now, were these engineers suffering from an internal psychological disorder, or from an external psychological disorder—one forced upon them by the environment?

Certainly it was external. But listen to the dialogue that I imagine would have occurred if one of these four engineers had visited a psychiatrist:

DOCTOR: *What seems to be your problem?*

ENGINEER: *Well, I feel blue all the time. I don't sleep very well at night. I have stomach pains sometimes and I ache, but my family doctor says I'm fine physically. He said I should consult a psychia-*

trist. I'm a little bit embarrassed about that, but I want to know what's wrong with me.

DOCTOR: *What's bothering you?*

ENGINEER: *I don't know for sure. I can't think of any specific thing.*

DOCTOR: *How about your job? Everything all right there?*

ENGINEER: *No, not really. I haven't been very happy at work. Not like I used to be. I can't seem to get the work done anymore. I don't know what's wrong.*

Remember, the psychiatrist is not aware of the information that we discovered in our investigation of the refinery's day-to-day operation. He's only seeing this individual employee. So he continues:

DOCTOR: *Tell me about your job.*

ENGINEER: *Well, I run a part of the Maintenance Department of an oil refinery, but I don't feel I'm doing a very good job. I can't control the men and there are too many breakdowns in the plant.*

DOCTOR: *How long have you felt this way?*

ENGINEER: *Ever since I got promoted.*

DOCTOR: *How long ago were you promoted?*

ENGINEER: *Oh, about a year ago.*

DOCTOR: *How did you do in your last job?*

ENGINEER: *Fine. That's why they promoted me.*

DOCTOR: *So what's different about this job that you can't handle?*

ENGINEER: *First of all I have more men under me and I have more responsibility. I work for a different boss . . .*

DOCTOR: *Do you like your boss?*

ENGINEER: *He's okay. He's down on me right now because I'm not doing a very good job. But usually he's OK, you know?*

Click, click, click. The thoughts flash through the psychiatrist's mind. Look through the history of his early relationship with his family. Perhaps a parent has died. Look at his relationship with his father. His reaction to authority. Possibly he needs to fail . . .

DOCTOR: *How do you get along with the men who work for you?*

ENGINEER: *I can't control them. I'm down on them because the work isn't getting done. . . .*

DOCTOR: *How about things at home. OK there?*

ENGINEER: *Hmmm. They're terrible. My wife says I'm depressed all the time. I've lost interest in sex. I sit and watch TV. Sometimes I just sit. I don't know what's wrong.*

Aha, says the psychiatrist to himself. Dependency problems . . . problems with another relationship. Fear of sex. Guilt about a marital indiscretion? Fear of intimacy?

And so it continues. The format of the psychiatrist's investigation assumes that the environment is reasonable and that the individual is malfunctioning. So the investigation will naturally proceed in a direction to discover what is wrong with the patient, a direction which is fundamentally off course in this situation.

PASSAGES

Not long after my experience at the refinery I heard about Gail Sheehy's book *Passages,* and its subtitle, *Predictable Crises of Adult Life,* hit me like a zap of electricity. I had been reaching out and grabbing for it, but the concept was always beyond my fingertips. I knew there had to be change occurring in adult life, but I couldn't characterize it; I just didn't know what terminology to use.

Then when I read *Passages* my reaction was, "Aha, at last someone has provided a road map." I didn't believe it was absolutely true, but it was a beginning: Adult life is like a map of Russia to someone with no knowledge of Russia—it was an undifferentiated glob. It's almost unpenetrable, but suddenly *Passages* provided hope. There could be other answers than what psychiatry had already put forth. Crises did not necessarily have to be explained by internal malfunctions or by precipitating events (such as divorce, death, or the loss of a job). There were other answers!

By this time, in my own search for reasoning, I had decided that even though psychiatry had taught me to ignore the external events of an individual's life, in favor of the internal system, it was conceivable that the external environment was a crucial determinant of adult happiness. The majority of therapists in this country do not agree. They believe the external environment is innocent and unalterable, so they doctor their patients to fit the environment. Exceptions are when a precipitating event is involved, but even in those cases the therapist's investigation is geared toward helping the patient cope and not adapt.

This is ego psychology, a third-generation derivative of Freudian theory, and it ignores the discovery that the environment, in a chronic, enduring, invisible manner, might be impossible or damaging and that there are periods of change in adult life (adult development) during which new values and motives shift the desire and meaning of an individual's life.

MODELS OF THERAPY

In fairness to my psychiatric education, I had been taught various models of therapy (in addition to Freudian psychoanalysis):

BEHAVIOR THERAPY—Assumes mental problems are the result of habit patterns (e.g., overeating) or the environment's reaction to specific behaviors (e.g., delinquency) or conditioned anxiety (e.g., fear).

COGNITIVE THERAPY—Assumes some mental problems are the result of the way people perceive or misinterpret their environment (e.g., overgeneralization—if one woman dislikes me, all women will dislike me).

EXISTENTIAL THERAPY—Invites people to explore their inner selves to gain a sense of meaning, purpose, direction, and therefore motivation in their lives.

FAMILY THERAPY—Assumes familial communication patterns can be reorganized and changed in a way that will help individuals adapt. It is largely based on structural and communication approaches which tend to reorganize or facilitate dialogue in the family and its structure.

While these models are extremely useful for specific problems, they lack general utility for adult developmental and environmentally induced problems.

SNAPSHOT VERSUS MOVIE

Without taking those two fundamental causes of unhappiness into consideration, therapists are trying to cure normal people, and that can't be done. It's like trying to cure adolescence with psychotherapy. Adolescence is a normal growth process. There are tools and exercises for helping a youngster cope through that period of life, but no one can prevent it from occurring, nor should anyone want to.

Nor should anyone want to block adult development. Mothers struggling emotionally when they enter the job market . . . 25-

year-old men doubting their sexuality . . . middle-aged men and women filing for divorce—to many therapists these are mentally ill people, but they might be normal. Until someone asks the questions "Could their problems be developmental? . . . Could their environments be impossible?" no one will know for sure.

To ask those questions a therapist needs to look at his patients through the developmental focus of a motion picture, rather than within the rigid framework of a snapshot.

A snapshot displays almost perfectly what has happened within the limits of the viewfinder. Everything stands still for that particular moment. An onlooker may conceptualize what has happened and he might be able to determine the mood and condition of the subject matter based upon the snapshot. He might even be able to perceive feeling and make some inferences. For example, if a boy in the picture is holding a ball above his head, the onlooker might guess that the ball was about to be thrown, but of course he could not be sure until the ball was thrown. That's the value of motion. An intelligent onlooker walks away from a movie knowing exactly what occurred. He gets an accurate impression of all the forces and interplay, and he doesn't have to make inferences.

LEVINSON'S LIFE STRUCTURE

The man who has done the most to convince some psychiatrists that environment and development are related factors in adult growth is Daniel J. Levinson of Yale University. He is one of the pioneers of contemporary adult developmental research and the first psychologist to provide a comprehensive model of adult growth. His model has not been universally accepted, and it does not include any mode of therapeutic utility, but it is a primary building block.

Levinson introduced the term *life structure* and defined it as "the basic pattern or design of a person's life at a given time." According to Levinson, an individual's life structure consists of a social cultural world (class, religion, ethnicity, family, political system, and occupation structure); aspects of self (fantasies, moral values and ideals, talents and skills, character traits, modes of feeling, thought, and action); and participation in the world (roles of citizen, lover, worker, boss, friend, husband, member of diverse groups and enterprises). These components are interrelated, as shown in Figure 1.

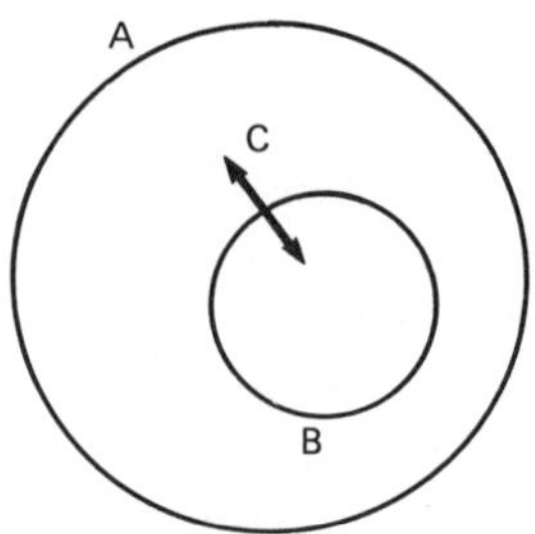

FIGURE 1. Life structure. The components—the social cultural world (A) or specific conditions or events of the time; aspects of self (B) that are either expressed and lived out or inhibited or neglected; and participation in the world (C) composed of evolving relationships and roles—are interrelated.

This, I am convinced, is the answer. The goal of modern psychiatry ought to be the development of a universally acceptable theory for adult life and to provide specific modes of therapy for its utilization. Traditional methods of psychiatry are not dynamic enough to treat the modern human psyche. That's precisely why I failed to help Ted Banks. If Ted Banks came to me today, I would still take a history of his life, but then I would immediately pick up the environmental realities that surround him: his choice matrix, his future, his idealized future, for example. I would not assume that he had made some dreadful mistake to arrive at a juncture of fear and depression.

Tips for Choosing a Psychiatrist

1. In the first three sessions you should feel that you like the psychiatrist and that he or she is positive toward you.

2. After three visits you should feel that the psychiatrist generally understands you.

3. At all times you should feel that the psychiatrist can help you and that his or her suggestions make sense.

4. By the end of three sessions you should feel mild to moderate improvement in terms of your symptoms or the way in which you view your problem.

5. The psychiatrist should be willing to entertain developmental views of adult life, which means that some adult problems are normal.

6. The psychiatrist should express some concern and interest about your external environment.

7. The specific training, affiliation, and theories of the psychiatrist are not as important as knowing that the psychiatrist is flexible, genuinely concerned, empathetic, and unconditionally positive in reacting with you.

I would entertain the possibility that he had performed so well in his career that he needed to be challenged again. His primary issue would be generativity versus stagnation, that is, he might need to get involved in something larger than himself—to move from being actor to director, to become a mentor for others, to seek satisfaction from events larger than life, to create a legacy for the world. To do this successfully, and without impeding his growth, he would need direction, but it could be provided only by therapy that was sensitive to his environment and personal development. For the most part, that is the aim of this book—to offer men and women alternative types of therapy that will provide meaningful direction to managing the transitions and crises of their lives.

CHAPTER TWO

Adapting to Life

"Society is inside of man
and man is inside society,
and you cannot even create
a truthfully drawn psychological entity
on the stage until you understand
his social relations and their power
to make him what he is and
not to prevent him from being
what he is not. The fish is in the water,
and the water is in the fish."

ARTHUR MILLER

Adaptation to change in life is the continuous struggle of every human being, and yet we've only begun to realize it or to understand how it occurs. People are forever experiencing cycles of happiness and unhappiness, and periods of doubt, fear, and loneliness, but rarely does anyone attribute these moods to physiological or biological phenomena. "That's life," we like to say, as we unwittingly adapt to life. Doctors and the media tell us that people who are happy more of the time are better adjusted than those who are not, so the mature, well-adjusted man (or woman) has become the ideal for everyone.

Now researchers are convinced the ideal man (or woman) doesn't exist, at least not in any traditional mold. He (she) is a popular myth. Recent literature in the fields of psychology and psychiatry define a human psyche more complex than that of the ideal man. It is a psyche that does not always respond to internal psychological rearrangement, but may require adaptive forms of treatment that are sensitive to both internal and external stimuli. Later in the book we will explore some of the adaptive treatments that are useful for individuals, most of which you can do on your own, but first it's necessary to outline some of the issues and effects of adult development.

STABLE AND UNSTABLE STAGES OF LIFE

Slowly and painfully the theory of a "compleat adult" is emerging in psychiatry, and the impetus behind it has been the research of several men and women, including Daniel Levinson, Roger Gould, George Vaillant, and Gail Sheehy. These researchers have identified age-linked stable and unstable stages of life that shape the course of adult life.*

The age limits of each era vary slightly from researcher to researcher, but according to Levinson, who wrote *Seasons of a Man's Life*, there are four eras of life:

- *childhood to adolescence, ages 0–22*
- *early adulthood, ages 17–45*
- *middle adulthood, ages 40–65*
- *late adulthood, ages 60 and beyond.*

These are the major structure-building periods of life, and as such they are called the stable eras. The three adult eras are interrupted by unstable stages, called transitions, and they commonly occur between the ages of 17 and 22, 28 and 33, 40 and 45, 50 and 55, and 60 and 65.

During stable eras, people create and enact life structures (see Chapter 1) which are intended to satisfy individual goals and desires.

Then, during transitional eras, life structures are reevaluated and oftentimes picked apart to satisfy more relevant or more urgent goals and desires. Once a life structure is created in a stable era, it is then perfected until the next transitional stage, and consciously or unconsciously, adults adapt to these cycles of life.

The Novice Phase

Levinson calls the first provisional stage of adulthood, the years between 17 and 33, the novice phase of life, and it requires men to face four basic tasks:

*These stages primarily shape the course of adult male life. Most adult developmental research has been conducted with men, so the findings are not conclusive for women, and even though it is anticipated that women's lives are similarly affected, we can't be sure.

They must form a dream, "a vague sense of self," says Levinson, "and place it in their life structure."

They must form mentor relationships with people who can guide and advise them.

They must pursue a career, developing skills and credentials.

And they must develop intimate love relationships, establishing a basis for affection, sexuality, emotional intimacy, dependency, friendship, collaboration, respect, admiration, and enduring commitment.

These tasks are in addition to those which may be undertaken during the age-related adult developmental transitions, the first of which we call the 20s transition.

The Twenties Transition

Between the ages of 17 and 22 most people need to take time to build a framework for leaving family and home and to make the preliminary leap into an independent adult world. In Western societies this is a critical developmental event. Without successfully mastering the 20s transition, a man can never learn to be independent, and that will undoubtedly create a variety of social and psychological problems for him later in life.

Although this can be a traumatic transition, it is usually accepted as an everyday occurrence, and it is probably one of the least painful. Generally a young man takes a look at his parents' life structure and he may choose to imitate it, or he may identify weaknesses in it and develop some alternative style. Quite often, much to the displeasure of parents, young men experiment with a variety of lifestyles before they settle down. At any rate, they are building a preliminary life structure, which they will then attempt to perfect later in their 20s, and the choice of lifestyles really matters little because by the age of 30, or thereabout, there will occur a second transition. In our culture we have some expectations about where a man ought to be by the age of 30, and as he reflects upon his first life structure, he gets a signal that the provisional quality of his 20s life is about to end.

In Levinson's words, "A voice within says, 'I am to change my life—if there are things in it I want to modify or exclude, or things missing I want to add—I must now make a start or soon it will be too late.' " Now the young man feels a need to dismantle the components of his life and prepare himself for the next stable period ahead.

The Thirties Transition

The Thirties Man

Desires:

—his wife to be more interesting but not to compete with him

—his children to be kept out of his way

—to make his mark on the world.

Fears:

—his wife's independence

—not performing as well as he would like to at work.

Sixty percent of all men experience moderate to severe crises at the 30s transition! At this time a man usually decides his life structure is not acceptable to him because it is either a copy of or a reaction to his parents' lives. In either case it is probably not satisfying his expectations, and so it is necessary to change in another era of transition.

During the 30s transition some men feel depressed, anxious, overwhelmed, lost, confused and even suicidal, depending upon the depth of the crisis and their own levels of maturity. Now a man realizes that indeed he is out of the home and on his own. Quite likely, he is married and has children, and he is not only worried about making it for himself, but for them as well. Sometimes he sees his marriage as an entrapment (which explains the high incidence of separation and divorce during the 30s) and he may blame his spouse or his children for his problems. Often he doesn't have close friends, or if he does, they may not be the type with whom he would feel comfortable sharing his troubles. And so the 30s transition is sometimes a period of loneliness and fear.

Once through it, however, a man begins to settle down again, and usually his goal is "to establish a niche in society," says Levinson, "to develop competency in a chosen craft and to become a valuable member of a valued society." Making his mark in the world becomes the most important task for him, more so than spending time with family or friends, and there is an intense, often enjoyable drive to fulfill the expectations of his own self. He is, as Roger Gould describes the 30-year man, "on the make" in every sense of the word.

The Forties Transition

THE FORTIES MAN

Desires:

—to experience intimacy and closeness

—to be part of the family.

Fears:

—his death.

Feels:

—stagnant and trapped

—highly self-critical.

By the late 30s or early 40s, however, the stability of life will be interrupted once again by the midlife transition. Eighty percent of men can expect moderate to severe crises during this powerful transition, and any man who is ill prepared to face it will likely suffer severe consequences for the remainder of his life.

For many men, the 40s transition is the beginning of upheaval in life. It is a period of in-depth examination and self-criticism, more intense than the reflective mood of the 30s, and it is often overwhelming and defeating. For a man to be as good as he can be, he must think that he's greater than he is. But having achieved for a dozen or so years, there is often a frightening, sudden loss of illusion during the midlife transition. When a man loses sight of his dream, in the clearing he often sees life for what it is. If what he sees is shallow and valueless, he will feel tricked and angry, having spent half a lifetime for naught. In defense, he will probably withdraw, although sometimes he turns to his family for comfort only to discover that his family doesn't seem to care. His children are teenagers, some are not even living at home, and those at home are more interested in their own lives than their father's. His wife may be gone as well, taking advantage of her freedom from a dependent family, working full-time or volunteering at the hospital or library.

The realization that his family isn't at home waiting for him is a shock for the 40s man. He begins to wonder why he had a family, why he's being rejected, why his life has fallen apart. And it's during these lonely moments that he may turn to another woman—infidelity is at its peak at this juncture of life—or he may try to drown his sorrows in booze or pills.

Sometimes, the 40s transition brings with it a pervading feeling about death, and this contributes to the anguish of upheaval. Typically the 40s man feels the world has suddenly turned on him. He used to think of himself climbing up the ladder, but now, particularly if he never made it to the top, he's descending rapidly, and he's petrified. At 30 he had options, but at 40 he wants to put himself in a holding pattern. He can't do it, and he thinks that somehow he failed. In that frame of mind it's difficult for any man to be optimistic or hopeful, and as a result many men suffer for long periods of time.

The majority of men, researchers say, resolve their 40s transition, many without ever realizing what happened, and they go on to build a third life structure, the quality of which depends upon the depth of resolutions during the 40s transition. "Some men have suffered such irreputable defeat in childhood or early adulthood and have been so little able to work on their tasks of their midlife transition, that they lack the inner and outer resources for creating a minimally adequate life structure," says Levinson.

Beyond Midlife

There are supposedly adult developmental transitions at about the ages of 50 and 60, but research here is sketchy and inconclusive. In fact, little has been worked out developmentally beyond midlife for either men or women.

WOMEN IN TRANSITION

Some of the most interesting data about women have been supplied by Gail Sheehy, the author of *Passages,* and Iris Sangiuliano, who wrote *In Her Time.*

Sheehy defines three basic types of women: *Caregivers* (or *nurturants*), who live to seek meaning and value from giving to others, according to Sheehy "a woman who marries in her early twenties or before and who at that time is of no mind to go beyond the domestic role"; *Either/ors*, who in their 20s choose either nurturant roles or work/accomplishment roles; and *Integrators* (or *super-women*), who try to combine marriage, career, and motherhood in their 20s.

The Thirties Woman

THE THIRTIES WOMAN

Feels:

—need to attach to a "stronger" individual

—she will drown without a man

—envy—she is on the periphery of adult world.

Her life centers around her man and all energy goes toward pleasing him, making a family for him.

We are writing mostly about the nurturant woman, about whom researchers have learned the most, and at the age of 30, in our society, she is usually a woman of lost identity. She has been taught to attach herself to a strong man, and if she doesn't by 30, she will. Even if she has been enormously successful on her own—she may have aced every course in high school and college and landed a high-paying job—she will still be attracted to a dominant male figure, because that is what she's been taught to expect.

Despite whatever consciousness raising may have occurred as the result of the women's movement, many women still stumble into dependency traps because belief systems, as we discussed in Chapter 1, are tremendously powerful and have been developed over centuries. As a result, the woman of 30 often faces periods of frustration and discontent.

Usually, she is occupied pleasing her man, caring for him, feeding him, making him a family, and happily so, but eventually, or all the while, she envies him. Once she loses contact with an adult world she surrenders her identity. Once realized, this is a dreadful, overwhelming feeling. She becomes a child-mother with no adult. She can be a parent to her husband, or a child to her husband as well as a child to her children, but she has lost her experience of being an adult with another adult. The tendency is for her to feel lonely, sometimes ugly, irritable, and unsettled, and in that condition she is afraid to approach anyone to talk about her troubles. Her husband is preoccupied with his career or his independence, her children are too young to understand, her family is too far removed to empathize, and she has not kept up with intimate friends or developed any new relationships. Rarely does she understand what's happening in her life and it's a natural tendency for her to assume she's mentally ill. If she goes for counseling or therapy, she's probably going to be treated as an abnormal patient, when in fact she is experiencing a normal condition.

The loss of identity has a devastating effect on women. Some of them never develop a strong sense of identity, some regain it, but Dr. Sangiuliano's research demonstrates that many women do form identity after they are married and struggle for a period of time. Men, on the other hand, form their identity prior to coupling and marriage, usually in adolescence.

Women in Midlife

Women in Midlife

Issue of self-declaration

Concern with loss of youth and appearance

High incidence of infidelity

Time many women enter (or reenter) the work force or seek additional education

Age at which most divorced women remarry

Most common age of runaway wives

Concern with mortality and death

Loss of illusion

Critical issue is achievement

The empty nest syndrome

There is a midlife transition for women, but not much is known about it. A married woman's midlife transition may occur at about the time of her husband's midlife transition, despite the probability of her being younger. This is a time of lost youth, especially for nurturant women, accompanied by a sense of emptiness as the children leave home for college, work, or marriage. It is not necessarily a sad transition, however, as a woman may feel jubilant about finally gaining freedom after waiting for so many years, sorting piles of clothing, cooking an infinite number of meals, and washing thousands of dishes. Now it's her turn to make a career, to have some fun, to live again, and she often feels it's her last opportunity.

TRANSITION AND MARRIAGE

One of the saddest commentaries about life in America is the scenario of the 40s transition man who seeks whatever goodness and comfort he believes remains for him from his family, only to discover that his family has scattered.

Not only does this contribute to the deterioration of family life, but it also makes life unbearable for many men and women as well. It would be easy to point fingers and blame men for bringing about their own fall, knocking them for not spending more time at home or taking an active role in family life, and it would be just as easy to turn around and blame women for not suppressing the urge to flee the family at about midlife, but in fact individuals are not to blame for this scenario. Much of the blame belongs to society's ignorance of adult development and the failure to recognize that age-related issues pop up throughout adult life. Now that research has begun to uncover patterns of adult living, many of the underlying issues which create trauma and result in deterioration can be exposed and hopefully overcome.

Two of the most destructive phenomena in married life are what I call "achievement as love" and "love as achievement" (see Figures 2 and 3). They are subtle, common occurrences, and when they are described it's easy to see how they detract from a couple's happiness.

Men generally ascribe to achievement as love, but it's becoming a common belief among women as well. "If I achieve, I'll be loved" is what a man thinks subconsciously. In grade school he knew

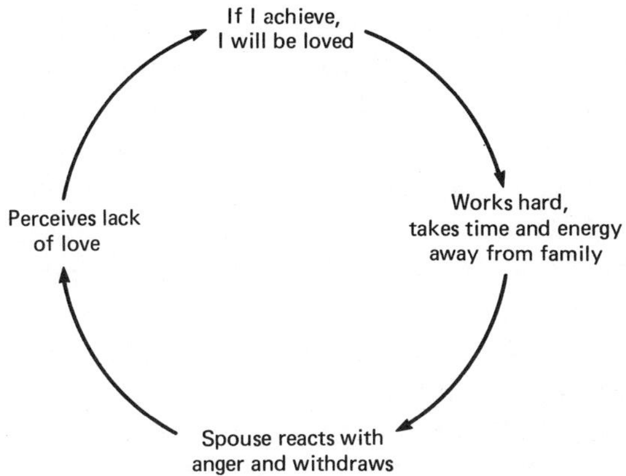

FIGURE 2. Achievement as love.

that if he earned good grades his parents would love him; later, if he played sports, his parents, relatives and friends would love him; and so at work, if he works hard and does a good job, his boss should love him, and so should his wife. What actually happens, however, is that his wife reacts with anger, or she withdraws from him, because he is taking time away from her and their life together. She's not getting the attention she wants and needs, and even though she may try to communicate that message, he perceives a lack of love. What does he know to do then? Work harder, of course, and so the cycle continues.

FIGURE 3. Love as achievement.

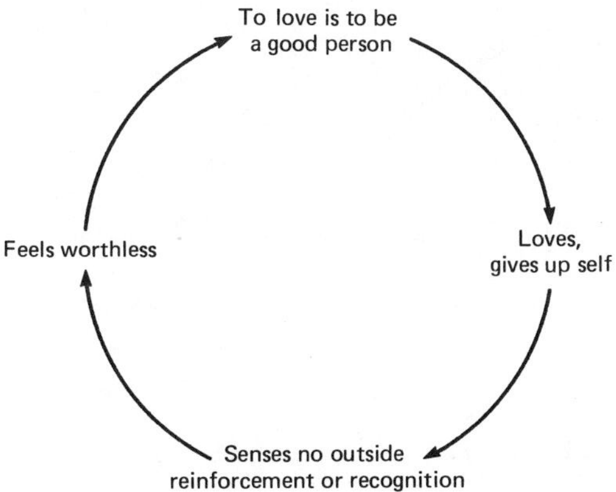

"Love as achievement" is most common among women because they are taught that to love is to be a good person. Frequently, then, a woman loves by giving herself up, even to the point of surrendering her identity. As a result, she senses no outside recognition or reinforcement, which signals achievement, and so it is natural for her to feel worthless. And how has she been taught to react to feelings of worthlessness? By loving more, obviously, and again the cycle continues.

These are vicious circles of interplay between husbands and wives and they are simply a result of socialization. Love is not achievement, nor is achievement love. Love gets love. Achievement gets achievement. And that is what we should have been taught.

Other adult developmental issues also contribute to happiness or unhappiness in married life. For example, marital satisfaction fluctuates throughout all of adult life, and this is normal. As shown in the chart in Figure 4, seventy percent of married people say they are satisfied at the outset of married life, but then that percentage rapidly declines. It falls consistently until the oldest child leaves home, when about 10 percent of married men and women say they

FIGURE 4. Family life is least satisfying at the launching stage: Percent of individuals in each stage of the family life cycle reporting that their present stage of the family life cycle is very satisfying (source: Rollins and Feldman, 1970).

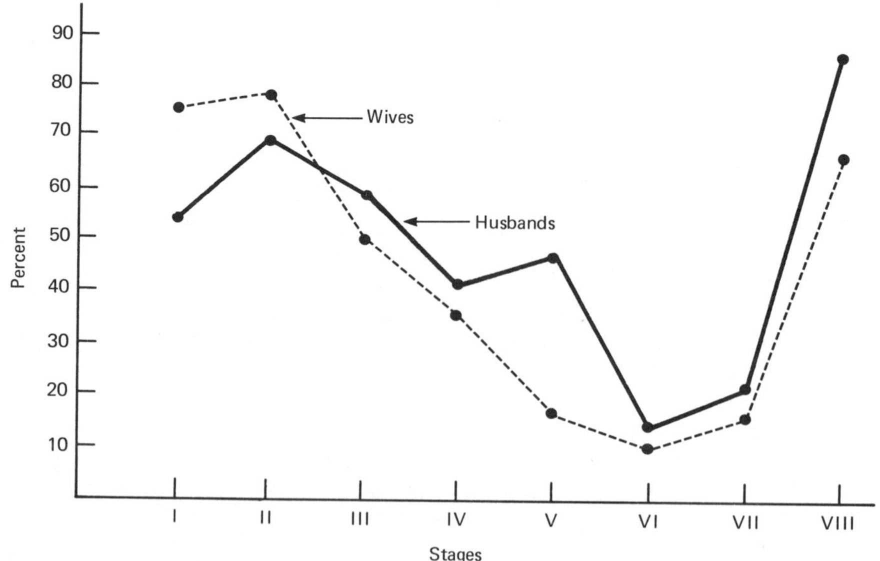

are satisfied, and then rises sharply after the last child moves out of the home. Eventually the percentage of satisfied men and women approaches 70 percent again, the level at the outset of marriage, and for women it often reaches 80 percent.

This understanding may not make married life any happier, but steep levels of dissatisfaction should be expected during married life, and they may even be worse than anticipated during times of adult developmental transitions.

TRANSITION AND THE ORGANIZATION

Adult development creates problems for individuals and marriages, and for companies as well.

The most serious threat to the company is reduced productivity. In my opinion, 70 percent of the male work force in this country is of limited effectiveness by the age of 40. It's not that men are lazy or undependable, but that they are often simply not capable of adapting to their adult development.

During the 20s transition, for example, the predominant issue for just about every man is compliance versus rebellion. A man who joins an organization during his 20s tends to relate the authority of the organization to the authority of his parents. If he rebels, he is purposely directed into a nonessential role where the organization can contain him, and if he rebels vigorously, he is fired. If he's overly compliant, however, he surrenders some of his independence and limits his potential effectiveness. From my vantage point, however, organizations lose about 10 percent of their productivity through rebellious or overly compliant employees.

There are many men who cannot make friends and they don't have the ability to form relationships which are necessary in the 20s when a man must visualize his dream and begin to pursue it. He can't build a meaningful career by himself, and if he can't make friends in the company, he will be less effective. My estimation is that about 20 percent of productivity is lost by men who cannot be intimate.

In the 30s transition another 20 percent of men prove ineffective when they are unable to resolve their inner conficts of self. They lack the ability to establish goals, and they are simply not as productive.

And finally, about 20 percent of men don't successfully negotiate their 40s transition. Like Ted Banks in Chapter 1, they lack the know-how to switch from personal achievement to something more challenging and rewarding.

America's business community can obviously benefit from a clearer understanding of the "compleat adult," and in Chapters 7–10 we discuss specific tools and plans of action that companies can utilize to help their employees adapt and to help them maintain productivity.

SEARCHING FOR ANSWERS

Since the mid-1970s, at least, dozens of researchers have dedicated their time to helping companies and people negotiate an improved quality of life. An adult's most valuable skill, without doubt, is the ability to create a world in which he can live and work comfortably and enjoyably. We live in an age of tension, indecision, uncertainty, self-doubt, and depression. Sometimes it seems we are in a perpetual state of crisis. To free ourselves we pop pills, chew nails, overeat, overachieve, and quite frequently die prematurely. What we overlook, many of us—the college professor, the corporate executive, the line supervisor, the beautician, the dock packer, the housewife and mother—is that we have the power to release much of this tension and to prevent many of our crises. By grasping control of the environment, we can predict patterns in our lives.

It's only in recent years, however, that people have realized they can control the environment. In the 1950s, social ethics made it clear that people should conform, and rather than attempt to change anything people accepted the environment for what it is. In many cases they worked on their intrapsychic environments but still failed to adapt to the world. The 1950s are history now, and the men and women of the late twentieth century are "born again," so the climate is ripe for new perspectives on the quality of life.

For the most part, the fields of psychology and psychiatry, the media, and the public in general have all been unprepared for a thorough understanding of adult development, but now we find ourselves on the threshold of a radical vista, and we've got to take advantage of that potential. Levinson and his fellow researchers have inspired a turning point in modern psychiatry. In a sense, they have invented the wheel without anyone knowing how to use it.

Even if we understand what they have discovered, and we accept it, how can it be applied?

Some therapists have answered that question by dismissing the idea of what I believe to be a comprehensive theory of life, and that is a defeatist opinion. In my own search for a deeper understanding, I founded the Center for the Study of Adult Development (CSAD) at the University of Pennsylvania in 1976. Once I realized that therapy is a process of conversion to a belief system, I had to explore additional topics, and the Center has made that possible.

Frankly, our explorations at the CSAD have not provided all the answers, but we are convinced that it is sometimes more efficient and beneficial to provide structures and techniques of therapy that lead patients to solutions for their problems, rather than analyzing their problems historically with the hope of discovering solutions. In my opinion, and the opinion of my colleagues at the CSAD, analytical therapy is inflexible and actually prevents a patient from experiencing, first-hand, a solution for his problem. After years of intellectualizing a problem in analysis, a patient may eventually feel what's wrong with him, and he may suddenly see the issues that created his dilemma, but he won't necessarily know what to do. And if he asks his therapist, "What should I do?" his therapist will respond, "Well, what do you think you ought to do?" because analytical therapy does not tell a patient how to act. He's got to find that out on his own.

Therefore, a more effective method of therapy, in many cases, is to help patients discover goals or solutions so that intuitively they'll satisfy their problems. It's much better if the exploration of the problem is itself the process that leads the patient to his solution, and once he *feels* what's behind his troubles, he'll automatically know what to do! This is adaptive therapy.

A MODEL FOR ADULT GROWTH

At the CSAD we have always practiced adaptive therapy but to do so we have had to develop a model for adult growth. It has been known for years that throughout life people are constantly forced to adapt, not only to environmental events—the death of a parent, a change of careers—but to social, developmental events as well, and so growth represents a necessary process of change. But how *do* people change? We have answered that question by studying transitional times, which are really critical periods of growth that bring to the surface many of life's problems, and we have developed an initial process of six basic steps:

1. *getting in touch with feelings*
2. *scanning the environment*
3. *exploring alternatives*
4. *making a choice*
5. *acquiring skills*
6. *obtaining feedback.*

First, people get a *feeling* that is the result of an unfulfilled need, motive, or value. If a person is unhappy, there's a reason for it, but even before he can discover the reason he must *feel* unhappy. This may sound so basic that you judge it to be ridiculous, but many people, especially men, do not know how they feel. They've never stopped to consider feelings, or they are incapable of describing them. They may simply announce to a therapist or spouse, "I am depressed," but they won't have the slightest idea of what "depressed" means to them.

Feelings are so important that probably 50 percent of therapy begins with the exploration of feelings. *How do you feel? . . . What's not happening in your life that you want to happen? . . . How does that make you feel?* These are the kinds of questions that therapists often ask their patients during first visits. Once the therapist gets his patient to realize how he feels, he can begin to question why, and this exploration often leads to goals or solutions that may satisfy the feeling.

Naturally many adults don't need a psychiatrist to help them get in touch with their feelings. People can usually explore their own feelings and then isolate the barriers that create unhappiness, or failures that cause dissatisfaction, but the importance of surfacing feelings cannot be underestimated, and no one should feel ashamed if he's incapable of doing it alone.

Scanning the environment is the second step. What resources does an adult have to solve his problems? What environmental factors are causing or compounding problems? These are questions that should be asked as soon as feelings are clarified. Many people, of course, don't ask these questions either because they don't know they should or because they lack the skill to scan their environment. Without an accurate assessment of the environment, it is almost impossible to realize solutions to problems.

It should not be surprising that many people have problems with this step of the growth model. A person's cognitive model of the world is often so powerful that he may pay attention only to selected elements of his environment and overlook others, and as a result he lacks a lot of information, which makes it difficult for him to change. Sometimes it's a matter of people not knowing the truth about their environment, or they have gathered distorted or inadequate information. At times, people simply don't know how to gather information about their environment. But common sense dictates that the more a person understands about himself and what's around him, the more likely he is prepared to adapt successfully.

Many people are not cognizant of the *alternatives* for problem solving, and rectifying this is the third step of the adult growth model. Often a man will say to his therapist, "I just can't figure out what to do about my wife (or boss, child, lover). I can't please her . . . what do you think I should do, doctor?" Some doctors will respond, "What do you think you should do?" and reflect the problem back to the patient, silently assuming that the patient has within his repertoire all the alternatives to solve his troubles. That's a fallacious assumption. Sometimes, certainly, the patient *does* know the alternatives, or he has it within himself to produce alternatives, but he's reluctant to change. Most often, though, people just don't know what to do. There are usually plenty of alternatives, but people need to be made aware of them.

Many people freeze when they have to *make a choice*, the fourth step in the model. How do people make choices? What are the criteria and methodologies? Neither laymen nor psychiatrists know for sure. Making a choice is a struggle and often a lonely, painful process. Whether or not an individual is good at it depends on his ability to understand his alternatives. If he's stuck at one alternative, he'll probably never get to the next, and I have discovered that many people can be helped to make decisions if they realize that every alternative they consider can have positive as well as negative results. On an unconscious level a person feels that something bad will happen if he makes a certain choice, and it may. But there are short-range and long-range effects connected to any choice, if he just thinks about it. Even when people understand the short- and long-range effects they still hesitate to make a choice because they're afraid to take a risk. There isn't much that can be said to comfort someone who's afraid of risk except to say that if he doesn't decide, he's going to remain in an indecisive, frustrated mood. People need to know that regardless of which choice they make, even if it's a wrong choice, it can be OK.

Frequently people make choices that are novel—obviously if the solution had been tried before the person wouldn't have a problem!—and therefore they need to acquire certain skills to satisfy the choice. *Skill acquisition,* then, is the fifth step of the growth model.

In many lives skill acquisition is routine. When a student goes off to college he learns how to control his study habits and his social life; when a woman accepts a new job she prepares herself to meet the challenge; when a man retires he must learn how to remain active; and so forth. But just as people won't allow themselves to be aware of their feelings and goals, they won't allow themselves to consider alternatives for goals which they don't feel qualified to fulfill. People don't generally consider skill acquisition part of the decision-making process, and if they don't realize they can learn specific skills, regardless of their limitations, then they will not permit themselves to consider an alternative that requires skill acquisition. They'll be blocked from further growth and remain unhappy unless they discover other alternatives for which they feel qualified. Many people accept this as a way of life, convinced there's nothing they can do to control their environments or to change the direction of their lives, and that's really an unfortunate attitude.

The final step in the adult growth model is *obtaining feedback,* the least-utilized component of the change process. No one changes, consciously or unconsciously, without monitoring progress. To do this a person looks for internal and external information that gauges how well he's performing. Relevant information, however, is often difficult to discern, and without good feedback people tend to give up.

I'm reminded of a man who was extremely controlling and domineering at home. He and his family had many problems, so they sought family therapy. Typically, in the early phases of therapy, as soon as the wife and children begin to open up, everyone is furious with the man of the house. And for this particular man, that was a jolt. At the very time he thought he was getting closer to his family—by seeking therapy—he discovered that they were even angrier with him. At that point, without insightful interpretation of the feedback, the man determined that his family really didn't love him, when actually he was experiencing a step forward. Accurately interpreting the feedback is critical in the growth process, and many people just don't know how to do that.

This model of adult growth is the fundamental underpinning of the CSAD's adaptive treatments that take into account both the internal and external environments. Through its utilization we have discovered that individuals experience change at an accelerated rate and with a significantly reduced level of turmoil. With it in mind, we proceed to the following chapters where we explain some of the most useful adaptive treatments available today.

CHAPTER THREE

What Transition Are You In?

"Lives change and the course of life
is filled with discontinuities.
What at one point in time
appears to be mental illness
at another point in time
may appear quite adaptive."

GEORGE E. VAILLANT

We don't know when the first adult transitions occurred, but if Adam and Eve really existed, they experienced transitions, and so does every man and woman today.

Until this chapter we have used the word *transitions* to explain unstable stages of life, and these are age-related, developmental transitions, but there are event-related, nondevelopmental transitions as well. They include death, marriage, divorce, birth, job promotion, and similar events which require adaptation. In a sense, they are similar to developmental transitions in that they are emotion-bearing events of life, but they are not necessarily age-related. However, people commonly experience combinations of developmental and nondevelopmental transitions—promotion at midlife, for example—quite disconcerting. This being the case, we think it's a good idea for adults to prepare themselves for the challenge of their transitions.

It is almost certain that every transition can be successfully bridged. Developmental transitions, by Levinson's definition, are unstable stages between two stable eras of life, so with time they must pass. And most nondevelopmental transitions can be dissected into various subevents, which in turn can be resolved. In neither case is the process simple, nor is it painless, but the point remains that you *can* do something about your transitions.

Unfortunately many people pay little notice to their transitions and they actually complicate life for themselves. People need to understand that an unresolved developmental transition at age 20 or 30 will surface later in life, and with increased intensity. Someone who fails to meet the challenge of transitions when they occur may sidestep some of the anxiety and emotional conflict involved, but the second time around it will be much more difficult and painful. The older people get, the fewer options they have available for solving transitions, so it's better not to procrastinate.

Nondevelopmental transitions don't always reoccur in life (some people get promoted only once, or they change careers only once, or they experience only one birth in their family), but some of them occur frequently enough (moving, job hunting, death of a family member, making friends) that people help themselves if they learn how to adapt to these transitions. For a clearer understanding of nondevelopmental transitions they have been classified as Mini, Midi or Maxi, according to their complexity.*

MINI TRANSITIONS

Every time you meet a stranger you experience a Mini transition. It may occur in a matter of seconds, but it happens, and probably without your ever realizing it. When you break off a friendship you experience another Mini transition, and it may be a bit painful, but you probably don't recognize it as a transition.

The Mini transition is your style for entering or exiting relationships, and your knowledge of that style can be very beneficial. Some people make friends in a matter of seconds. By looking at another person or listening to him speak, some people know intuitively whether or not they'd like that person for a friend.

Other people need more time to develop friendships. Even when they recognize they want a particular person for a friend, they may not know how to attract friends, and the whole process is scary and complicated. Some people, as a matter of fact, are never able to make friends!

Similarly, some people can end relationships with a telephone call and other people can't. And it doesn't necessarily mean that if you make friendships easily you break friendships easily. Many

*Thanks to psychiatrist Charles Seashore for the use of these terms, taken from his presentation entitled *Coping with Stress and Transitions.*

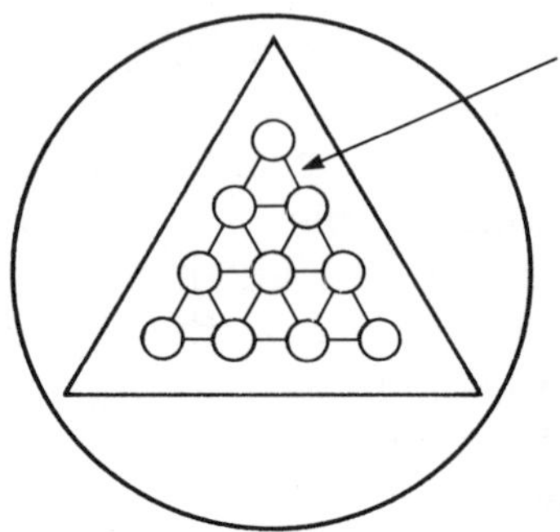

FIGURE 5. Mini transitions—the link between you and others.

people collect "bad" friendships simply because they lack the skill to end relationships. And even people who can end relationships often do it so clumsily that they alienate themselves from prospective friends.

The Mini transition is the least complicated of the three types, but for many people it is excruciating and for some it is impossible. Its importance, however, should not be underestimated.

In a longitudinal study of Harvard sophomores, George Vaillant discovered that the major difference between men who were considered psychologically mature and those psychologically immature was the quality of their friendship patterns.

Men with good friends get along better with their wives and children, they are physically healthier, they are less likely to use drugs and they consume less alcohol, they take more vacations, and they get farther ahead professionally, earning higher incomes. In general, they find their lives more satisfying.

People who can't make friends not only mature more slowly but usually feel lonely and are withdrawn. If you are such a person, you probably need therapeutic help, individually or in a group, because it is imperative that you make friends and it is almost impossible for you to learn to do so on your own.

Most people can make friends, but the level of pain that accompanies the ordeal of meeting new people and then building rewarding friendships with them often depends upon an individual's ability to regulate distance in relationships. At times you have to let yourself get close to another person, and at other times you have to withdraw. Certain people at certain times want openness and vulnerability from their friends, and at other times they need support from afar. And if you can't regulate distance, you probably aren't able to form meaningful relationships.

For married people this weakness presents a serious problem. There are times in every marriage when distance must be increased or decreased and the husband or wife who can't control distance will have difficulty getting through transitional times. Suppose, for example, that a wife has to go to school for a year before she reenters the work force. At times, by necessity, she will need to be more distant from her family. If her husband can't tolerate increased distance because it makes him feel insecure, he will fight her return to school and block her growth process, even though he may not realize what he's doing. He reacts this way not because he doesn't love his wife or disapproves of her desires, but because he simply cannot adapt to distance in their relationship.

The problem is just as bad when the couple needs to be close—during an economic pinch or a death in the family, let's say. Married people need to draw comfort, support, and energy from one another, and if one member can't provide closeness, the relationship can't be entirely rewarding. Fixed-distance relationships usually become sterile relationships and make very unsatisfying marriages.

The ability to regulate distance also improves your skill to terminate relationships. If you can't end relationships, you spend a lot of time with people you don't like or admire or enjoy, and this time keeps you from seeking quality friendships, an alternative you may not have ever considered. You probably don't feel the freedom to experiment with other relationships, but the company you keep makes you feel miserable much of the time.

Each person must judge his own friendship pattern, but some of the exercises discussed later in the book are intended to help you know when you need to make new friends and how to help yourself create a more rewarding circle of friends. This is not to say that the pain of making or breaking relationships will be reduced significantly, but getting through Mini transitions is a process that most people can improve.

MIDI TRANSITIONS

When a man is promoted to the next highest level in his organization, some of his peers suddenly become his subordinates and some of his superiors become his peers. At that time, as the man's position in the organization changes, so does his position in life, and he experiences a Midi transition.

When a housewife and mother of many years sends her last child to school and decides to work part-time, she changes her relationship with her husband and children, as well as her position in life, and she experiences a Midi transition.

In both of these instances the process of making the change from an old to a new or different role in life is a Midi transition.

Bridging Midi transitions, because it depends on the ability to make and break relationships, often requires the acquisition of new skills. If you don't know how to make new friends or to regulate distance in relationships, you are going to have problems every time you enter a situation that alters your position in life. At the same time, if you don't enrich your personal understanding and competency, you are asking for trouble.

Imagine that you are promoted without the ability to regulate distance. You would feel very lonely among your newly found set of peers and uncomfortable with your subordinates, and you might have problems exerting your qualities of leadership.

Similarly, a woman who enters the work world and is expected to manage without any formal training or introduction may find out that she's having more problems on the job than she can handle. She'll probably end up feeling awkward, unwanted, and incapable.

Men and women who learn to solve these Midi transitions diminish many feelings of self-doubt and loneliness, and they avoid more complicated issues.

While Mini transitions occur and may be resolved in a matter of seconds, Midi transitions require a minimum of three months, and

FIGURE 6. Midi transitions—changing your role or position in life.

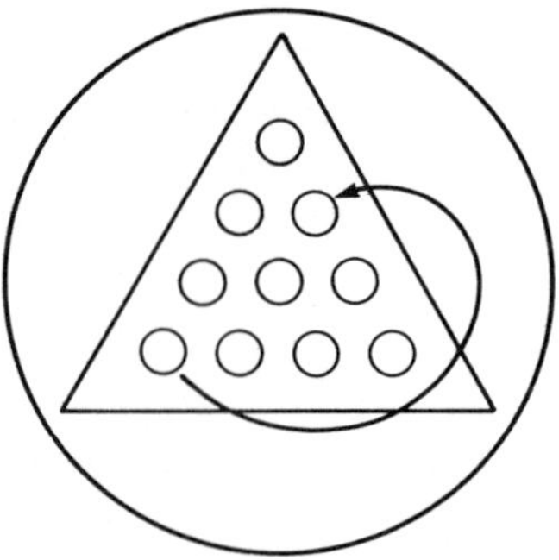

only after they last nine months is there reason to be concerned. When you accept a new job or added responsibilities at work, it may require three months to resolve the process of change that's involved, to understand your altered role in life, and to make new relationships. During this period it's natural for you to feel unsettled and hyper, and even depressed for a while, but if you meet the challenge of the transition, these feelings should not persist.

Depression is the most dangerous feeling during the Midi transition—or any transition—because it often causes people to doubt their capabilities and then give up without really trying hard enough or long enough. People who are depressed think they're feeling low because of their new position in life, but by surrendering too soon their depression often intensifies and leads to serious psychological illness.

Realize that during Midi transitions it's normal to undergo a period of unsettled nerves. You can't prevent it, but you can lessen the impact if you prepare yourself for the challenge of the transition. Many of the exercises presented in the next several chapters will help you get through your Midis.

MAXI TRANSITIONS

The most troublesome transition of all is the Maxi transition because it changes the meaning of life. It occurs when you move to a different environment, when a baby is born into your family, or when a member of your family dies. It happens when you change your style of living in any dramatic way.

When a 40-year-old man decides he's going to give up his business career and go teach in a college, or when a 32-year-old married woman decides she's going to quit managing her employer's office staff and have a baby, they are going to experience Maxi transitions.

The bottom line is meaning. "Is this what I want for myself? . . . Is this what I want for my family? . . . What does all of it mean?" Those are the forceful questions of a Maxi; without this change of meaning, the transition is a Midi.

Maxi transitions require at least eighteen months to resolve and frequently they require three or four years! During that time it is natural to feel empty and out of place and only your ability to

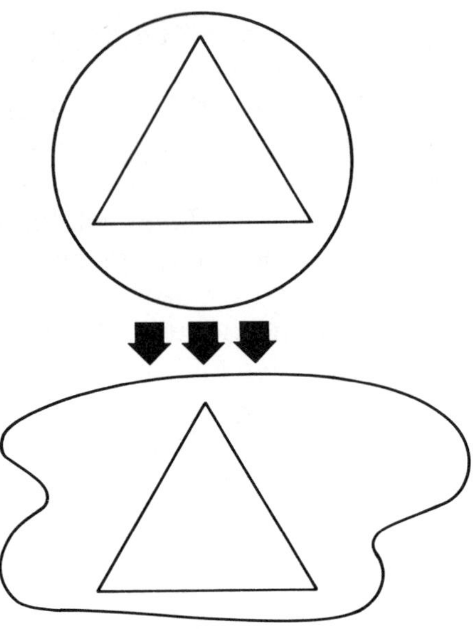

FIGURE 7. Maxi transitions—a change in setting or meaning.

bridge this transition can determine whether the experience will be prolonged and dreadful or relatively short and beneficial. The Maxi is torturous much of the time because it forces you to scrutinize the meaning of your life and it sometimes leaves you with the feeling that nothing at all has meaning for you. That attitude often leads to serious psychological or physiological illness, and sometimes both.

Developmental Transitions Are Maxis

Adult developmental transitions always reflect upon meaning and therefore are Maxi transitions, not illnesses!

The actual onset of an adult developmental transition is not as predictable as that of an event-related transition. Because people of the same age are at various levels of maturity, their adult developmental transitions may occur earlier or later, and sometimes significant external events occur which precipitate adult developmental transitions.

There are, however, some indicators for forecasting these transitions. If you sense less control and safety in your life, a change in your relationship with other people, or a speeding up or slowing down of your life time frame, then you are a likely candidate for an adult developmental transition.

Most of the transitions which we discuss in this book are Maxis, and the process of bridging each of them can be vastly improved through the exercises that are yet to come.

MONITOR YOUR BEHAVIOR PATTERNS

By now you've probably concluded that you and most people you know have experienced an infinite number of transitions. Most likely you have resolved the majority of your transitions without even knowing what you were doing, but that doesn't mean your transitions have been painless or easily resolved or that you have resolved them effectively. It does imply, however, that when you are conscious of your transitions you can control much of the difficulty that it takes to resolve them. As a matter of fact, you can do a better job of resolving your transitions if you monitor your behavior patterns during transitional times.

The next time a stranger enters your life, be aware of how you approach him and respond to him. Regardless of whether or not you'd like to become friends with him, mentally (or on paper) note your thoughts and reactions. What is your behavior pattern? Every transition is an opportunity for you to act out your behavior pattern which you began constructing very early in life. Whether you know it or not, the way you make friends today is influenced by the way you made friends your first day in grade school. You began to establish a pattern for making friends even before grade school, and since then you have added to that pattern and refined it until now it is a fixed and stable mode of your expression. You repeat your behavior pattern time and again. You probably relate differently to a child than you do to an adult, and differently to a middle-aged man than to a senior citizen, but those are variations of your behavior pattern and you rarely deviate from your mode of expression.

By charting behaviors you can predict your patterns for future transitions, be they making friends, moving to another city, finding a job, having a child, etc. It's important to analyze your patterns because you may discover that your behavior is preventing you from achieving desired results.

Also, analyzing behavior gives you an opportunity to consider alternative approaches for the various problems that arise in life, and so it is a basic step for improving your ability to resolve transitions more efficiently.

DON'T RESIST TRANSITIONS

People do try to run away from transitions, but it just can't be done. They seem to think it's easier to be miserable in the ways they know than happy in ways they don't. Habitually, they cling to their identity even when they are wrong.

Many people are convinced they're ugly, though very few people are. Intelligent people are certain they're ignorant even when evidence says they're not. Self-identity, as safe as it may be, is the number-one enemy of transitions. You can't grow mentally, emotionally, or spiritually if you're not willing to change your opinions of yourself at appropriate points of life.

For similar reasons people try to resist transitions because they think they're odd for wanting to be different. A man who wants to be a nurse may not pursue that goal if his environment won't support him—say, if he fears he'll be labeled gay. He'll conform to society and suppress his inner desire even when he knows the fulfillment of his dream is essential to his self-development.

Yet another reason for resisting transitions is lack of knowledge. "My father (or mother) never went through transitions so why should I think that I do?" is an oft-quoted remark, particularly regarding adult developmental transitions, which leave many people baffled and scared. Much of this resistance is beginning to erode, as researchers continue to probe the phenomena of adult life and share their findings with the media and general public.

Resisting transitions, for whatever reason, is senseless. It's like forfeiting an opportunity to get ahead, to create, to feel excited and satisfied. Transitions will change your life, with or without your consent, and if you want positive results, you must meet the challenge of transitions with a spirit of optimism and confidence and with the knowledge and skills that invite emotional maturity and growth.

YOUR LIFE CHART

Facing the challenge of transitions is easier when you know what transition you're in, but often that is the problem. You may have determined, from our discussion of Mini, Midi, and Maxi transitions, that you're in a transition, but some transitions are subtle, obscure, or camouflaged, and as such they are difficult to identify. They create problems without your ever knowing they exist.

If you recall our model of adult growth (see Chapter 2), which we said helps people adapt to change in life with greater ease, you'll remember that many people cannot get in tune with how they feel and so they lack the insight to quickly identify transitions. Even people who can pinpoint how they feel often say they are confused about life, or about what's bothering them in life, and so they too overlook some transitions.

One way to protect yourself from this problem is to evaluate the dimensions of your life. The best exercise for doing this involves constructing a Life Chart—a diagram of your life that provides a historical explanation of who you are, like the one shown in Figure 8. Anyone can draw a Life Chart, and everyone should. It takes about forty minutes. You need a large sheet of paper (at least 10 by 15 inches) ruled off in half-inch squares (You can buy graph paper in office supply stores or you can make your own.) and three marking pens of different colors.

Position the paper horizontally in front of you. Along the left-hand margin place a zero at the midpoint of the vertical axis. Above the zero, number up the vertical axis from +1 to +10. Below the zero, number −1 to −10. Then, across the bottom of the paper, number zero through whatever age you are now.

Now you're ready to plot the dimensions of your Life Chart: achievement, affiliation, and satisfaction.

Basically, *achievement* is related to sports, occupations, performance, and status. It is a sense of improving your competence and worth. Graduating from high school, finding a job, getting married, winning an award, climbing the corporate ladder, giving birth—all are achievements for certain people. Not everyone has the same sense of achievement.

Affiliation describes the nature and quality of your relationships with family, friends, and associates. What relationships do you have and of what quality are they? That's affiliation. It's possible to know many people and feel disappointed about your affiliations, and vice versa. The state of your affiliations is determined only by you.

Satisfaction is independent of affiliation and achievement, but it usually reflects those dimensions. Satisfaction answers the question "How content am I?" at any given point in life.

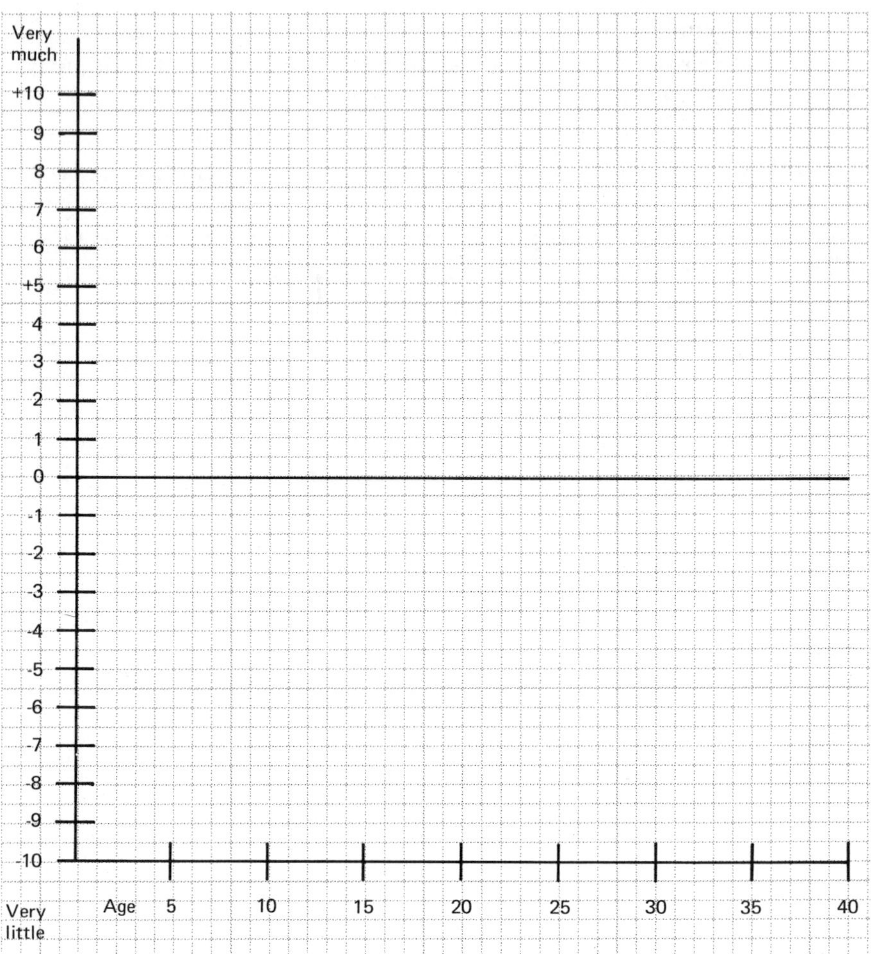

FIGURE 8. Life Chart.

Begin plotting your Life Chart from the left side of the paper. Ask yourself the question, "How would I rate my achievement at age *1*?" Try to remember as far back into your childhood as you can, but don't be concerned if you can't remember anything before age 4 or 5. Some people can remember how they achieved at age 2 or 3 and almost everyone has at least some idea of how they performed during the earliest years of life. Whatever your rating, plot it above the corresponding age on your chart.

If, for example, you believe your achievement at age 2 rated a +5, then mark a dot on the horizontal line across from +5 and above age 2. If at age 9 your achievement then fell to a −4, mark a dot on the horizontal line across from −4 and above age 9. Don't fret over these judgments; simply consider the question and make an evaluation. Then, with one of the marking pens, connect these two plot marks. Continue plotting your achievement until you reach your current age.

Then ask yourself, "How would I rate my affiliation at age . . .?" and plot that line with a different-colored pen. Finally, ask, "How satisfied was I at age . . .?" and plot that line with the third marking pen. Each of these lines should be a different color so that you'll be able to tell one from the other.

You could add a fourth dimension—power—but it's not necessary. Many of our corporate and organizational clients prefer to include this fourth line, and if you use it, ask yourself the question "How much power (to effectuate change) did I have at age . . .?"

ANALYZING LIFE CHARTS

It may be helpful for you to consider several Life Charts of people in various transitions. The following Life Charts belong to clients who have attended the Transition Planning Workshops sponsored by the Center for the Study of Adult Development in Philadelphia, and while names and certain incidents have been changed, the Life Charts are real in all other respects.

A Typical Thirties Transition

Susan Masters is a 32-year-old divorcee who came to our workshop depressed and frightened. She had grown up in a medium-sized midwestern town where her father worked as an accountant for a national corporation and her mother was "a typical housewife." Susan was the second of four children, her parents made her feel loved and accepted. She remembered that the first years of her life were rather happy. Her kindergarten experience was warm and eventful and in grammar school she performed well, earning "mostly As and Bs."

Then, at the age of 15, two disturbing events popped up in Susan's life. First, her father was promoted and her family had to leave the Midwest and all their relatives and friends for a large, eastern city; and second, she broke up with her boyfriend. "I wrote

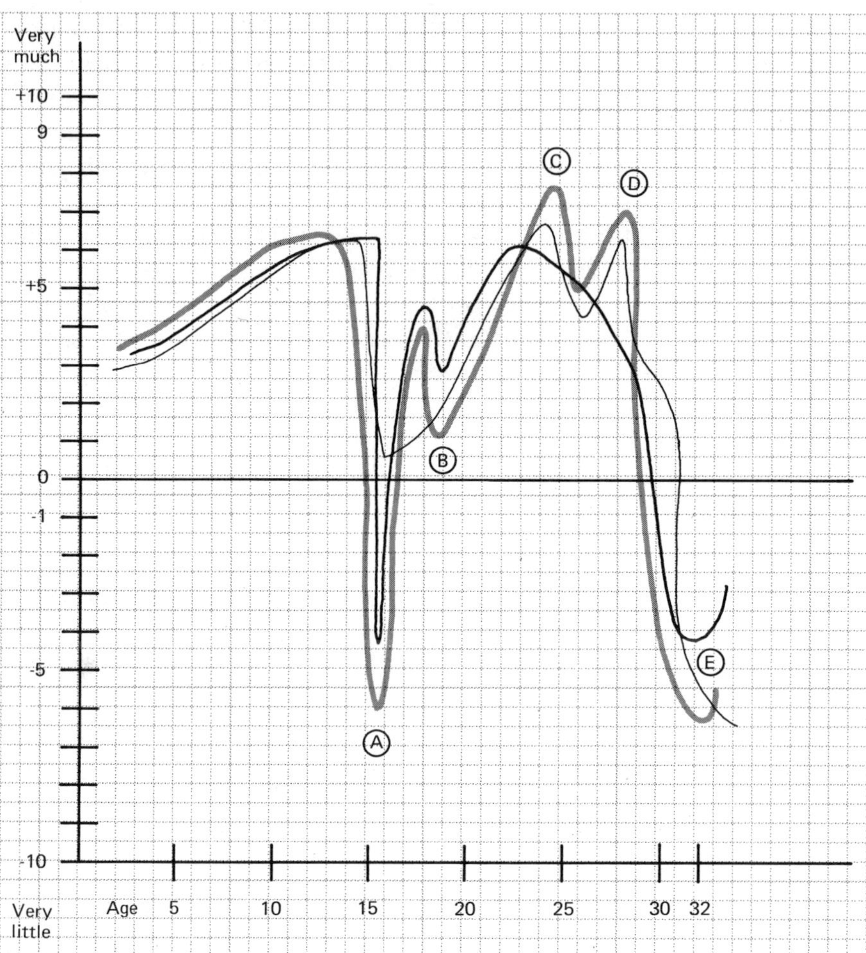

FIGURE 9. Typical thirties transition.

him for a long time after we moved," Susan said, "but it just wasn't the same. A lot wasn't the same after that move. My parents fought all the time, or so I thought; I didn't have any friends, my grades really suffered (point A) and I was miserable a lot of the time." At age 15, Susan rated her level of satisfaction a −6, her affiliation −4, and her achievement +1.

Eventually life got better for her. She found another boyfriend and her grades shot back up to normal, and her three lines responded accordingly.

In college Susan had an affair that was rather disappointing and she felt "hurt, then guilty once it was all over" (point B). He was the first man to sleep with her, and she thought they would get married after college, but then it just didn't work out.

She met other men, naturally, and right after she graduated she did get married and that represented a peak achievement in her estimation (point C), and it was soon followed by a second peak achievement: the birth of a son, Tommy. That gave her a tremendous burst of satisfaction (point D).

Not long after Tommy's birth, however, Susan's life began to deteriorate. She had worked, even before graduation, as a buyer in a department store, but once Tommy was born she became a mother full-time. That left her at home with a child and "a neighborhood full of older women" with whom she couldn't relate. "My husband was tied up in his career and he was going to graduate school, so he really didn't know what was happening. I tried telling him but I don't think he could understand. I was dissatisfied with our marriage and I got the feeling he wasn't very happy either. He was angry a lot and he made me feel worthless. I figured this was the way it had to be for a while, but then the truth came out. My husband told me he was sleeping with another woman and that was the end of our marriage" (point E).

At our workshop Susan was still dissatisfied with her life, but now also very confused. She had done everything right, she thought, and yet she was unhappy and angry, and she needed to know why.

From her Life Chart several observations were immediately noted: she was recovering from a divorce—a Maxi transition—but nothing was wrong with her personality. She could make friends and she could recover from transitions without a lot of difficulty (obvious from the rapidity with which her lines recovered and moved above the zero point). What she needed, essentially, was to get out into the world and redirect herself. The main issue was recovering from her divorce, and there was nothing in her background to suggest that she couldn't successfully adapt.

Adult Developmental Transition

A 41-year-old physician, Steve Stone, came to our workshop very unhappy with his life and "distrustful of therapy." He had grown up in Philadelphia, the oldest of three children, and his father worked in a hardware store while his mother was a schoolteacher.

As a child, Steve had been much closer to his mother, who was warm and nurturant and always praising Steve for his many accomplishments, while his father was very strict, often spanking the children for minor offenses. Steve remembered that his first nine years of life were relatively happy, but then he contracted tuberculosis, and his parents had to send him to a sanitarium for about a year (point A).

For six months Steve was miserable and lonely, and he resented his mother for not keeping him at home and caring for him. Once he met a friend, though, the remainder of his stay in the hospital "wasn't all that bad." He lost a year at school, however, and when he returned he was shy and reticent. But gradually his affiliations improved and his satisfaction shot up with his straight As.

At 19, while Steve was in college, he went through a miserable period when a girlfriend "dumped" him (point B). Later, though, he met his future wife, a registered nurse, and they married at about the time Steve graduated from medical school (point C).

Following his internship, Steve opened a private practice and for many years experienced a high, rewarding sense of achievement and satisfaction (point D). His relationship with his wife deteriorated slightly once they had children, but despite any problems at home Steve thought he had a fairly satisfying life. He was busy all the time, to the exclusion of his social life, but he loved his work.

Then, at about age 39, Steve lost his mother when she suffered a heart attack. He became depressed (point E), and nothing could draw him away from feeling that his life was stagnant. His relationship with his family worsened; at work he "just didn't seem to care." Finally, at his wife's urging, he went for therapy.

First once a week, then twice a week, Steve visited a therapist who focused on his sense of abandonment by his mother. For six months his therapy centered around that issue, but improvement was minimal. He was on three different antidepressants, and nothing seemed to help, until a colleague told him about the Transition Planning Workshop. Steve checked with his therapist who agreed to let him attend.

His Life Chart revealed a parallel between his mother's death and his earlier illness (point A), and that's why his therapist knew to focus on the issue of abandonment. But his therapist

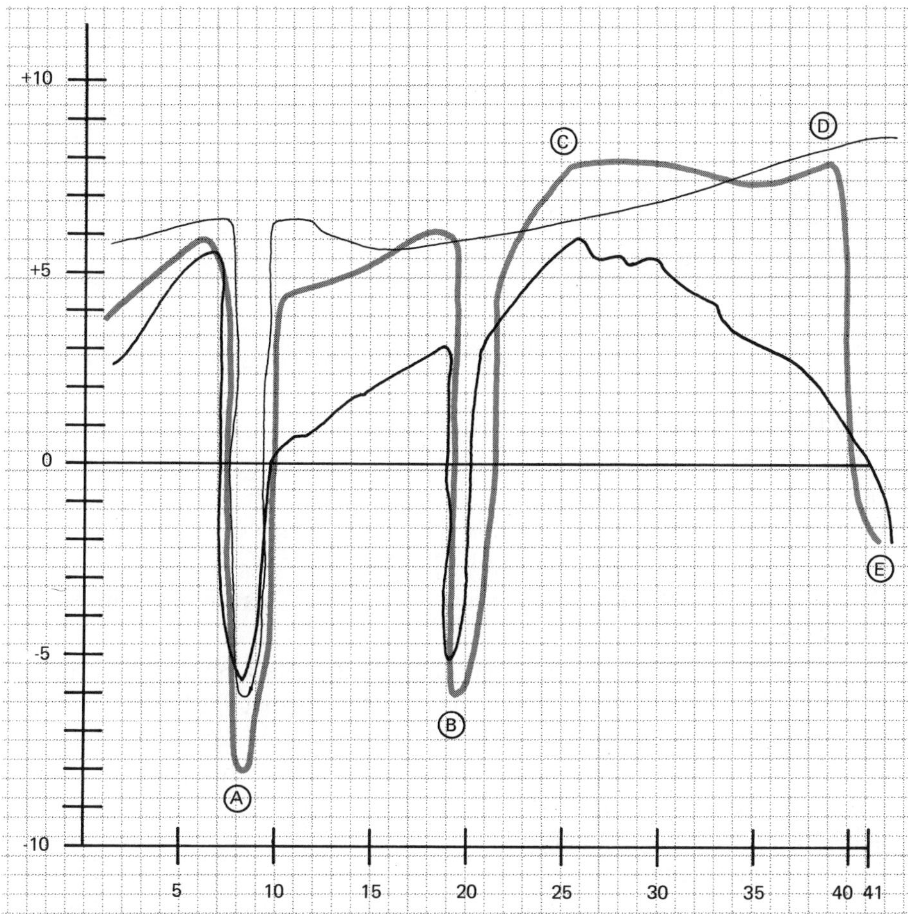

FIGURE 10. Adult developmental transition.

missed the issues of Steve's midlife transition. In many of Levinson's subjects, "marker events"—death, divorce, tragedy—initiated the midlife transition. In Steve's case, his mother's dying made death suddenly real to him, and it required some evaluation about the meaning of his life.

By focusing so much time historically, Steve's therapist had stolen from him the adaptive energy that was necessary to make the midlife transition. He needed to find intimacy and challenge. He needed to develop the latent qualities and components of his life which would provide him satisfaction once again.

In the workshop, without anyone saying a word to him, Steve's problem became obvious. He left individual therapy and joined a group session and within six months he had redirected his life. He spent about eight weeks with a career counselor and clarified his desire to work in a poverty clinic, which he later undertook with the support of his wife and children. One year after the workshop his satisfaction was at a +8 and his depression had vanished. He stopped in the center one day to say hello as he was taking his family on their first vacation in ten years.

External Trauma with Some Internal Component

Hawthorn Bydon III was the product of a stable and grave if somewhat socially fading southern family. His great-grandparents had been members of the southern aristocracy; his grandfather was a doctor; and his father, Hawthorn Bydon II, was a prominent attorney. At age 35 Hawthorn Bydon III was nervous, confused, and depressed. His employer referred him to our Transition Planning Workshop.

On the weekend, Hawthorn plotted his Life Chart. Until first grade he had considered himself happy, but after that he never did well in school (point A) and his opinion of himself changed. "I just wasn't as smart as my two brothers," and in fact his IQ tested at only 110. However, he had two saving graces. He was a natural athlete, and he was likeable.

"I was a star runner, and I was very well coordinated, so I played a lot of football and baseball and everybody liked me. I was the local hero. I got a sports scholarship to a local college and I played well there, too, but I was never big enough to play pro ball."

Three years after college graduation Hawthorn married "a girl I knew all my life." At the time he worked for a national company with a branch office in the South. He was a salesman, a good one, and by the age of 33 he was promoted to regional sales manager, which meant he had to move to Philadelphia (point B). That's when his serious troubles began.

His wife was unhappy in the North, and she finally returned home with their two children. On the job, Hawthorn wasn't in control and was upset a lot. "I just couldn't get the hang of it. There

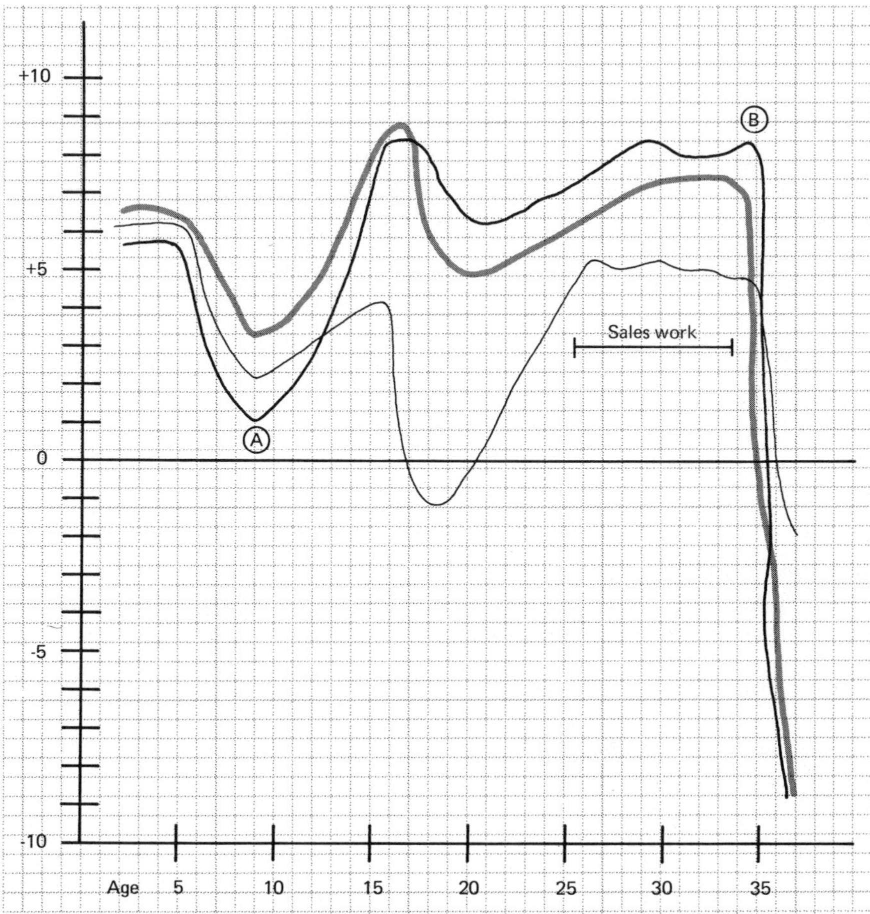

FIGURE 11. External trauma with some internal component.

was so much to do that sometimes I just didn't know where to begin." He became progressively unhappy, and that's when he was referred to the Center for the Study of Adult Development.

Obviously Hawthorn was in two Maxi transitions (geographic move and wife/children leaving him) and a Midi transition (promotion) as well. His life was changing in many ways, he was confused about what it all meant, and he felt he had neither the time nor the know-how to figure it all out.

Working with people he didn't know was apparently a problem

for him because in a familiar environment he was usually fairly satisifed (his satisfaction line dropped below +4 only once prior to his move North). Adding to his troubles were the facts that he had lived in the shadow of his family—never developing an independent sense of self-worth—and had never before managed people.

During the course of the workshop Hawthorn made a decision to remain in Philadelphia and adapt to his new environment. He went into individual therapy to help him negotiate his wife's departure and also enrolled in a management training course.

Within six months his work performance improved and he realized that he liked being away from his parents' shadow. One year after the workshop his satisfaction was higher "than any point in the last ten years."

Early Life Trauma

Douglas Menton was a 23-year-old graduate student in psychology when he came to the Transition Planning Workshop. He had grown up in a large industrial city and was the product of a broken family. His parents had separated when he was 4 years old (point A). A year after the separation his parents got back together, but they never got along. "My father drank a lot, and he was violent sometimes," Doug recalled, saying that he had often seen his mother "black and blue." To Doug, his mother was a "depressed and haggard woman" and he didn't consider himself close to either of his parents, or to his younger sister for that matter.

Despite problems at home, Doug was a gifted student and athlete. He was bright and tested well, and he continued his stellar performance right into college (point B).

He had many friends, but he never talked with them about his personal problems, and he said he didn't feel close to anyone. "Anyone who likes me can't really be worth a damn," he thought. Generally speaking, Doug had been dissatisfied since the age of 4, and he lived with an enduring sense of deep anxiety.

Without a doubt, Doug had an intrapsychic problem that would require in-depth therapy. Both his enduring sense of dissatisfaction and his lack of response to environmental change showed a disordered person, desperately in need of help.

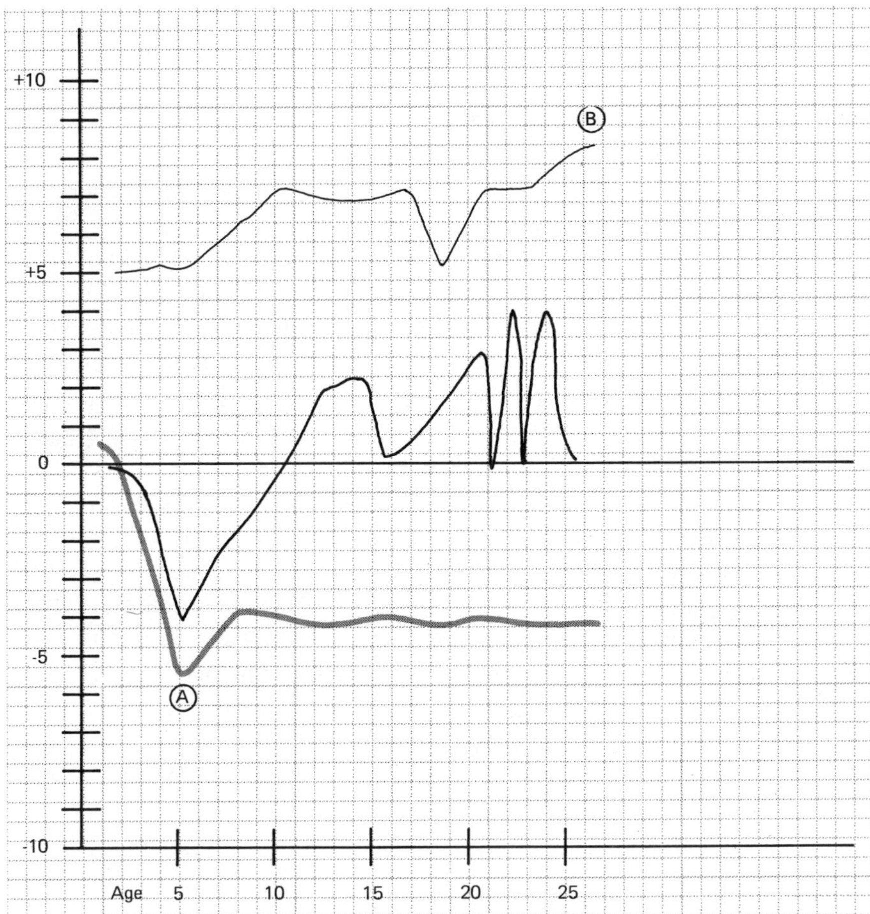

FIGURE 12. Early life trauma.

During the workshop, however, Doug experienced a sense of closeness "unlike anything I can remember." He found the people in the workshop sensitive and warm to him, and that helped him formulate some ideas about his own self-worth. Later, he lost that sense of closeness to the group, but he was on his way to a better life. We referred him for intensive psychotherapy, and about nine months after the workshop his satisfaction had advanced beyond the zero point.

You may or may not have identified similarities in your own life and the preceding case histories. They are examples of common patterns which we've observed at the Center, but they may not relate to you now or in the future. What's more important is your Life Chart, and hopefully you will take time now, or in the immediate future, to construct your own.

Once you have, take a look at the satisfaction dimension of your chart. That line reflects your level of life satisfaction or dissatisfaction, and it is often the most revealing. If the line follows your achievement line, you derive satisfaction from achievement; if it follows your affiliation line, then you get satisfaction out of affiliations. It may also follow both the lines, and in that case your satisfaction derives from both dimensions.

Possibly your satisfaction line takes a course of its own and ignores the paths of affiliation and achievement. If the satisfaction line is declining, there's possibly some external, environmental issue taking place in your life. Trace the line back to its peak—what happened at that peak in your life? It was the beginning of your dissatisfaction. If no obvious environmental event occurred at that point, then you may be in an adult developmental transition, and your problems are related to your age.

If your satisfaction line is chronically below the zero point, you may be suffering from some intrapsychic problem that will require psychotherapy. For most people, however, that is not the case.

If your satisfaction line is ascending to your present age, that indicates you are adapting. You were in a transition, but now you're on your way out and you've probably solved your problems. Knowing what you did can be helpful in future transitions!

In some Life Charts the satisfaction line reflects achievement and then suddenly switches course and follows affiliation. This is common among men and women. We have found that between the ages of 18 and 22, a man begins to derive more satisfaction from achievement than affiliation, but then some men, at about the age of 40, reverse that direction again and seek more affiliations than achievements. A woman's line of satisfaction seems to reflect affiliations until about the age of 35, and then sometimes achievement becomes more of a critical motivation.

The Life Chart is a perfect exercise for scanning your internal environment, which you may recall is part of step 2 in our model for adult growth. Once you've constructed your chart you should discover a pattern in your life, and it should help you fit many of the pieces of your life into context.

GOAL SETTING

Another good exercise for scanning the internal environment is goal setting, which helps people determine their source of dissatisfaction by looking at what they want from life.

Plot your Life Chart first, then try to set some goals. But get yourself into an appropriate mood. Relax. Find a quiet spot, sit down, and close your eyes and just breathe calmly for a few moments. Then ask yourself the question, "What do I want to do in my lifetime?"

Now don't be afraid to jot down whatever thoughts come to your mind. If you want "to be a millionaire," "solve marital problems," "buy a farm," "live abroad," whatever, put it on paper. No one else is going to see this list of goals, so let go of your identity and be honest.

Some of the goals people have listed during our workshops include:

- *learn a better method for discovering my talents*
- *improve my relationship with my spouse*
- *improve my relationship with my children*
- *become more assertive*
- *become a better decision maker*
- *become an independent person*
- *find a job or career*
- *gain some insight to myself*
- *plan my career*
- *make many friends.*

Try to be as specific as possible in listing your goals. It's OK, as many of our clients have said, to desire more insight about yourself, but to what end? Is it to explain why you're unhappy in your marriage? Or why you haven't been promoted?

The more specific your goal, the better, but don't get stuck during this exercise. List any goal that comes to mind.

Writing out your goals forces you to consider your expectations. You had to feel a need before you could recognize a goal. That need may be a dream, a desire, or a whim, but it is real to you and if you realize it as a goal, then it becomes a possibility.

Occasionally we've had clients who were not able to conceptualize goals, but this has happened only rarely, and in those instances the people were frightened of their expectations. They didn't think they could accomplish them, and that's a natural judgment, but hopefully that's not a problem for you.

As soon as you have listed several goals, assign a number of importance to each. Use a scale of 1 to 5, with 1 being minimally important, 3 moderately important, and 5 very important.

Some people try to change everything at once, and that's virtually impossible, so they become discouraged and give up. As a result, they become depressed. So if you assign values to your goals, you can then work on one goal at a time.

This process of goal setting should help you establish direction for your life, but you can also relate these goals to your Life Chart. Has your past life been directed toward reaching any of your goals? If not, that may explain why you are dissatisfied!

In this chapter, hopefully, you have learned to improve your ability to feel and to scan your internal environment. In the next chapter we'll explore ways to help scan your external environment—the component of life which often gets overlooked.

CHAPTER FOUR

Scanning Your Environment

"It is the function of the social character
to shape the energies of the members of society
in such a way that their behavior
is not left to conscious decisions
whether or not to follow the social pattern
but that people want to act
as they have to act and at the same time
find gratification in acting according to
the requirements of the culture.
In other words, the social character
has the function of molding human energy for
the purpose of the functioning of a given society."

Erich Fromm

Society consistently teaches people to be self-critical. From the moment a child begins to understand he is taught to turn inward to improve himself and his lot in life. "Think about what you're doing before you do it," parents tell their youngsters. Then once in school, teachers reinforce this self-examination when they say, "Don't worry about the other children, worry about yourself!"

By the time some children become adults they are so internalized that they never think to inspect their external environments for the cause of a problem. This is a time-honored coping strategy that works in some instances, but like any strategy, at the wrong time it is self-defeating. People must stop thinking they can't control their external environments. They can!

Following are several methods that will help you scan your external environment.

YOU TELL ME, I'LL TELL YOU

Most people know a variety of information which they never reveal, and for different reasons. Sometimes the information is purposely concealed because it's privileged—let's say to a family or an organization—but at other times the information is withheld because no one has ever asked for it. Often the format of exchange controls the flow of information, and the person who develops a network for information sharing is at an advantage.

In many cities across the country, *networking* is an operative word, particularly among women's groups. Networks vary from the 900-plus Washington Women's Network, a class of professional women in the nation's capital, to less formal, smaller groups of men and women who get together periodically to exchange information. The emphasis is on exchanging information.

Networks are not social groups, though they are a form of social activity, and they are not mutual-aid societies. They provide a forum for the exchange of information and at the same time offer support and opportunities to members.

A network may begin on a one-to-one basis by simply approaching someone in your company or neighborhood and sharing concerns. This often leads to revealing information that may be of use to you. More practically, however, a network ought to include at least a half-dozen members who share common interests but who are not in direct competition with one another. (No two members should work at the same occupation or within the same department, perhaps.) For example, a group of writers might get together to talk about ideas, proposals, contracts, editors, etc. Or a group of businesswomen might meet to discuss common problems and career opportunities. Or housewives might form food co-ops or babysitting circles.

By this method you establish a network of people who agree to provide one another relative information. Allies supporting each other is the idea.

HISTORY TAKING

Whenever you're confused by an environmental problem, one of the easiest and quickest ways to understand what's happening is to take a history. This is similar to plotting a Life Chart except you are now examining an event or series of events, and not a life. History taking could have benefited the zone engineers at the oil refinery in Chapter 1. By this method they would have expanded their frame of reference to clearly identify the forces in the external environment that were creating their problems.

If your job is bothering you, begin your history taking by locating the person who held the job before you. Compare notes with that person and find out if his feelings in that job were similar to yours. Was he frustrated? If so, why?

Then, what were his responsibilities? Find out how those responsibilities may have been changed through the years. Has the relationship of your job to other jobs in the company been altered in any way? Has the authority of the job been increased? Has it been diminished? The answers to these questions may point to the cause of the problem you're experiencing.

An excellent example of how jobs are changed by the external environment occurred in the mid-1970s when Congressman Wayne Hays of Ohio was stripped of the chairmanship of the House Administration Committee. You may remember that the congressman's mistress blew the whistle on him, and that was the end of his long career in Congress. It was also the end of a silent but powerful committee chairmanship.

Eventually some congressman may be appointed to that committee chairmanship without realizing how the committee traditionally operated. As a result, he's going to be frustrated and possibly ineffective. For years the congressional bureaucracy in the House of Representatives revolved around the power base of Wayne Hays's committee, and the loss of that power distorted the balance of the bureaucracy. If some future chairman should try to expand his power base, he will be challenged by his colleagues, and even they may not know why they're reacting so strongly, but they will be irritating to the chairman. Until the chairman identifies the history of his colleagues' resistance, he's going to be troubled. He won't necessarily have to expand his power base to be more effective, but he will need to restore the bureaucratic balance.

History taking is also useful to families. Members of a family frequently withhold information simply because they haven't been asked for it, or they're afraid of hurting another member's feelings. But when the balance of the family is distorted—perhaps when the father accepts a new job or the mother goes to work full-time or Grandma moves in—people are going to be unhappy. By asking each family member for his interpretation of what went wrong within the family, a solution often becomes obvious.

OUTSIDE OBSERVERS

A person's lifestyle—his approach to friendships, the way he rears his children, his attitudes about sex—is usually the product of folk wisdom. "Your children will treat you the way you treat your parents," "Clothes make the man," "First impressions are lasting impressions," "You can't tell a book by its cover," and other such gems of knowledge influence lives and sometimes create turmoil.

Asking a friend to observe your lifestyle—or to listen to your explanation of your lifestyle—is an effective methodology for problem solving. An outside observer can frequently discriminate the relevant environmental variables in your life because he's naïve when it comes to your belief system. Think of a friend (or a couple) who is close to you—someone you know pretty well—and ask yourself, "What's really causing his (or their) unhappiness?"

It doesn't take long to answer the question, does it? It won't take your friends long to answer the same question about you. They're not always going to be correct, because they may not be aware of certain psychological issues or other environmental forces in your life, but they can often lead you to discoveries that will help you redirect your life.

Exchanging this kind of information can be risky, of course, and people seldom use it. But if you can trust a person to tell you what he sees wrong with your lifestyle, and not resent the person afterward, you will find this exercise to your advantage.

EXPERTS

Experts comprise another grouping of outside observers, but they're usually not friends. Businesses and marriage partners consult experts in times of crises or at the onset of potential crises. Experts in business and marriage are often able to identify a variety of environmental variables that are so subtle they are overlooked. Experts have the knowledge and training to question employees, or husbands and wives, without alienating them or otherwise making matters worse. As paid professionals, experts are usually more effective than ordinary outside observers, and they can readily be located through the Yellow Pages of a telephone directory.

Social support is a second determinant of human behavior, equally as forceful as belief systems, and its presence in your life is critical to your maturity and physical well-being, as we'll discuss in Chapter 7. You cannot make transitions without social support, or at least you can't do so without a lot of suffering, and the Social Systems Map is your guide to personal social support. It shows how you are supported in the four major quadrants of life—family, friends, work, and community (including religion and leisure)—and it can be constructed in a matter of minutes.

We have provided the Social Systems Map structure (Figure 13) so you can plot your map as you read along. Think of yourself as the intersection of the quadrants and in some or all of the quadrants there may be people who affect your life. Remember, you may not have people in every quadrant of your life.

The idea is to identify the people in your quadrants and position them on your map with a dot. The closer you feel to a person, regardless of how the person feels about you, the closer you should position that person to the intersection of the quadrants. Use initials (or titles/relationships) to identify each of the dots.

If you have a relationship with someone in more than one quadrant—say, for example, that you and your boss are tennis partners—then position that person in both the community and work quadrants, and connect the two dots with a line. By the way,

FIGURE 13. Social Systems Map.

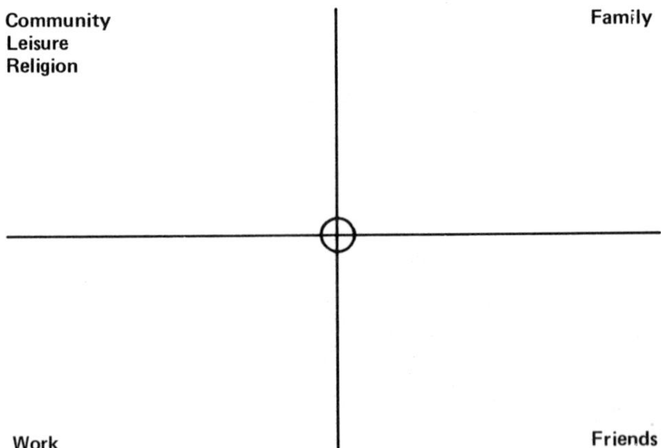

the people in your community quadrant are not necessarily friends. Friends are people with whom you discuss your personal life, and people in the community are sometimes acquaintances whom you see at church or whom you visit occasionally for a drink or to play cards.

As soon as you have positioned the people on your map, draw a circle around the inner core of your group so that your map resembles Figure 14. Your inner circle may or may not resemble the one in the figure, and that's not at all important. Your inner circle should reflect the people who have the greatest influence upon your identity. Supposedly people don't need other people to tell them who they are, but in fact that's another myth of adult life. All people are subject to and influenced by the opinions and actions of others, especially when they are close.

Consider the lives of Lee and Ann who had married right after they completed business school and were now in graduate school. They were both competitive and anxious about their studies and they were often critical of each other's mistakes on examinations and in classroom settings. Their Social Systems Maps looked like the map shown in Figure 15.

Each had tremendous impact on the other's identify—without knowing it, of course—and so they were making each other feel horrible. Their marriage deteriorated, and so did their performances at school. The cycle they were caught in is illustrated in

FIGURE 14. Sample Social Systems Map.

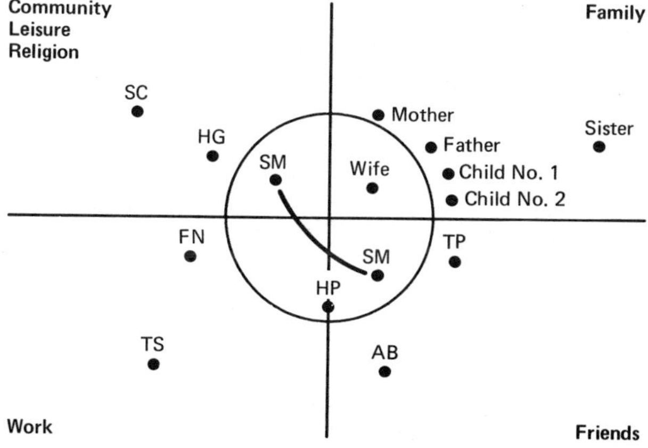

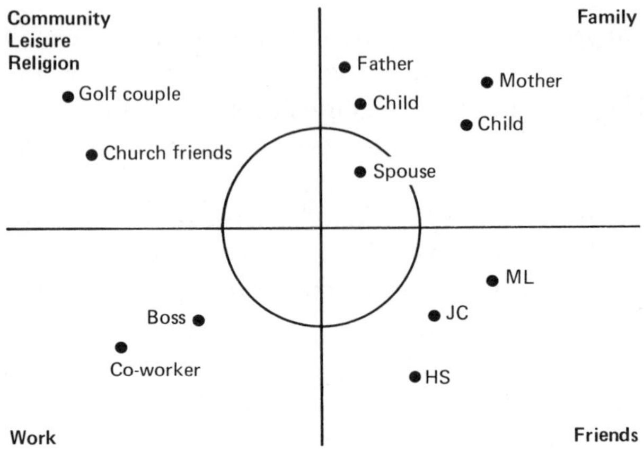

FIGURE 15. Lee and Ann's Social Systems Map.

Figure 16. Not only were they putting each other down, but they were participating in a "closed dyad," which was inescapable without their conscious effort.

Closed dyad disease, as it is called, occurs when the inner circle includes just one other person, usually the spouse. This makes a marriage inflexible because as soon as one partner needs to change or develop, the other partner resists. Why? Because all his (or her) security—identity—comes from one person: the spouse. People don't like uncertainty, and so it's natural to resist change, even if it's positive, but closed dyad disease makes it extremely difficult for a marriage to be adaptive. It is not, contrary to what many people believe, the *ideal* marriage.

FIGURE 16. Closed dyad cycle.

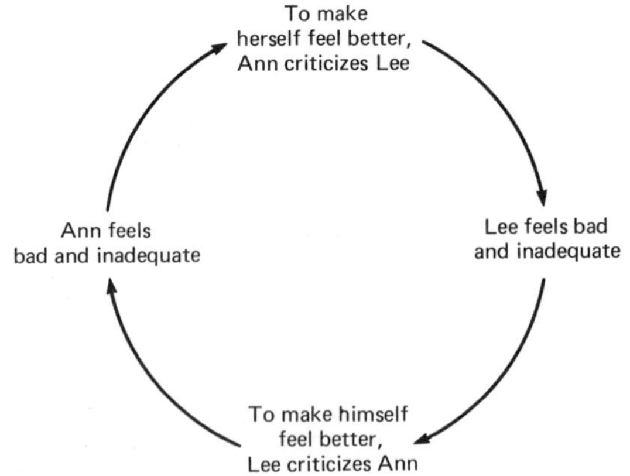

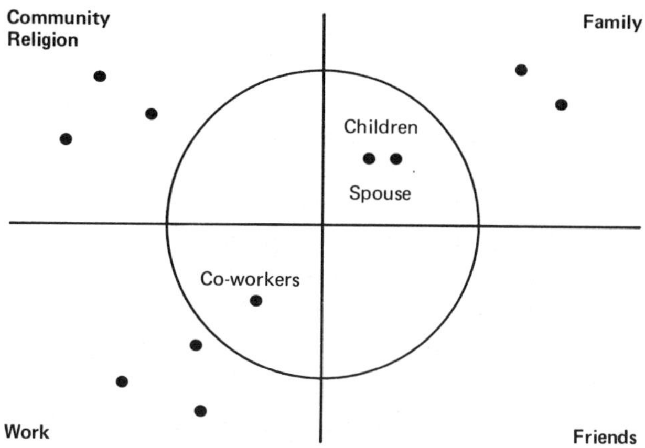

FIGURE 17. Margaret's Social Systems Map.

We did say that not all of your quadrants will necessarily include people. For example, Figure 17 (above) illustrates the Social Systems Map of a client we'll call Margaret. Notice that her friends quadrant is empty, and that's an indication of what her problem might be. She complained of loneliness and a feeling of stagnation and said she couldn't understand it because she was happily married with several children and "always on the go." Still, she thought something was missing in her life.

Obviously she needed friends, but she had difficulty meeting people. Until she put someone in that quadrant, however, she was going to continue feeling lonely, so she knew how to begin working on her problem. If this is similar to your Social Systems Map, ask yourself why that particular quadrant is void of people, then start to do something about it.

Remember, you have the right to bring new people into your social systems, or inner circle, as well as move them out. It is *your* life. Structure your social support to enrich your life, not to impoverish it.

FORCE FIELD ANALYSIS

One of the most popular and useful exercises for scanning your external environment is force field analysis, developed by the late social psychologist Kurt Lewin. This tool helps you conceptually define and clarify the forces that work against you in life, and it's enormously valuable during a transition.

People are used to thinking in single-force causations: "The reason my wife left me is because she's selfish." "The reason my boss won't give me a raise is because he's tight with money." And so on. But the world is more complicated than that, and when people can't understand it they tend to simplify it by generalizing. Force field analysis, however, takes a complicated situation and dissects it so that its simplification is specific and accurate.

In any situation a combination of two sets of forces tends to alter the situation or hold it stagnant. For example, imagine that you want to switch careers. On either side of the issue there will be a set of forces. Let's call those on the left the *pro forces*—they want you to switch careers—and those on the right the *con forces*—they want you to stay put. At all times the forces are pushing at each other (see Figure 18), and you're caught in the middle where you feel encouraged some days and discouraged other days. If the pro forces are stronger than the con forces, eventually you're going to

FIGURE 18. Force field analysis chart.

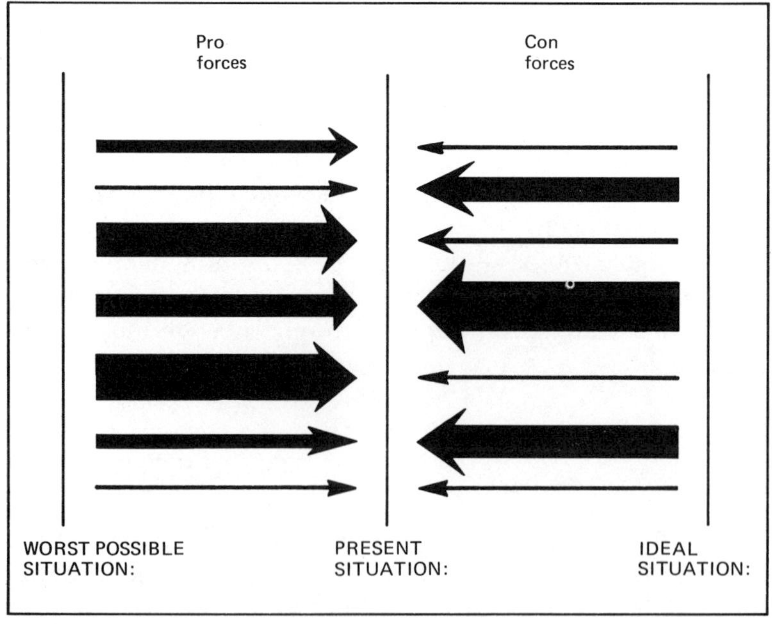

find another career, but the con forces might win out and your goal will have to be suppressed or you will continue to suffer.

In life, the con forces often *are* stronger, or they appear to be stronger, and they create countless problems both psychologically and physically. You could eliminate much of the stress and frustration of solving problems if only you broke down the components of the situation and analyzed each of them independently. That's force field analysis!

A man in one of our workshops said he was having trouble finishing his Ph.D., and he thought he might have some psychological desire to fail at life, so he wanted to know what was wrong with him. His Life Chart showed no pattern of failure, however, and the force field analysis chart he built looked like Figure 19.

His present situation, as you can see, is that he's enrolled in a Ph.D. program. His ideal situation, his goal, is to earn the degree; the worst possible situation, of course, is to fail the program. The forces involved, represented by the arrows, are of various sizes and weights. Those pushing away from the ideal are the con forces and those pushing toward the ideal are the pro forces.

Each of the con forces has been identified: lack of money, lack of time, a critical, nonsupportive adviser, and lack of a dissertation topic.

FIGURE 19. Sample force field analysis chart.

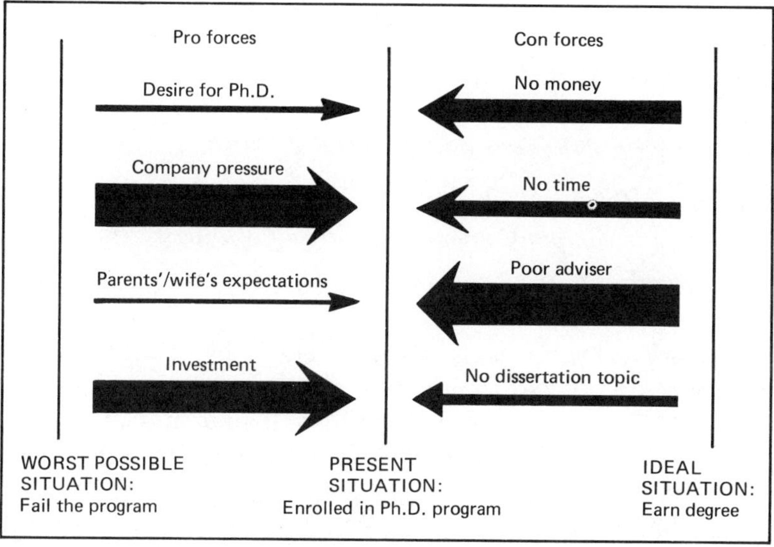

The pro forces are his desire to earn a Ph.D., his company's insistence that he complete the program, his parents' and wife's expectations of him, and the amount of time/money already invested.

People often try to achieve their goals by adding more pro forces, and sometimes that produces change, but usually it just adds more tension. It causes the con forces to shorten and fatten, and eventually they may snap and make matters even worse. More often a better strategy is to eliminate the con forces.

Every force is either changeable or unchangeable (labeled C or U in the illustration) and those that are changeable—lack of money, lack of time, lack of a dissertation topic—can be eliminated.

Our client can borrow money, perhaps, or apply for a grant or scholarship; he can rearrange his time to better suit his needs; he can certainly come up with a dissertation topic if he gets some encouragement and support and spends some time thinking about it.

Of all his restraining forces, only a critical, nonsupportive adviser is unchangeable, and it's even possible that he could do something about that if only he investigated the possibilities.

By eliminating some and preferably all of the con forces, our client makes progress toward his goal and gains an increased sense of control over his life. He'll feel motivated to do something about his situation and he'll feel better overall.

In this case, our client's decision was to begin by eliminating the restraining force represented by lack of money. He developed a strategy and decided to:

1. *go to a local bank and inquire about a loan*
2. *ask his parents if they could lend him some money*
3. *consult his company's personnel office for a loan*
4. *consult the school's financial aid adviser.*

To his surprise, his strategy worked. The bank granted him a loan and his parents offered to advance him a small amount of money. The school's financial adviser didn't have loan money available, but he did arrange a tuition reduction in exchange for a few hours of work/study time.

Time had been a con force as well, but his company offered him the opportunity to work three-quarters-time, at full-time pay, providing that he remained with the company for at least one year following graduation.

Once the financial pressure was lessened, the other con forces were easily eliminated—even his adviser became supportive—and our client graduated eighteen months after the workshop.

There's nothing magic about force field analysis, and it doesn't work in every situation. It's valuable because it takes a complicated problem and displays it in easily understandable terms. It then points the way to factors that are changeable, but it's up to the individual to follow through and make the necessary alterations.

PROGRAM EVALUATION AND REVIEW TECHNIQUE (PERT ANALYSIS)

Quite often, people can't follow through. Even when they clearly see the pro and con forces at play in a given situation, people still have trouble solving the problem, and so there's another exercise which is extremely helpful during times of transition and problem solving. It's called PERT (program evaluation and review technique) analysis.

PERT analysis, developed by the United States Navy Special Projects Office in 1958, is frequently used as a management tool in industry. In an abbreviated form it has some applicability in day-to-day life.

While force field analysis helps clarify all the conflicting forces in a given situation, PERT analysis helps you zero in on one or two con forces and eliminate them.

People often need help working through a problem that includes a series of steps and related activities. They can usually advance from one step to the next—from A to B, let's say—but when they have to mentally juggle a series of steps and related activities, the process becomes jumbled and frustrating. At that point, when people are most confused, they tend to give up without solving the problem. PERT is a useful tool in this regard because it not only makes concrete plans but it also provides direction and it can be used to provide social support and feedback, two of the essential steps necessary for adult growth.

PERT analysis sounds difficult and is a bit time-consuming,

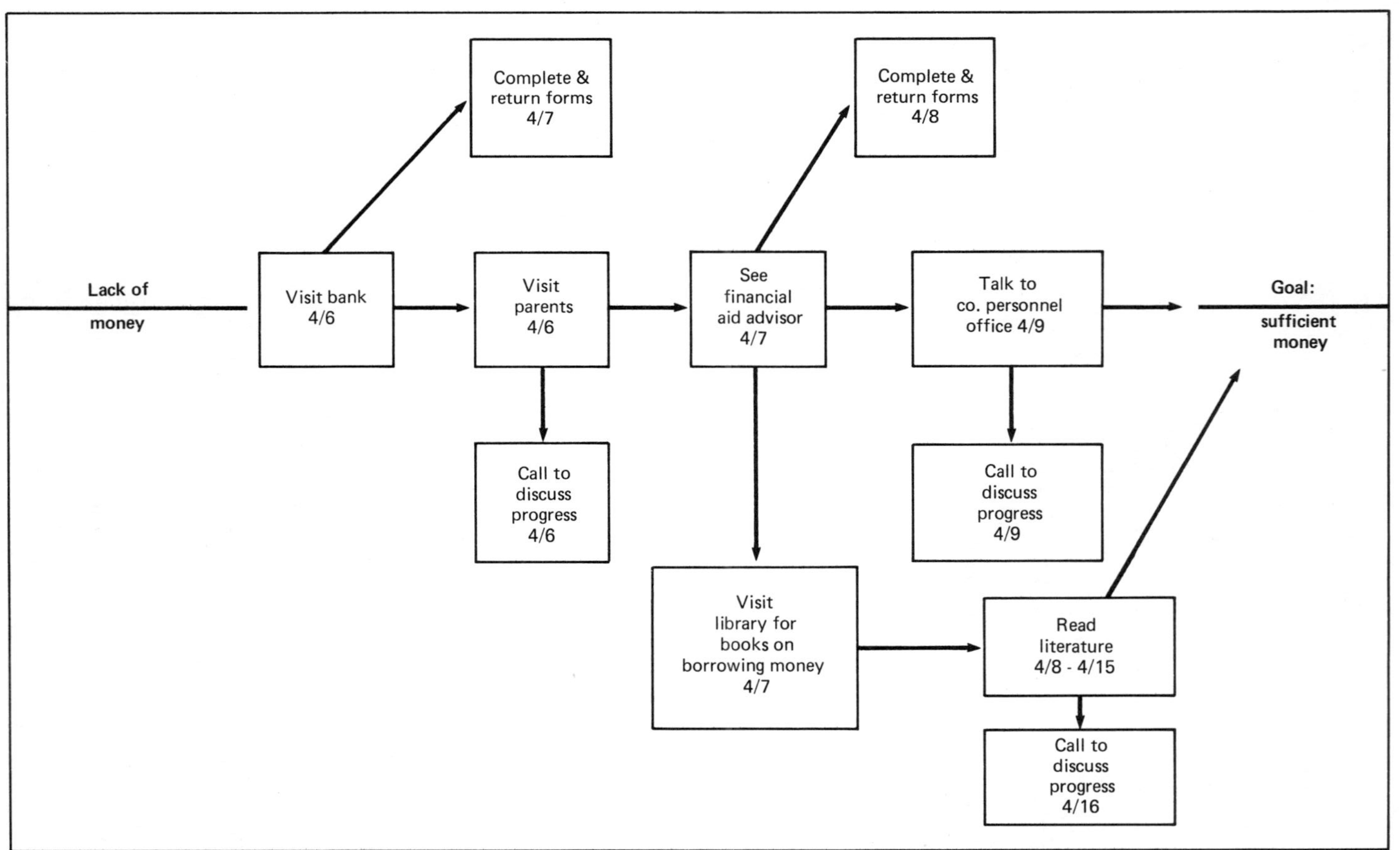

FIGURE 20. PERT analysis chart; circles represent events at stated times or dates and arrows represent processes or behaviors.

but it's really simple and worth the effort. As an example, let's return to the client who had difficulty completing his Ph.D. program. Before he left our weekend workshop, he drew a PERT chart to discover how to eliminate the con force represented by lack of money. As you can see, he began his chart by indicating a lack of money and across the page he listed his goal, sufficient money. Between these points he included a variety of events to occur during a period of time, and he connected the events with arrows. This provides self-direction.

Since he lacked money, his first step was to investigate additional sources of money. He decided first to visit his local bank and inquire about a loan, then his parents, his school's financial aid adviser, and his company.

Each of these possibilities required a certain amount of time; as shown in the illustration, he assigned a completion date to each event. Some of the events required several steps, not all of which were known to him when he drew this chart. When he visited the financial aid adviser, for example, he was asked to complete a batch of forms, and at the bank there was paperwork to be completed before he could be considered for a loan.

You'll also notice that he periodically built in some check points to monitor his progress. We encourage people to tell friends or acquaintances what they're trying to achieve and then invite them to act as monitors. This provides motivation as well as social support.

By plotting each step and then following his own plan, our client would eventually arrive at a conclusion. He may not eliminate the con force by the end of his venture, of course, but unless he tried he would never know if it could be done.

PERT analysis is not a practical solution for all problems, but it is an invaluable tool in situations that involve a series of concurrent developing processes. Many people simply can't conceptualize all the steps necessary to arrive at a goal, and the PERT chart makes conceptualization possible.

SATISFYING OUR MODEL

When used properly, force field analysis and PERT analysis are the two most effective exercises for satisfying the adult growth model of Chapter 2. When you identify pro and con forces you actually surface feelings (the first step of the model). Scanning your external environment (the second step) is the primary intent of both exercises, and as you focus on the external events that cause your troubles you are often led to alternatives (the third step) which suggest skill acquisition (the fifth step). Feedback (the sixth step) is a function of both methods, although the Social Systems Map is the best tool for identifying social support.

WHAT ABOUT CHOICE?

We didn't mention choice (the fourth step), which might be considered the most important step of the model, because it presents more problems than any of the others. It requires another exercise.

Even though some people think they don't have many alternatives in life, in our society people are victims of overchoice—too many alternatives. Because of that, it's easy for a person to get stuck trying to make a choice. Perfection has something to do with the problem. So does fear. People are so concerned about doing what's right that they become confused and frustrated and eventually they just give up.

Sometimes people can't juggle all the variables that must be considered in making a choice, and sometimes they don't realize that every choice includes positive and negative consequences, so they are immobilized.

If this sounds like a familiar problem to you, the following is an exercise that will help you make choices.

Choice Chart

This exercise lets you examine the positive (desirable) and negative (undesirable) consequences of an alternative as well as their impact over a period of time.

One of our clients was a 37-year-old man who had a challenging career and a happy home life. One day he received an offer to become vice-president of a company, but to take the job he would have had to move his family to a city fifteen hundred miles away. He didn't particularly want to move—he wasn't fond of that part of the country—and his family didn't want to move, but the offer represented a substantial salary increase and it was a jump up the corporate ladder. Trying to decide what to do threw this man into a tailspin. He became irritable and couldn't function after a while. Finally, he came to the CSAD for counseling, and we asked him to construct a Choice Chart. His chart looked like this:

	Stay at Present Company	
	Positive	*Negative*
short-term	Won't have to move	less salary
	Less disruption to family	less status
	Continue with present friends	
	Like co-workers	
long-term	Like future potential work in present company if get promoted	disappointment if give up opportunity
	Present company has better future	

The client was instructed to assume that he decided to reject the offer, and then he was to ask himself:

"If I don't take the job, what will happen?"

"What will happen immediately?" [short-range]

"What will happen within nine months to a year?" [long-range]

"And are these positive or negative effects?"

Then he listed his responses accordingly. Once the chart was completed, the major issue of the situation became obvious: Would his present employer promote him?

He thought he could deal with the disappointment of "passing up the opportunity" if he had a better income and more status, so the next step, even before he rejected the offer, was to speak with his employer.

When he told his boss that he was thinking about leaving the company, the boss was surprised and a bit alarmed. He had plans for his employee, but they wouldn't evolve for another six months, or perhaps a year. That was enough to relieve our client, and he immediately turned down the offer.

The Choice Chart won't help you decide in every instance, but it can relieve some of the fear that accompanies decision making. People feel frightened about making decisions, and because they don't decide they remain frightened. Eventually fright leads to the conclusion that they're psychologically ill, and that takes away self-confidence and makes the decision process all the more painful and complex. People must realize that there is some risk involved in every decision, and if they don't take risks at least some of the time, they're going to remain indecisive and upset.

THE EFFECTS OF ADAPTIVE THERAPY

With a few exceptions, the exercises and tools presented in this book have been tested in the Center for the Study of Adult Development's Transition Planning Workshop (TPW), a two-day event usually taking place over a weekend.

Three months after every workshop the center conducts a follow-up study. The percentages below indicate the number of people who experienced a "moderate to sufficient" attainment in the corresponding categories:

Self-awareness	88.2%
Management of emotions	64.7%
Relationship with spouse	80.0%
Values clarification	75.0%
Future job/career clarification	87.5%

In addition, the center administers symptoms scale questionnaires prior to the TPW and three months after each workshop. In the five areas measured—depression, anxiety, obsessive-compulsive behavior, oversensitivity to interpersonal situations, and somatization (tendency to experience bodily pains that are psychologically caused)—the average participant has reported significant improvements.

Without a control group, it is not possible for the center to claim for certain that these benefits are a result of TPW. However, in a later study involving a control group and conducted by Bell of Pennsylvania (see Chapter 7), similar changes resulted.

The preceding exercises are intended to help you explore your external environment. They won't necessarily solve any of your problems, and they definitely won't free you from having to experience transitions, but they will advance your psychological awareness and maturity.

They can do much more than that, of course. Several of the

exercises are guides to what has occurred in your life (or environment); others are plans for what ought to occur, based upon your own expectations. As such, these exercises can be enlightening. They can help you live a less complicated, more fulfilling life.

Once you've scanned your external environment, you're better prepared to make the transitions that lie ahead, and as you probably know, a multitude of transitions await you.

In the next two chapters we'll discuss some transitions of life and work and talk about how you can successfully adapt to them.

CHAPTER FIVE

Transitions of Life

"Most of us as individuals
often act as though we think the future
is something that happens to us,
rather than as something we create every day.
Many people explain their current activities
in terms of where they have been
rather than in terms of where they are going.
Because it is over,
the past is unmanageable. Because it has not happened,
the future is manageable."

HERBERT A. SHEPARD

Scores of articles and books have been published about marriage, separation, divorce, death, and other events of life, so our interest is not to repeat what has already been written but to look at several of these personal issues as transitions. We have glossed over points that others have spent chapters discussing, and have focused on what is new and useful about these transitions of life.

MARRIAGE

As you've probably concluded, marriage is a Maxi transition, altering peoples' expectations from the instant they say, "I do."

Actually, marriage begins to affect expectations even before the ceremony, frequently during the period of engagement, and that's when the earliest problems of this transition arise.

While two people are dating they usually have a relatively informal relationship—even though they may feel strongly for each other—and their expectational rights are relaxed. As they become more involved, however, and serious about a future together, the expectations of the couple, and often of their families, become more of a concern.

Consider, for example, a man without a bank account who spends his entire paycheck on a toy computer for himself. Let's say

Leaving Home

One of the most critical events of early adult life is the process of leaving family and home. The population of clients at the Center for the Study of Adult Development tends to be older than 22, so we have had limited experiences with this transition, but two points seem to stand out.

First, for young adults going away to college, it is important to visit the college campus beforehand, if possible, and become familiar with the environment prior to enrolling and beginning classes.

Try to imagine the kinds of situations you will encounter and how you will handle them: studying in a noisy dorm, dating, getting up on time for an early class, socializing, etc. If you know people who attend this college, talk to them and find out what they think it's like. The more you understand and anticipate about a situation, the better you'll be prepared to adapt.

Remember that distress in the first three to six months of this process means nothing in terms of how well you will do. You are simply going through a transition that requires time for you to adapt.

The second and probably more important point is that once you've been away you should not return home for more than six months—just enough time to refuel, so to speak, and then you should do this only once. Whenever children leave the family and then return months or years later to live for any extended period of time, it is almost always to serve some family function. Maybe the parents can't get along without a third person in the house. Or maybe this child has always been close to one or both of the parents. Maybe the parents can't stand the feeling of growing older and seeing their last child leave home for good.

The persistent push on the part of parents needs to be toward independence, and in many instances it's up to the young adult to see that this transition does occur.

---

that in situation A the man has been dating the same woman for three weeks; and in situation B he was married just the week before. Now imagine the woman's response, her family's response, and his family's response in each situation. And to make this even more interesting, what if he's 18? 25? 35?

Obviously, in different situations, and at various ages, the man's behavior will be judged differently. If he's 18 and dating for three weeks, his behavior may have little relevance. No one may even notice. He's a young man without obligations to this woman.

But if he's 35 and dating three weeks, there are going to be many brows raised and questions asked. "Why doesn't he have a bank account?" . . . "Is this how he spends all his money?" . . . "What kind of responsible husband will he make?"

If he's 25 and married, his wife will react strongly, her parents may get involved, his parents may get involved, and the toy computer may be remembered as the cause of the couple's first major fight in married life. Behind it all? Expectations.

Marriage affects meaning and behavior in ten critical areas which call for attention and understanding if people expect to adapt in this transition. These areas are:

1. *dependence (one person caring for another); independence (one person caring for himself); and interdependence (taking care of each other, but possible only after both have developed a secure sense of independence)*
2. *intimacy*
3. *commitment*
4. *roles and responsibilities*
5. *sex*
6. *relationship with parents*
7. *children*
8. *friends*
9. *money*
10. *religion.*

Issues surrounding most and probably all of these areas will continuously arise during the years of marriage, and since the adaptive process of the Maxi transition requires a minimum of eighteen months, and possibly three years, couples who get divorced in the first two years of marriage, when most marriages fall apart, aren't always giving themselves a fair chance.

Unfortunately, little is known about the adaptation process of marriage, and there is no specific model for making the transition. Coming up with a model will require additional study and effort. But since conflict resulting from expectations is one of the major underlying factors involved in the marriage transition, couples who are skilled at resolving conflict will have the best chances of succeeding in matrimony. For this reason it's helpful to treat the marriage transition using a conflict negotiation model that is widely utilized in industry.* At the CSAD we teach negotiation to executives who can use it in management training, and many of them later tell us that their marriages improved after they learned the model!

Psychiatry has traditionally taught people to deal with conflict by expressing feelings, but that theory is inadequate. One night early in my psychiatric education, I stood before a church group and voiced the notion that fighting benefits a marriage. All of a sudden a man stood up and interrupted my speech.

> *"You say couples should fight. You say people need to free themselves from unconscious problems and fight, and that then the marriage will be OK?"*
>
> *"Yes, that's right," I said. "If you love each other, you will fight to a better level of understanding."*
>
> *"Well, my wife and I have tried all that, and we just end up hurting each other."*
>
> *"Maybe you're not getting deep enough into the understanding," I offered.*
>
> *"Sometimes we spend hours and just go around in circles."*
>
> *"It's possible you have some unconscious conflict in your relationship."*
>
> *"Well, we've both been in therapy for about two years and we're only getting worse!"*

At that, our dialogue ended because obviously I wasn't helping this man. I suggested that he and his wife seek marriage counseling, but honestly I didn't know if that would help. It occurred to me that either the man didn't want to be helped or he was incapable of being helped or the advice I gave—to fight—was either inaccurate or incomplete.

The man had, however, confirmed a problem that I now frequently treat. Many couples who experience problems in their marriages go into therapy only to discover that their problems intensify. Why? The typical therapeutic explanation is that as they

*The material on pages 89–94 is based on the Conflict Management Survey authored by Jay Hall and published by Telemetrics International, 2203 Timberloch Place, Suite 104, The Woodlands, Texas 77380. Copyright 1969, 1973.

get in touch with each other's feelings, they discover they don't really want to be married. But that's not always the case; there's another possibility.

Just as husbands and wives come from different cultures, so in a sense do therapists. At last count, there were more than 140 theories in psychiatry. So what if a therapist teaches a husband one theory and a second therapist teaches his wife a conflicting theory? Remember, there's no satisfactory method for determining which of two or more theories is true, or more effective, so how will they know if they're being led to the wrong belief systems?

Possibly, when a therapist asks a couple to simply express their feelings, he is contributing to the problems of the marriage. What can happen when a man and woman express their feelings is illustrated in Figure 21.

How do they break this cycle? They may continue expressing their feelings without any resolution. As the man said, "We spend hours and just go around in circles."

So if there is to be progress, the model for resolving conflict must be more than simply the expression of feelings. There must also be an understanding of why those feelings exist. It is the understanding that clarifies the meaning of behavior.

Conflict negotiation, the process that we recommend for the marriage transition, produces understanding, and it often helps couples resolve their conflicts *after* they have expressed their feelings.

In most conflicts, two concerns are basic: Concern for the

FIGURE 21. Cycle of expression of feelings.

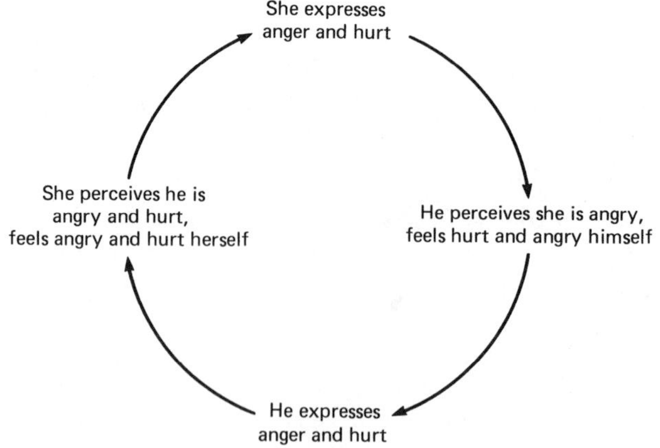

satisfactory resolution [*goal*] of the conflict and concern for the relationship, as shown in Figure 22.

In the illustration, the 9 represents the most concern (for either the relationship or the goal of the conflict); 5 represents moderate concern and 1 the least concern. There are five practical positions on this grid, and each represents a solution for conflict.

Creative problem solving is, of course, the ideal solution. It attempts to satisfy both of the parties involved.

Compromise satisfies both somewhat, but it is not as desirable as creative problem solving.

Preserving the relationship requires one or both parties to give in, for the good of the marriage, but the problem still exists.

Win-lose is a power strategy which may resolve the immediate conflict, but contributes to later, more serious problems.

And *avoidance*, requiring withdrawal by either husband or wife, is the least desirable of the solutions. It undermines an otherwise potentially satisfying relationship because the communication process stops, the feelings remain, and the problem is locked into a frozen relationship. These five positions are shown in Figure 23.

Here's how the conflict negotiation model works in a marriage: Both parties express their feelings when a conflict surfaces. This requires more than simply uttering feelings, and it does not mean shouting at each other. Some people may prefer to write out how they feel in advance of a discussion; others want to collect their thoughts and then talk.

As the husband shares his feelings, the wife has to concentrate

FIGURE 22. Conflict negotiation chart.

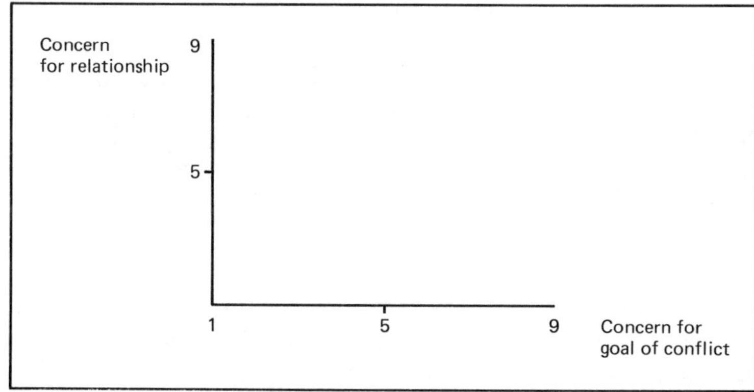

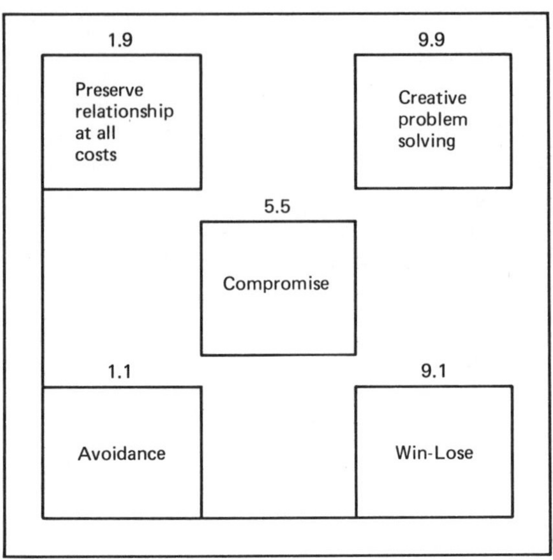

FIGURE 23. Conflict negotiation chart showing typical outcomes (based on 1969 conflict management survey for Teleometrics International, Texas conducted by Jay Hall).

on listening to what he's saying; and then the roles reverse. People are usually not good listeners, and in an argument much of the conflict could be resolved if husbands and wives would just stop to hear one another.

The next step is to resolve the conflict with a creative solution.

If that's impossible: Compromise.

If that's impossible: Preserve the relationship.

If that's impossible: Try to win.

If that's impossible: Avoid the issue.

The trick is to reframe the problem so that a solution is possible. For example, consider the various solutions, and their implications, for a conflict that arises almost every night in America when a husband habitually comes home late for dinner:

AVOIDANCE
Usually nothing is said by either the husband or the wife. There may be some comments made by one or the other, but generally feelings are suppressed and the issue is avoided. Neither husband nor wife benefits, and the relationship suffers as well.

WIN-LOSE
WIFE: *You're late again.*

HUSBAND: *I had to work late.*

WIFE: *If you're not home on time tomorrow, I'll never cook another meal again!*

PRESERVE THE RELATIONSHIP
WIFE: *You're late again.*

HUSBAND: *I had to work late.*

WIFE: *I know, but I love you, and so couldn't you get home on time for me?*

COMPROMISE
WIFE: *You're late again.*

HUSBAND: *I had to work late.*

WIFE: *Could you try to get home on time at least two nights a week?*

CREATIVE SOLUTION
WIFE: *You're late again.*

HUSBAND: *I had to work late.*

WIFE: *I'm sorry you have to work late. Could you call me before you leave the office so I know when to expect you?*

For some couples, a creative solution might also mean bringing some work home, going to work earlier in the morning, looking for another job, moving closer to the office, catching an earlier ride, etc. But the couple has to invite the possibility of a solution.

This is a simple example, and not all problems can be solved as creatively, but couples who use this model say that it is thoughtful and successful. It provides a scheme for the expression of feelings, and it offers alternatives to prevent a stalemate.

Not all marital conflicts are immediately solvable, of course. There are deep fears and longings that sometimes require in-depth attention. Some people are so traumatized by childhood relationships that they marry with irrational expectations and they cannot control themselves. In these instances, psychotherapy is usually necessary to help the individual get a better grip on life.

There are marriages in which conflict is not a problem, by the way, but that doesn't mean those marriages are any better. Unexpected consequences often arise from issues of total agreement, sometimes without the couple even realizing it. For example, imagine two people who had been taught responsibility to the point of being overly cautious. What would you expect to happen in their relationship? They probably wouldn't take any risks, they would be predictable beyond doubt, and after a while they might not have much fun.

Even responsible people need entertainment and enjoyment, but these two, by their silent agreement, would end up blaming each other for their staid marriage. In such a case, a marriage counselor or other expert could hopefully analyze the relationship and point out the couple's problem.

It's pretty clear to anyone who counsels married people that most marriages fail not because of unconscious motives—they fail because couples lack the skills to be married. Society expects married people to know how to be married, and yet very little emphasis is placed on formally training men and women to be husbands and wives. How do they learn? By example, of course. They may not approve of the way their parents lived their married lives, but what alternatives do they have? And where would they learn them?

Fortunately, in recent years, a variety of services and adult education courses have been devised for married people to enrich their relationships and for single people to learn about the marriage transition. Before they can be helpful, though, people have to be willing to acknowledge that they don't always know the answers!

Marriage Enrichment

In the last ten years a variety of marriage enrichment programs have been developed across the country, partially out of a need to slow down the rate of divorce, and also out of concern for family life. These programs are generally designed for couples of all ages who want to improve their relationships, and they're available in most cities and towns.

Marriage Encounter is one of the country's oldest marriage enrichment movements, founded by the Roman Catholic Church and adapted by many other faiths including Baptist, Jewish, Methodist, and Episcopal. The weekend experience is for couples with good relationships who want to deepen and grow in their awareness of one another and of their marriage. On the weekend couples learn a specific technique of communication which they can use in their daily lives to continue their discovery and appreciation of each other. The atmosphere of the Marriage Encounter weekend is one of growth. Husbands and wives reach out to one another in terms of their goodness and attractiveness. The couple builds upon their sense of importance as the weekend helps them explore important areas of their relationship.

Marriage Enrichment, conducted under the auspices of the United Methodist Church, also focuses on enhancing communication skills between husbands and wives. Like *Marriage Encounter,* it is open to people of all faiths.

Many family counseling agencies include marriage enrichment programs. In Philadelphia, for example, the Jewish Family Service, Family Service of Philadelphia, and Planned Parenthood all offer programs to enrich family life. Hospitals, colleges and universities, churches and synagogues, and parents' organizations offer similar programs as well.

The Couples Learning Center

The Couples Learning Center is a program of the Institute of Exploration of Contemporary Life, a nonprofit educational corporation created in Pennsylvania in 1976.

The purpose of the center is to create and conduct courses and seminars for couples so that they may continue to grow as a couple and to enhance their skills, their understanding, and ability to creatively deal with life as a couple.

It is an educational alternative to marital therapy which is often too late to be effective, says director Dr. Matti Gershenfeld. It is an alternative to eroding despair, as couples who want to stay together are blocked in their desire to "have things better" but don't know how to change.

Individuals and couples as well as community, business, governmental, and educational organizations can contact the Couples Learning Center to design special programs for them.

Some of the courses and programs offered by the center include Transition Stages for Women: Coping with Work, Men, Life-changes; The ME Generation: Healthy or Pathological?; The New Dilemmas of the American Couple; The Contemporary Couple; Parenting and Step-parenting; How to Make a Two-career Marriage Work Better; Your Family: Discovering Its Hidden Assets; Stress Management for Men and the Women in Their Lives; and Sexuality in the Life Cycle.

The Couples Learning Center is located at 180 York Road, Suite 102, Jenkintown, PA 19046; telephone (215) 884-4664.

TWO-CAREER MARRIAGES

We know even less about the adaptive process of two-career marriages than we do about marriage in general, and this is a serious problem because for the first time in American history there are more two-paycheck marriages than traditional marriages.

Couples in two-career marriages face all the problems of single-career marriages, but with different twists. Problems often surface around the following issues:

POWER: *As women begin to make money they enjoy more leverage in decision making at home, and that includes the area of sex. Studies have demonstrated that an increase in the earning power of a woman directly reflects upon her ability to say no to sex.*

ROLES: *It used to be that men worked and women stayed at home, but that's not the case in a two-career marriage. As a result, men and women have trouble discovering their own identities and understanding the expectations of their partners.*

INTIMACY: *Women in two-career marriages may be more assertive in their sexual demands and refusals. They feel they have more to share with their husbands, but if maintaining dominance is important to a man, this becomes a sensitive issue.*

NURTURANCE: *Husbands in two-career marriages sometimes lose the practical nurturance provided by wives, and they must learn to help out at home. While he was used to her listening to his woes of work, now he must listen to her as well. Working wives need more basic care and attention.*

COMPETITION: *Working wives compete with their husbands, and serious problems occur when wives are more successful than their men.*

CHILDREN: *If a husband becomes more of a nurturant parent, problems with children can be held to a minimum, but if he's not willing to take up some of the slack of his wife's absence, the children may feel abandoned and the wife may feel guilty.*

SEX: *Women who work often pay more attention to how they look; as a result they may be more attractive, not only to their husbands but to other men as well! Sometimes this makes husbands wonder, "Am I good enough for her?" and they may feel threatened by other men admiring their wives.*

GUILT: *Working wives are vulnerable to feeling guilty about liking their jobs as much as they do their families. Husbands of working wives often feel guilty about not making enough money to support their families.*

Many couples in two-career marriages come to the CSAD for counseling, and a typical case is the story of Doug and Cathy Laurienco.

They were both 37 years old. Doug was a successful lawyer, with a six-figure income, and Cathy was a training director in a local hospital.

When they were first married Cathy was in graduate school and they had a happy relationship, but then Cathy went to work and all hell broke loose. For four years, before they arrived at the center, their marriage was on the rocks, but they didn't know why.

Shortly after Cathy started working Doug developed physical complaints; when he went to the family doctor, nothing was found wrong with him. The doctor put him on tranquilizers, which made him sleepy and irritable at night, particularly when he had a drink or two, and Cathy often saw him in frightening, unprovoked fits of temper. Their marriage turned into one long argument, it seemed, and it looked like it would end in divorce.

Initially Cathy came to the center on her own, and every time she mentioned her marriage she burst into tears. She loved her husband and children, but she just couldn't imagine what had gone wrong, and she was scared.

Later Doug went into therapy on his own, and occasionally we would bring the couple together with two therapists, but while they seemed to make individual progress their relationship didn't improve. They fought, the family was upset, and none of their problems was getting resolved. In spite of their desires—Doug had also said he wanted the marriage to work—it looked like a midlife divorce was in the offing. But one point bothered me about this marriage.

As I often do in marriage counseling, I assigned Doug and Cathy the task of going away together for a weekend alone. They did this several times and invariably they returned ecstatic. Within a day or two, though, life was back to horrible. How could that be? If they were so angry with each other, how could they get away alone and come back so much in love?

We decided that one of three problems could be happening in this marriage:

1. *Outside forces were overstressing the relationship.*
2. *The relationship was poorly organized so as to overstress the couple.*
3. *They had outgrown each other, or didn't like each other for whatever reasons.*

Their weekend experiences seemed to argue against the third problem. When they were alone they had a great time. So it was either number 1 or 2.

In organizational theory, numbers 1 and 2 are common problems, and they respond to three basic strategies:

1. *Increase resources—that is, hire more people to get the work done and relieve the stress.*
2. *Plan and organize more effectively.*
3. *Simplify—that is, eliminate some responsibilities.*

If these strategies work in organizations, they can work in marriages as well. Some people react negatively to using systems theory and organizational theory in marriage, but just as marriage is an emotional institution, it is also a functional system. Married people are, in a way, running little organizations.

So I asked Doug and Cathy to list the forces or factors that prevented them from exercising these solutions in their marriage, and I wanted them defined as forces outside the marriage or inside the marriage. They listed:

OUTSIDE FORCES

1. *Cathy's desire to take on new things to make up for lost time.*
2. *Doug going outside the home to compensate for Cathy not being home.*
3. *Both having a high sense of morality and responsibility, thus always helping other people.*
4. *Cathy's identity as a "modern woman."*
5. *Competition with each other.*
6. *Both being performance-oriented.*

INSIDE FORCES

1. *Both having a high sense of responsibility to children, and disagreement on how to rear and discipline the children.*
2. *Cathy's need to feel that a strong mate is taking care of her.*
3. *Cathy's ambivalence and inconsistency about marriage and emotions.*
4. *Being at different points in individual therapy.*

5. *Different styles of living: Doug likes to work now and enjoy himself later; Cathy likes to intermix responsibility with pleasure.*
6. *Doug's being tired of the financial role of managing money.*
7. *Both reluctant to spend money on themselves for resources (maid, housekeeper, carpenter, etc.).*
8. *Both lacking commitment to marriage, which produced a sense of a temporary living arrangement.*

As Doug and Cathy produced this list they experienced a tremendous rush of euphoria—at last they recognized some of their problems. They (and I) could understand why they fell in love every time they went away alone—they liked each other! Once someone removed the pressure and responsibility of their marriage, they were easily in love again.

To work on their relationship Doug and Cathy decided to implement the three-step organizational plan. They hired resources to help relieve their workloads at home; they started planning their time together; Doug tried to be at home when Cathy couldn't be; they eliminated some of their responsibilities to other people and functions, and so on.

They didn't solve all their problems in one session of therapy, but they're no longer in therapy. They left feeling they had a plan for their marriage and with it they would try to make their relationship work.

SEPARATION AND DIVORCE

When marriages don't work, they often end in separation or divorce, and that has been the trend in the second half of the twentieth century. Almost half of all American marriages end in divorce, and the percentage continues to climb. Economic conditions, increased mobility, relaxed morality, expectational and developmental changes are all contributing to the staggering rate of separation and divorce.

In our experiences at CSAD, divorce is the result of two basic processes: A deterioration of the couple's relationship, and/or developmental changes in one or both of the partners.

Contrary to popular belief, married people probably aren't any more dissatisfied today than their parents were twenty and thirty

Help for Single Parents

Unwed pregnancy, death, and divorce often result in single parents who struggle alone with their problems rather than ask for help.

Granted, help is often not available. Unwed mothers are frequently censured, as are divorced mothers and fathers, and the image of widowhood strikes a note of fear in many adults.

The burdens of single parenthood are too numerous and taxing for any one individual, and such individuals must therefore depend on friends and community for support.

Finances are usually a burden for single parents. In addition to the normal outlays for clothing, food, medical, and school expenses, a single working parent of a small child must also pay a sitter. Some assistance is available through Aid to Dependent Children (ADC), but it's usually minimal, and only certain parents qualify.

The physical burden is also very real in the home of a single parent. After working all day he or she comes home to children who need to be fed and bathed and put to bed, and in between he or she needs to talk to someone. Regardless of the single parent's physical state, he or she must be attentive to the children in their times of illness and emotional need.

Most burdensome of all is the single parent's psychological trauma. He or she feels guilty for what has happened to his/her family. At the same time, single parents accept the responsibility for the family. He/she is left without another adult who can share the joys and problems of life. So the single adult is lonely much of the time.

Regardless of how single parenthood has occurred, it is a community's responsibility to respond to its people in need. Parents Without Partners (PWP) is a national group of single parents with chapters in most large cities and towns. Your telephone book probably includes a number, or you can write to PWP at 7910 Woodmont Avenue, Washington, D.C. 20014, or call (301) 654-8850.

If your community doesn't have a PWP group, single parents can still get together. Sharing their burdens and thoughts may provide compassion and understanding, two important needs that are rarely supplied in the life of a single parent.

For many single parents their basic need is social, so a picnic in the park or a weekend camping trip might be of interest to them. There are many other ways in which single parents can support one another. They can babysit at a fraction of the regular cost, they can be adult companions, they can shop for one another, and they can pool their home maintenance skills. The possibilities, of course, are endless.

Single parents, whether they are single by choice or circumstance, are people in need.

years ago, when divorce was less common. Studies during the last twenty years show no significant change in the level of marital dissatisfaction. What's happening, though, is that more and more couples are deciding to end relationships that don't live up to their expectations.

Hopefully the divorce rate will sputter and decline, but there's not likely to be a drastic change in the coming decades. Realistically, society will always produce some rate of divorce, and for these reasons a model for separation and divorce is as much a safeguard as it is a psychosociological guide.

No two divorces are alike, just as no two marriages are alike, but every divorce consists of similar issues and problems that must be confronted. By looking at the common elements of divorce, rather than focusing on one divorce, we have developed an adaptive model that prepares individuals for the separation and divorce transition.

Reaction to Separation and Divorce

Phase	*Length of Time*	*Characteristics*
Crisis	3–6 Months	Feelings of stress, guilt, embarrassment and fear
Consolidation	3–6 Months	Feelings of anxiety, loneliness, isolation; reassessment of life
Adaptation	6–9 Months	Feelings of adjustment about new life and personality; a feeling of rebirth
Restabilization	6–9 Months	Feeling happy about self and life in general with intermittent resurfacing of issues
Growth	End of transition	Planning the future

Psychologically, there's no such thing as a "quicky" divorce. A marriage isn't over when one partner moves out of the apartment or house, or when the judge in a court of law voids the marriage license. Divorce is not a stagnant condition, it is a psychosociological process that is active for a minimum of eighteen months and perhaps as long as three years.

The initial reaction to divorce is *crisis*, and it's the most painful of the five phases of the transition model. The issues of crisis include a sense of loss of family, failure as spouse, parent, man or woman, and overwhelming embarrassment and fear.

Pain in the crisis phase stems from guilt and loss. A person feels responsible for hurting his spouse, children, members of his family, and social network. "What do they think of me?" "What did I do wrong?" "How could I make such a mess of my life?" "How could he (or she) make life so horrible?" "What will happen to me now (socially, psychologically, professionally)?" "Who's going to take care of me?"

Those are some of the nagging questions that pop up in the crisis phase, which lasts for at least three months from the moment of separation and may continue for as long as six months. Any longer than that, and there's reason to be worried.

The answers to the questions in crisis evoke embarrassment and fear, but it's a mistake to avoid these questions. People remarry hoping the hurt will go away, or they simply refuse to confront the issues. It's understandable that this happens, but the result is almost certain to be disastrous. Experiencing the pain lays the foundation for stability in the future. In a sense, crisis is like mourning after death. Cut it short and it tends to prolong the grief for maybe five, ten, or more years.

Everyone in the crisis phase of divorce is scared. There's a feeling that the pain will never end, or that it will hurt too much, but no one has ever been injured physically or psychologically because they experienced psychological pain in limited doses and with sufficient outside support. In crisis, you *must* experience the pain. Don't overlook your social environment as an outlet. Your Social Systems Map, which we discussed in Chapter 4, is useful to you now. Use it to identify the people in your life who can help discharge the pain. Lean on a friend—or many friends. Ideally, they should be single friends, or friends experiencing your same issues.

There are also experts who can help you now. Look for them in hospitals, clinics, and social service organizations. In many cities there are consciousness-raising groups for women and men.

Children and other members of your family may also be understanding and supportive, so let them be. Don't make assumptions about your family and friends. By thinking that they're going to reject you, you often create that very response. A woman who thinks her parents won't support her during a separation and divorce is likely to withdraw from them and block their opportunities to be supportive. In turn, her parents become angry at her distance and unavailability and they do reject her or become less supportive of her. The woman in this case produces the very reaction she fears.

While it is important to experience pain in crisis, it is equally important to establish your own nest. Set up your own household independent of your spouse or ex-spouse. Usually this is more difficult for a man because it's often the first time he's had to arrange his own living quarters. But it's an essential step that leads to the establishment of identity and the satisfaction of the psychological issues involved in crisis.

Again, if you need assistance setting up house, consult your Social Systems Map. Someone in your network can help you. If not, you haven't developed a satisfactory social system, and you need to spend some time making new friends.

Loneliness frequently begins to set in near the end of crisis and the onset of *consolidation.* It's a feeling of not being able to survive. "Will I ever feel better?" "Are my kids going to hate me?" "Will I ever see them?" "What do I do if I see my ex?" "Will people like me, for *me?*" "Who are my friends?" "Will my friends tolerate my depression?" "How do I make new friends?" "Who pays when I date?" "*Will* I date?" These are the issues of consolidation, a phase that lasts from three to six months.

Now you must establish a variety of defenses for your loneliness and isolation. The fundamental misunderstanding in this phase is that creating a social system will occur by itself. It won't. You need to deliberately establish a social network. You must consciously present your own image to the world and reach out to certain people who you want to make your friends. This isn't a pleasurable task. During the consolidation phase there's generally little pleasure, but the reason you form a social network is to feel comfortable again.

Once you begin to form your social network, you enter the phase of *adaptation* and you begin to feel good about yourself. New skills become critical to you now as you're confronted with the problems of overchoice. Many new avenues of exploration and lifestyle are possible for you, but only you can make the decisions.

At first this is difficult because people fear freedom. People who went right from high school to college and then into marriage never experienced the sense of autonomy that happens during a divorce, and they're going to feel guilty about it.

You may feel undeserving, but now you've got to catch yourself or you'll slip backward. Throw yourself into the skills that will carry you forward. They might include learning how to entertain people, if you're a man, or where to buy a new car, if you're a woman. You may also need to learn a new vocabulary, a new style of dress, and a different set of manners. You'll have to seek this information on your own, but again, use your Social Systems Map for friends who can help you.

Also, now is the time to use force field analysis and PERT analysis to provide alternatives, skills, and feedback.

You'll also find information in magazines and books, and there are experts nowadays who can teach you almost any new skill.

After six to nine months, adaptation gives way to *restabilization,* and you're actually happy about your new life. Hopefully, you realize that you've experienced a severe, emotional event in your life and that your personality has changed.

During these six to nine months take the opportunity to put your newly acquired skills to work. Date, socialize, learn to trust and love again, and develop relationships. Get yourself settled and make priorities that suit you. Decide who you will see and when. Establish sex values for yourself and understand the consequences of those values. In time, you'll begin to feel secure.

Finally, your transition comes to a conclusion at *growth,* which actually is another beginning. This is the planning phase that follows all the trauma, self-doubt, and questioning of separation and divorce. Now take time to evaluate yourself and your goals. Will you marry again? Do you want children? Should you change jobs? Move to another city?

At last, you conceptualize your life as a totality, and you can enjoy yourself again!

There are numerous pitfalls during this transition, and the most serious is another relationship immediately following the divorce. This is almost always a mistake. It blocks the acquisition of new insights, techniques, and skills that are essential for your readaptation to life.

We have discovered that people frequently marry during their first adult transition phase when they're trying to exit the family, and as a result they never have an opportunity to complete one transition before they enter another. If you are one of those people, and you divorce, you take a dreadful risk when you enter a second relationship without solving the separation and divorce transition.

Not only will you face the issues of separation and divorce in your second relationship as well as the issues of marriage, but you'll also relive your first adult transition. The second relationship, which you hoped would prevent loneliness and fear and erase your guilt, will likely become a copy of your old relationship because you haven't experienced any growth. Until you do, the second relationship cannot be satisfying. You *need* to feel lonely and guilty, you *need* to be afraid, and that will make you a more mature, experienced adult.

THE FINAL TRANSITION

Death is an extremely difficult transition for a variety of reasons. It is the final transition for the dying person, and because most people generally have little experience with it, death has become a sterilized and traumatic event.

Just as life has meaning, death has meaning, and in fact some people never see the meaning of their lives until they are confronted by death. So it is a transition that requires patience, understanding, and support.

The foremost authority on the social and psychological issues surrounding death is Elizabeth Kubler-Ross, who has defined five stages of the dying process:

1. *denial*
2. *anger—why me?*
3. *bargaining*
4. *depression*
5. *acceptance.*

It's important that these stages be clearly understood not only by the person who is dying, but by the people around him as well. Obviously this is a different transition for the person who is dying than for family and friends, but the level of trauma associated with death greatly depends upon personality, ethnic background, life history, ability to adapt, and psychological maturity as well.

Most families, upon discovering that one of their members is dying, try too early to confront the different issues that arise in the mind of the dying. As soon as a family member is diagnosed to have

Similarities of Death and Divorce

Two women were talking about single parenting at a church group when one asked the other, "How did your husband die?"

"He didn't," the other woman responded, "I'm divorced."

"Oh," said the first woman, "well, I didn't ask for my situation, God took my husband from me."

For some reason people assume that with divorce a person has control of his marriage and life, but with death there's an innocent victim.

It is true that death is a more stressful phenomenon. A University of Washington School of Medicine report said that the loss of a spouse registers a 100 percent stress impact upon an individual, and this is higher than the rate for divorce, retirement, or pregnancy.

Understandably, the widowed person is often caught in a financial web, a legal tangle over property and insurance, and he or she is lonely, afraid, and depressed. Underlying it all, of course, is the pain that accompanies death.

The divorced person shares some of these same difficulties, even though he or she doesn't experience the same level of stress. The divorced person also experiences a shattering of self-image and carries around large doses of guilt that the widowed person might not necessarily know.

There are as many similarities as differences between the divorced and the widowed. Both experience emotional trauma, and both, if they are to continue functioning, must create new lives. To do that they need courage and determination, companionship and understanding, and neither of them will be able to escape the pain, fear, and isolation that accompany these transitions of life.

cancer, for example, and is told that he has a limited number of months to live, the family, in its horror, tries to talk about death when in fact the first stage of the dying process is *denial.*

When a person is told he's going to die of some disease, in just about every case he first thinks he'll be saved from death somehow, and as long as he's being treated for his condition or is in a period of remission, he denies that he is going to die.

He may become withdrawn, adding a silent sort of tension to the family atmosphere, or he may even be optimistic, making his denial obvious, but unless the family knows what's going on, there's bound to be a lot of confusion and sorrow. A dying person cannot be deprived of denial.

Eventually, the dying person may acknowledge he's going to

die, but then he enters the *anger* stage, and this is difficult for many families to accept.

The dying person may blame one of the family members for his death, causing family arguments and deep hurt, or he may blame doctors or God for bringing about his final transition. Even though it may be painful to endure, families need to understand that the anger must be vented, and it will be.

In *bargaining,* families sometimes try to interfere when they hear the dying person making a deal with God. The irrationality of this stage is obvious to everyone except the person who is going to die, and it won't help anyone if it's stopped. Not even the dying person can control himself at this stage of the transition.

The family's presence is most critical during the stage of *depression.* Dying people fear abandonment—they are scared to die, but they also don't want to be left alone. The idea of someone dying is so noxious to some people that they can't cope with the thought, and they tend to stay away from someone who has been told he's going to die. The depression probably can't be prevented, but the anguish of the transition can be reduced if family, and friends as well, support the dying person through his depression.

Support is what often helps a dying person arrive at the stage of *acceptance,* when much of the anger and resentment are over and he is just waiting to die.

Not everyone who knows he's dying experiences these stages of development, and those who do experience them don't always arrive at acceptance. Some people may die while they're in anger, or in depression, but the important point is for families and friends to realize that the transition is normal, that at different times they

---

For Widow and Widower

Many support groups for widows and widowers are being formed across the country, and to find out if there is one in your area contact local churches, YMCAs, county group services, hospitals, and medical offices.

Some programs are limited to people up to age 50, for example, while others are for those 50 and older. They usually meet once or twice a month on a year-round basis and charge a nominal fee.

Typical evenings include a social gathering plus a special presentation. Topics covered include relevant issues of concern: legal, psychological, emotional, child/parent relationships, sexuality, etc.

---

must not interfere, and at other times they should not hesitate to get involved.

After the death, the family's transition continues and may involve levels of low or high grief. The more opportunity a family has to anticipate the death of a member, and the more grieving that is completed prior to the death, the less difficult the adaptation following the death.

One danger to the family is not grieving. In some cases, when death does not come as a shock or surprise, there may not be any grieving, or it may be only momentary. In other cases grief should be expected and experienced. People try to deny grief—they busy themselves in projects, for example, or they just don't think about their loss—and that can create psychological and physical problems as well.

Families should plan to grieve, together when possible, and realize that adaptation after a death in the family may require weeks or months.

During a time of grief, it's useful for people to consult their Social Systems Maps to identify support. With adequate social support people can pass through this transition with a reduced amount of anguish, but when support is not available, prolonged difficulties may arise and therapy may be required to help a person readapt.

Dying is a frightening process, as is the adaptation that must occur after the death, but it's a transition, with a beginning, middle, and end, and as such it is normal when people know what to expect.

CHAPTER SIX

Transitions of Work

"There is nothing wrong with retirement
as long as one doesn't
allow it to interfere with one's work."

Ben Franklin

Every December when Americans make New Year's resolutions the betterment of self "in my business or job" is always at the top of the list. People pledge to stop smoking, save money, stop drinking, and improve character, but betterment in the workplace has been *the* priority among Americans since at least 1935, according to the Gallup poll.

Americans, particularly men, believe they are supposed to work, and even if work bores them they don't like to admit it. They complain about jobs and bosses, and they fuss about coworkers and working conditions, but it's not often that they'll say work bores them. Work is a way of life and brings with it a degree of status and meaning. To be a worker is to be productive. To be a worker is to be a provider. And in America, that's what a person should be! Or so it's believed.

If the Gallup poll had been founded prior to 1935, say before the Industrial Revolution, or even in the earliest years of the twentieth century, it probably would have revealed that betterment of self "in my business or job" was not a priority. "To get a good job" or "to get a well-paying job" would certainly have been among the top ten resolutions at the turn of the century, but the idea of bettering one's self at work would not have been so important. Work served a more utilitarian purpose then. Man was made for work and not work for man.

But since the Industrial Revolution, the spawning of America, and two world wars, the nature of work has changed. It is still utilitarian, but now work must also be gratifying, and when it's not, it's irritating, boring, and counterproductive, regardless of who's willing to admit it.

Nowadays men and women go to colleges and trade schools and in a matter of a few years prepare themselves for jobs that they expect will meet their emotional and materialistic needs for a lifetime. If eventually their work leaves them feeling unsatisfied, they tend to think they somehow failed to follow the proper course in life. Sometimes they know their jobs are wrong for them, or they know that in a different office, or with different people, their jobs would be more suitable for them, but many times they blame themselves for the drudgery they call work.

It's OK to feel unhappy about a job, but many people refuse to believe it. They suppress their thoughts of disappointment, work even harder to improve themselves, but they never quiet the feelings of failure and disappointment. This unhappiness complicates life for a lot of people. They feel confused and worthless, and during times of developmental transitions, they are often depressed and overwhelmed by the weight of their troubles.

Every week, thousands of American men and women complain to therapists about their jobs, and few of them think they're normal! "There's got to be something wrong with me," said one patient at the CSAD. "I'm 32 years old and I don't know what I want to do with my life. Look at my father—he's 60 and still working after 40 years."

What he failed to mention was that his father hated his job for 25 of those 40 years, and he did not recognize that his father started out in a different era, when opportunities for education and career were limited.

Ask a dozen men of 60, "If you were given the chance to choose a second job or career and begin working all over, would you select your present job or career?" and the percentage of men who answer no will be surprisingly high.

The late twentieth century is an age of overchoice in which people of all ages and backgrounds have the opportunities to do almost anything they want, if they want it bad enough. The same man or woman who wants to be a family practitioner also wants to be a lawyer, or a journalist, or a senator, or a business executive.

The problem today is not *will* I find a career that suits me, but which career? Choosing is the stumbling block for many men and women.

And sometimes people choose wrong, but in a modern society they can choose again, if only they're not made to believe they're abnormal. In an age of overchoice, when work has to be fulfilling and productive, it's very likely that a man or woman will wake up one morning and say, "I'm bored with my job, I want to do something else."

If you are such a man or woman, and you decide that only an expert can help you find out what's wrong, you may spend months in psychotherapy and never know you're normal.

The effects of work and organizational life are not clearly understood by all psychiatrists and social scientists. Freud said a healthy adult works well and loves well. Menninger related work to a sense of mastering. And in some circles these thoughts prevail.

But the desire to change jobs or careers, almost regardless of age, is a normal desire. Some people may be chronically dissatisfied due to intrapsychic problems, or they may require some historically focused psychotherapy to get at the root of their work dissatisfaction, but the vast majority of people don't need that. They simply need effective career counseling.

If your psychiatrist searches historically for the roots of dissatisfaction in your life, he may discover something, and he may be able to help you, but if he doesn't consider your adult development and your external environment, he's not effectively helping you with your problems of work. He may conclude your problem is that you need another job, but if he doesn't look at the developmental and environmental issues at play in your life, another job is probably going to end up as unpromising as the one that has you depressed.

Like so many other problems, changing jobs or careers doesn't require a pathological model to arrive at a satisfactory solution. A developmental model is usually more beneficial. From the outset, a developmental model assumes you are normal and then explores alternatives that might possibly alleviate your boredom and unhappiness.

I remember a patient who came to me the first year of my private practice. Charlie Kleaver was a 23-year-old white-collar employee in an accounting department and he was having problems in his personal life and work life as well.

When he was graduated from college in a small central Pennsylvania town near his home, Charlie was recruited for an entry-level job by a major manufacturing company. He had a passion for numbers, he was very meticulous (obsessive is the psychiatric label I had learned to apply), and the company assigned him to the accounting department to review expense vouchers for a large portion of the sales force. The job was in Philadelphia, so Charlie found an inexpensive apartment and began to establish himself in his new environment. He was a modestly attractive, medium-build young man who expected to set the world on fire, and he wanted to begin in the City of Brotherly Love.

Not long after he moved and started working, however, Charlie ran into problems.

Worst of all, he hated his job. It was boring to sit all day and review expense vouchers, and occasionally it was frustrating. Every time Charlie found inconsistencies in the vouchers, which was the one purpose and pleasure of his job, he was afraid to report them. If he discovered that a salesman requested more reimbursement than he was entitled to, either on purpose or by error, Charlie was supposed to correct the voucher and the salesman would receive less money.

That made some salesmen angry, and certain ones would visit Charlie's boss, who seemed to keep different rules for different people. Unfortunately he wasn't willing to spell out those rules for Charlie. He just expected Charlie to know them, and if Charlie violated one of the rules, the boss became displeased.

Despite Charlie's unhappiness, he needed a job, so he tried to make do. He figured that eventually he'd get promoted or transferred, or he'd try to find another job.

At the same time, Charlie had personal problems. This was his first experience away from home, and he didn't make friends easily, particularly with women. If he met a woman, he clung to her, became very dependent on her, and as a result ended up losing her. He was usually embarrassed to tell his women friends about his job, and so most of the women he met thought he was a run-of-the-mill guy without much future.

I began Charlie's therapy by exploring his past. He had had a very satisfying childhood, with plenty of love from his parents, but his father wasn't at home a lot of the time because he worked in the coal mines. In fact, at the time of therapy, Charlie was very concerned about his father who was chronically ill as a result of his work.

I followed Charlie's story through high school and college and then reviewed his feelings about his present situation. He was frustrated, angry, and lonely. So as a good psychiatrist I encouraged him to express those feelings, and he did.

He told his boss his job bored him and he shared his feelings of loneliness with the women he met. Both had adverse consequences. His boss told him that if he didn't like his job, he should look for another one; and the women dropped him almost on the spot.

I then decided to work on Charlie's career. He prepared a resume and mailed it to more than fifty companies and got a few responses but no interviews. He tried the want ads, and that resulted in two interviews, but no offers.

The thought occurred that he might need practice interviewing for jobs, so I conducted several exercises for him, and finally, after he answered additional newspaper ads, Charlie got a job as an assistant manager in a supermarket.

At first, he seemed to like the change, but in a short time he became dissatisfied again. At that point I concluded there was something wrong with Charlie—some reason why he didn't like to work, and I began an in-depth exploration of his identification with his father's illness. I knew that Charlie was disturbed about it, and the fact that the sickness resulted from the coal mines made him angry, so I worked around those issues.

Eventually, Charlie arrived at the conclusion that while his father's illness was unfortunate, there was not a thing he could do about it. And it was then, about two years after he had started therapy, that we terminated our relationship. Charlie had improved somewhat, but he was still dissatisfied with his job.

Years later I realized I had made several erroneous assumptions about Charlie Kleaver and about the nature of organizations and jobs as well.

I mistakenly thought Charlie knew what he wanted to do with his life, that he was aware of his skills, that if he exposed himself to the job market and wanted to work some employer would notice him and offer him a satisfying job. My most naive assumption, however, was that organizations structure reasonable jobs.

Also, I assumed quite mistakenly that self-esteem is essentially an internal phenomenon—that people either have self-esteem or they need therapy to clarify whatever happened earlier in their lives to deprive them of self-esteem.

But Charlie's lack of self-esteem was externally caused. Self-esteem comes from a sense of competency, status, appreciation, and success at work, and that's what was missing in Charlie's life. It was normal for a young man who had what he thought was a boring, impossible job to feel bad about himself and to communicate his sense of low self-esteem to others, verbally or nonverbally. There was nothing wrong with Charlie, except what I couldn't see!

The traditional psychiatrist within me would ask, however, "Then why couldn't he find a better job when he tried? That's the key. Anyone could have a bad job. Certainly it would make him feel bad, but why did the interviews go sour and why didn't anyone offer him a better job, and finally, when he got a different job, why didn't he like that one? Obviously his unconscious will not allow him either to find a job he likes better or to be satisfied with *any* job."

But there was another possibility. Maybe Charlie's search strategy was wrong. Could it be that the process he utilized to find a job made it almost impossible for him to find one that would caress his self-esteem? Certainly! But I wasn't aware of that possibility for several years, not, in fact, until Richard Bolles wrote *What Color Is Your Parachute?*

In Bolles's book, which we use at CSAD and recommend for people with career problems, he quoted studies which revealed a job seeker can expect to get one to four interviews for every hundred resumes he mails. Some companies receive as many as 250,000 resumes a year, and on the average, companies invite one job seeker to interview for every 245 resumes they receive!

With those kinds of odds, choosing a career and pursuing it can easily become a nightmare. As Bolles says,

> *You . . . go into Shock, characterized by a slow or rapid erosion of your self-esteem, a conviction that there is something wrong* with you, *leading to lower expectations, depression, desperation and/or apathy. This assumes, consequently, all the proportions of a major crisis in your life, your personal relations and your family, leading to loneliness, irritability, withdrawal, where divorce is often a consequence and even suicide is not unthinkable. (One major executive career counselor did a survey of 15,000 clients, and discovered*

*that 75% of them were either facing, in the midst of, or just out of, a marital divorce.)**

As a buffer to this agony, and as an alternative to traditional approaches to job hunting, Bolles has devised a method for job seekers that finds a satisfying job for the majority of people who take the time to try it. The method helps people clarify their work interests and skills, match those skills to specific kinds of jobs, and then locate companies that offer jobs to satisfy their qualifications and expectations.

At CSAD, staff member K. C. Baldadian has modified various career-planning methods and developed a program for our clients who need to make career decisions.† We encourage our clients to plan their own careers, and with minimal guidance this is easily possible. You can do it as well!

LIFE CHART

Begin with a Life Chart (see Chapter 3) and add a projected line to it to indicate the path you expect your life to follow in the future. Hopefully the projection is on the upswing!

What has to happen in your career to meet that projection? After studying the possibilities, and perhaps talking about your ideas with a friend or your manager, you can begin to make some preliminary career decisions.

PEAK EXPERIENCES

Glancing at your Life Chart you will spot several peak experiences in your life. These are activities that provided meaning and pleasure; moments when you enjoyed living and being you.

*From *What Color Is Your Parachute? A Practical Manual for Job-Hunters & Career-Changers*, 1980 Revised Edition, by Richard N. Bolles, © copyright 1972, 1975, 1976, 1977, 1978, 1979, 1980 by Richard Nelson Bolles. Used by special permission. Those desiring a copy of the complete book for further reading, may procure it from the publisher, Ten Speed Press, P.O. Box 7123, Berkeley CA 94707.

†K.C. Baldadian has written an unpublished workbook entitled *Self-Directed Career Planning*, copyright, 1980, in which she discusses these various career planning methods. Available through the Center for the Study of Adult Development, 3910 Chestnut St., Philadelphia, PA, 19104.

Make a list of those peak experiences and next to each one mark the needs that the experience fulfilled and the values that it satisfied. For example, if you had presented the valedictory at your high school graduation, your Peak Experience Chart might resemble this:

PEAK EXPERIENCES

Experience	*Need/Value*
1. Presented valedictory	Recognition, prestige, public acceptance; high achievement, excellence, social recognition.
2.	
3.	

After you list several peak experiences you'll probably discover some similarities in the need/value column. Those common denominators are significant. If you can find a job that will provide those needs and values, you'll probably have found a rewarding job.

CAREER ALTERNATIVE FILE

Throughout your career it's a good idea to assemble a career file.

Whenever you learn something about a job that may interest you, write it down and put it in the file. Clip interesting articles pertaining to the people, jobs, and departments that interest you. You never know when these bits of information might be needed.

The more information you have at your fingertips, the easier the decision-making process becomes. When you want to apply for another job, a promotion, or a transfer, you'll be knowledgeable about the field of interest if you collect data in advance.

A career file can also help keep you up to date on what's happening in your field or related fields: problems; new products; changes; who the successful personnel are and why; who the key personnel are in various companies and departments; content; jargon—all become a part of your career file.

Career information has many purposes. It can help you screen out jobs that are not suitable for you; it can increase your career credibility with a future supervisor; and it gives you the added advantage of forethought and knowledge which helps keep you prepared for the unexpected.

But that's getting ahead of the exercises. Ask yourself, "What have I accomplished?"

This is no time to feel inhibited. Society frowns on bragging, but it's time to toot your horn. No one is going to see what you write anyway, so feel free to express yourself. List your accomplishments. They are a key to your future success in career development, so take your time and write out what you have done well and what you have liked doing.

Here are a few directions to help you list your accomplishments:

- *Look at your Life Chart and Peak Experiences Chart and identify your most satisfying or most important accomplishments. Choose at least a half-dozen.*
- *Write a step-by-step detailed description of each accomplishment.*
- *Use the pronoun* I.
- *Use the following guides for describing your accomplishments:*

  What did you accomplish?

  Whom did it benefit?

  What did you most enjoy about it?

  Who were the people involved?

  What were your feelings during and after?

  How did you accomplish the task?

  What was the result?

  What was the environment like?

  What objects were used?

  What did you do well?

  How did you see yourself in this situation?

  What did you learn?
- *Begin with accomplishments in your present job.*
- *Other areas to consider include personal, academic, extracurricular (hobbies, organizations, sports, etc.), and other work-related (paid and unpaid) accomplishments.*

HISTORICAL SKILLS INVENTORY

Each of the accomplishments you described above made use of certain skills. You possess a unique combination of skills which you use in whatever work you do. Visualize those skills now; list them and rate them using the chart below.

HISTORICAL SKILLS INVENTORY

Each of your accomplishments made use of certain skills. List your accomplishments, skills, abilities, and talents used and rate your proficiency for each according to this scale:

1. Inadequate—Awkward
2. Adequate to finish the task
3. Skillful—Competent
4. Very skillful—Very Competent

Accomplishments	*Skills, Abilities, Talents Used*	*Rating*
______________	______________	______________
______________	______________	______________
______________	______________	______________
______________	______________	______________
______________	______________	______________
______________	______________	______________
______________	______________	______________

A COMMENDATION

Before you actually begin sizing up jobs, you've got a speech to write. Pretend you are about to retire and your fellow employees are throwing a party to bid you farewell. Your best friend has been asked to give a speech about you to a crowd that knows you well. What would you want that speech to reveal? Take some time now and write the speech.

Finished? OK, now look over the speech and ask yourself, "What can I do to increase the likelihood that such a speech could be written about me?"

Your answer is a good clue to what can be done to increase the likelihood of success in your personal career planning.

These exercises are good for appraising yourself and getting to know more about yourself, and the information provided arms you with increased knowledge that gives you greater control over your career future. Once you become aware of what you like to do, what you do well, what motivates you and gives you greatest satisfaction, you should be able to visualize the kinds of jobs or careers that will make you happy. The next step is to aim for those jobs or careers.

A way to begin is to match your personality to a job. The most important variable in career development is the person/job fit. People and jobs must be compatible, otherwise work becomes unsatisfying, boring, frustrating; it leads to lowered self-esteem, and it causes psychological and physiological problems.

According to John L. Holland, author of *Making Vocational Choices: A Theory of Careers*, people can loosely be classified into six different personality types, as can jobs. They are:

INVESTIGATIVE: *Likes jobs using observational, analytical, and evaluative skills; has scientific and mathematical abilities; seeks to understand and control physical, biological, and sociological phenomena; values intellectual pursuits. Often described as analytical, cautious, independent, intellectual, introverted, modest, rational, reserved.*

REALISTIC: *Likes working with machines, tools, animals, agriculture; has mechanical abilities, athletic abilities; values tangible, concrete things like money, power, and status. Often described as humble, honest, materialistic, conforming, natural, practical, shy, stable, thrifty.*

ARTISTIC: *Likes jobs that create art forms or products; has innovative or intuitional abilities as well as writing, musical, or artistic abilities; enjoys language, art, music, and values aesthetic qualities. Often described as complicated, emotional, expressive, idealistic, impractical, independent, intuitive, nonconforming.*

SOCIAL: *Likes working with people to inform, train, service, cure, civilize, and educate; has human relations skills; has interpersonal and teaching skills; values, moral, social, and ethical activities and problems. Often described as convincing, friendly, generous, helpful, idealistic, kind, responsible, social, tactful, understanding.*

CONVENTIONAL: *Likes conventional jobs using clerical, computational, and business system abilities; prefers working with data, systemizing and ordering it. Often described as conforming, careful, conservative, inhibited, obedient, persistent, unimaginative, efficient.*

ENTERPRISING: *Likes jobs using leadership, interpersonal and persuasive speaking abilities; prefers working with people to attain power and/or money. Often described as adventurous, ambitious, attention-getting, energetic, impulsive, optimistic, self-confident, popular, managerial.*

Examine each of these personality types and determine where you belong. It's natural for you to resemble more than one type, by the way.

MATCHING JOBS TO PERSONALITY TYPES

Jobs can be categorized by the same six personality types. Begin with the job you have now. How can it be described in terms of personality? How well does it match your personality type? If it doesn't match, this may not be the job for you!

So what are some other jobs that interest you? They might include your present work, or maybe not. They might be jobs within the company where you're now employed, or they may not have any relationship to the kind of work you're now doing. That's not important. Just list a few jobs that interest you and evaluate them in terms of your personality, interests, skills, and experiences.

GATHERING CAREER INFORMATION

After you put together a list of possible jobs, how can you find out more about them?

You should analyze potential careers and jobs in the same way that you analyzed accomplishments and experiences.

There are many resources you can use to find information about specific jobs (for example, job descriptions, career resource libraries, experts, job postings, want ads, training and development programs, etc.), but your best resource is a person who is successful and knowledgeable in your field of interest. If you don't know any such person, contact the personnel department of a company where you would like to work and find out who has the job you'd like to have. Then set up an appointment for an interview.

You're not going to the interview to get a job, remember, you're going to ask for information and guidance from someone you consider an expert in the job of interest.

Before you go for the interview gather as much information as possible about the job from other resources.

Prepare a list of questions that you want to ask. Know what your objective is, and try to make your questions interesting to answer. Some sample questions include:

1. What is your typical workday like from start to finish?
2. What are the best educational and/or occupational routes that I might take to get into this particular field?
3. What skills are most important for your kind of work?
4. Tell me something about the equipment, tools, and knowledge you use in your job?
5. What are the greatest satisfactions you get from your job?
6. Who are the people you serve?
7. Why is there a need for your services?
8. What is the future growth potential in this field?
9. How flexible and mobile could I be if I had a job like yours?
10. How secure is your job now and will it be in the future?
11. What are the most important factors contributing to your success?
12. What are some of the difficulties, negatives, or problems of your job?
13. Is there any personal advice you have to offer someone interested in this field of work?
14. Could you give me the names of other people in this field who might be able to provide me with additional information?

GETTING THE JOB

Now, how do you get one of those jobs? To answer that question you can begin with the force field analysis that we described in Chapter 4. It will help you look at possible career goals in terms of the pro forces which are encouraging you to facilitate change in your life and the con forces which are barriers to your career plan. The barriers must be removed to get the job of your choice.

Make your force field according to the directions that we provided earlier, but in addition to marking forces changeable or unchangeable, also indicate whether they are internal or external forces.

Internal pro forces may include personal strengths, for example, while internal con forces are shortcomings such as lack of skills, knowledge, training, experience, etc.

External pro forces are people or things that can help you get your job; while external con forces are the obstacles that block your progress.

Once you've constructed your force field you can then make a Career Action Plan, similar to PERT analysis, as demonstrated below.

CAREER ACTION PLAN

Career Statement: I want to be ______________________

Internal or External Barriers: ______________________

Action: ______________________

Barriers to the Action: ______________________

Method of Barrier Removal or Reduction: ______________________

Who or What Can Help: ______________________

When: ______________________

If, for example, you wanted to be a counselor but didn't have a degree, your Career Action Plan might look something like this:

Career Statement: I want to be a counselor.

Internal or External Barriers: Internal barrier—I don't have a master's degree in counseling.

Action: Go back to graduate school to get my master's in counseling.

Barriers to the action: No money.

Method of Barrier Removal or Reduction: Find out about my com-

pany's tuition reimbursement program; use savings or a loan for the payment till I get my reimbursement.

Who or What Can Help: Personnel; my bank.

When: Today; when needed.

So you must plan the events that will be necessary to remove the barrier. And then do the same for other barriers as well.

Eventually, with direction and determination, you will prepare yourself for the job or career of your choice. And unless you've changed your mind about the kind of work you want to do, or you've experienced some developmental movement away from the values and feelings that led you to this job, the end result should be satisfying work.

This method, as well as those of Bolles and others, is a developmental solution for the Maxi transition of career planning. It surfaces feelings, scans the environment, and produces alternatives for decision making. It points out skills that may have to be acquired, and it provides feedback. Granted, the method is time-consuming, but for people who need to make career decisions, it works.

One point needs to be clarified. You should not assume that unhappiness with your job is always a result of boredom. I remember a high-powered salesman who came to our Transition Planning Workshop thinking that he was tired of his job. He wanted to do something else, he said, but he needed help to make the decision.

However, once he plotted a Life Chart and experienced some of the other exercises of the workshop, he discovered that his job wasn't his problem. It was his marriage. He could have sat through months of therapy and switched jobs for ages, but he wasn't going to feel any better about working until he resolved his marital conflicts. In this case, the client had failed to clarify his feelings.

At the Center for the Study of Adult Development, we have also discovered that some people, even after they know why they're dissatisfied, are still incapable of making career or job decisions because they're afraid to look for another job. They may be afraid of interviews, or they may believe they're too old for another company, or they lack the necessary skills.

Quite frequently these people think there's something wrong

with them, but of course usually there isn't. If they constructed a Social Systems Map (see Chapter 4) and identified several people with whom they could discuss their fears and consider their alternatives, they might be able to help themselves. They may also need to seek career counseling, and if they are suffering from some deep-seated emotional disturbance, then therapy is certainly advisable.

WORKING WITHIN THE SAME COMPANY

If it's your job that makes you unhappy with your career, and not your company or the career itself, then you probably don't like the values, tasks, and/or social environment of your position. There are some ways you can help yourself.

First rely on the tools you've learned in this book. Scan your external environment, and you may discover that within your company there is another job that attracts you. In that case, go after it.

If that doesn't work, try to enrich your present job as a second attempt. Don't assume you have to put up with what you have, or that you must find another job in another company. Don't assume that your boss knows what's best for you, or that you don't have the right to alter your job to make it more satisfying. Give yourself a chance to evaluate what you do that satisfies and dissatisfies you, and then appproach your boss with a plan for making your job more fulfilling. That should also make it more efficient!

Of course, if you work for a small company, or one in which you are not granted any flexibility of workstyle, then you may have to seek work outside the organization. In that case, conduct a thorough search using the tools and exercises we've already described.

GETTING PROMOTED

People in organizations are often transferred to new jobs in the same location that are the result of promotion or lateral movement. If that happens to you, remember that you're in a Midi transition and allow yourself three to nine months to adapt.

During this period of time you're going to feel intermittently insecure, inadequate, and off-balance. You may encounter some sleepless nights and marital arguments, but that's all part of the transfer package.

In addition to some standard methods for stress reduction, which we'll discuss in the next chapter, here's the best strategy for tackling a new assignment:

- *Don't accept a job you don't want. Not so many years ago refusal to accept a promotion or lateral movement often meant an employee would be fired or never moved beyond his current place in the company. With rare exception that's not the case today. Whatever the consequences might be for refusing a job, they're almost never as bad as taking a job you're not prepared to accept.*
- *Take some time to think it over. This isn't always possible, but when you can, thinking it over will help in two ways: you'll have more time to check out the job, and more time to get a frame of reference about the job before you begin.*

  Use as many techniques as you can to scan the external environment. Take a history of the job, ask questions of people who know about the job, and try to find out as many of the good and bad points as you can. This will lead you to a quicker, sounder decision.

  Once you begin the new job, you'll lose some of the perspective you had as an onlooker, so it's important to set yourself up for the experience. Basically, know where you're stepping before you move, and thus maximize your options.
- *Hold power and gather information. Don't step into your new role and make off-the-cuff decisions or judgments. Ask questions first, get familiar with the people, and wait as long as you possibly can to make decisions.*

  When you do make decisions your subordinates are going to judge you as either uncompromising or compromising, unsupportive or supportive, unethical or ethical. You want these people to see you as someone who respects ideas and who plans to involve as many people as possible in areas of responsibility and decision making.

A good method for holding power and gathering information for someone promoted to a supervisory position is a staff meeting where each of the key employees is requested to draw a Lifeline (similar to a Life Chart) of the department or unit. Ask the employees to draw the ups and downs of the department and to label and explain critical events (points where the direction of the line changes radically), such as the one shown in Figure 24.

We can see that in the last five years Boss X was hired and at the time the department's productivity record was in a decline. At point B Boss X instituted new sales techniques which boosted productivity for about a year. Then, at C, a competitor cut into the market and sales went into a second decline. One year later, at D, you were promoted into the job.

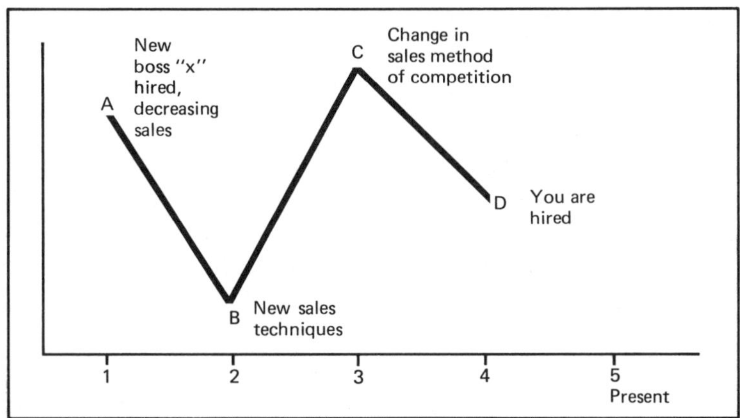

FIGURE 24. Lifeline.

As the employees describe the events, you will learn more about the workings of the department and departmental personnel than any individual could have told you.

Now assign the employees to small groups of three to four people and ask them to list:

1. *the administrative style of their previous boss*
2. *the strengths of the department at the moment*
3. *the problems of the department*
4. *improvements that they think would boost morale and productivity.*

Ask a member of each small group to report the finding of the group. People talk more openly in small groups, and spokesmen for groups speak freely because they are simply reporting a list. They feel responsible to their group and report whatever was said, and if someone reacts unfavorably to it, they can disclaim the idea. "I was only reporting for my group, I don't necessarily agree."

In your role, however, you should not react to any of the points. Ask questions if you like, but don't offer information or give away your reactions. As a result of this exercise, you will improve your understanding of how your people perceive their jobs and you will have had time to develop your method of operation. At the same time, you're holding on to your power. So when you do make decisions they will have been chosen carefully and with the complexities of your department in mind.

RELOCATING TO ANOTHER CITY OR COUNTRY

When you are transferred or move by your own choice to another locale for work, you undergo a Maxi transition that may require as many as three years to resolve. The complexity of the transition and the consequences to be endured depend primarily upon your state of mind and the condition of your family. You may or may not experience prolonged illness or physical ailments following your move.

In a study conducted in the mid-1960s, psychiatrists T. H. Holmes and R. H. Rahe developed the Social Readjustment Rating Scale for predicting illness and injury.*

They assigned life change units (LCU) to common events of life. Death of a spouse, for example, equaled 100 LCUand retirement 45. They then discovered that "of the life crises between 150 and 199 LCU, 37 percent had an associated health change. This association rose to 51 percent for crises with scores between 200 and 299 LCU, and to 79 percent for crises with scores of 300 LCU or more."

Social Readjustment Rating Scale

Rank	*Life event*	*Mean value*
1	Death of spouse	100
2	Divorce	73
3	Marital separation	65
4	Jail term	63
5	Death of close family member	63
6	Personal injury or illness	53
7	Marriage	50
8	Fired at work	47
9	Marital reconciliation	45
10	Retirement	45
11	Change in health of family member	44
12	Pregnancy	40
13	Sex difficulties	39
14	Gain of new family member	39
15	Business readjustment	39
16	Change in financial state	38
17	Death of close friend	37
18	Change to different line of work	36

*Reprinted with permission from *Journal of Psychosomatic Research, II*, T. H. Holmes and R. H. Rahe, "The Social Readjustment Scale," Copyright 1967, Pergamon Press, Ltd.

19	Change in number of arguments with spouse	35
20	Mortgage over $10,000	31
21	Foreclosure of mortgage or loan	30
22	Change in responsibilities at work	29
23	Son or daughter leaving home	29
24	Trouble with in-laws	29
25	Outstanding personal achievement	28
26	Wife begin or stop work	26
27	Begin or end school	26
28	Change in living conditions	25
29	Revision of personal habits	24
30	Trouble with boss	23
31	Change in work hours or conditions	20
32	Change in residence	20
33	Change in schools	20
34	Change in recreation	19
35	Change in church activities	19
36	Change in social activities	18
37	Mortgage or loan less than $10,000	17
38	Change in sleeping habits	16
39	Change in number of family get-togethers	15
40	Change in eating habits	15
41	Vacation	13
42	Christmas	12
43	Minor violations of the law	11

People who relocate may engender up to 310 life change units! They include:

Changes in work responsibilities	29
Outstanding personal achievement (promotion, awards)	28
Change in living conditions	25
Change in residence	20
Change in work hours or conditions	20
Change in children's schools	20
Change in recreation	19
Change in church activities	19
Change in social activities	18

For people who move overseas this transition is intensified. One researcher working with foreign service employees has concluded that after three moves people can no longer feel attached to a community, and as a result they experience a lot of unhappiness in their personal and professional lives.

Little empirical work has been conducted about the best strategies to manage this Maxi transition, but a few points may be helpful.

It is important to mourn the loss of the city or town you are leaving, if you feel attached to it, just as you would mourn the loss of a loved one. Experience the pain of leaving; otherwise you'll find it difficult to adapt to your new locale.

You can alleviate some of the pressure that may result from your change in financial status (38 LCU) and your home life, which may include arguing with your spouse (35 LCU). Be extremely reluctant to accept a company-initiated relocation that will create financial hardship for you. Surprisingly, some companies expect their employees to cover all but direct moving expenses, and families often lose money selling and buying homes, transferring children to new schools, and meeting higher living standards in a new location.

Your raise in salary, provided the move includes a raise, may not be sufficient to offset your real costs.

It's also important to have your spouse's cooperation and agreement before you move. Without cooperation your spouse is going to blame you either overtly or covertly as the hardships of the transition unfold.

Often covert blame is played out on the children, and that has a polarizing effect on the family, or it causes the children to slip into bad habits at school or into delinquency problems.

So before you make any commitments, discuss the transfer with your spouse, and provided you're in agreement, explore the possibility of you and your spouse traveling to the new locale in advance of the move, at the company's expense. If it's not possible for both of you to go, your spouse may wish you to go alone and search for employment, housing, church, schools, etc.

Your family may also need to spend time learning a language, studying a new culture, and reading about their new "home" in anticipation of the move. Failing to take the time to negotiate these matters at home will only aggravate your adaptation, if not make it impossible.

Finally, while your relocation is a Maxi transition, it involves a Midi transition at work, so you'll have to be careful to allocate time to both family and office. Ignoring either arena will create problems.

WHAT IF YOU'RE FIRED?

In a constantly changing work climate where needs and desires fluctuate with a stormy economy, some people are bound to be fired. But not all firings are the result of incompetency or personality deficiencies.

If you are fired, don't assume you're worthless. Why were you fired? Ask yourself that question even if you asked your boss and he gave you an answer. There are reasons for firing people that have nothing to do with the individual.

Remember the "Saturday Night Massacre" after Nixon had ordered Archibald Cox to "cease and desist" trying to obtain the White House tapes? When Cox dug in for the fight Nixon ordered him fired, but it took two resignations from key administrative people before someone finally lowered the hatchet.

In any situation, the economics of the company could have resulted in a pink slip, or general reorganization could have meant that several people had to be let go.

You might have lost your job because your department was eliminated, or because your company didn't like risk takers, or conformists, or people who write certain kinds of memos, or who wear blue jeans, for that matter. Many people are fired without knowing why, and this can create an overwhelming degree of shame and dissatisfaction.

So if you're fired, take the time to sort out the cause. The very reason one company fired you may be the reason another company will hire and promote you. And if the firing had nothing to do with your job performance, it's important for your self-esteem that you be aware of it.

If the process of exploring why you were fired is painful because it shows some weakness in your performance, the discovery may eventually be of benefit to you in another situation. It should also help you decide whether or not to use the organization or any of its members as references.

On the other hand, if you've been fired numerous times, you may have some internal psychological behavior problems that can be resolved in therapy. It may be a problem of relating to authority, to other people, or to planning. In any case, your own Life Chart should offer some clues to this discovery. If you suspect you have a psychological problem, by all means consult a therapist.

One final comment may be helpful. Immediately after you're fired construct a Social Systems Map and figure out who you can lean on during this time of crisis. Contact those people without delay. The longer you wait, the stronger your tendency to avoid them, and if you give them a chance, you'll be surprised at how supportive and helpful people can be in times of need.

RETIRING—CALLING IT QUITS

Why do people fear retirement? Ask a few people in their 40s and 50s and they may say, "I don't want to be a senior citizen," "I don't want to quit working," "I don't want to die." Some of them may laugh off the question with "Fear it? Why I can't wait till I'm 65. It'll be the time of my life."

It *can* be the time of your life, but only if you plan for it. One of the greatest predictors of successful adaptation to retirement is the ability to anticipate oncoming changes, and nowhere is that more important than at retirement. Just about every working man and woman will have to retire, and you owe it to yourself and your families to anticipate the changes that will occur in your life.

Retirement is a potentially fatal Maxi transition, and a quick glance at the functions work provides makes it obvious why retirement is so critical:

- *Economic returns that are a means to other ends—notably, work is instrumental for survival*
- *Opportunities to contribute to society*
- *Opportunities for interaction with others*
- *Personal identity*

Why Retire at 65?

H. C. Lehman concluded in *Age and Achievement* that man's creative capacities are not always greatest in early or middle life. In his exhaustive research project, Dr. Lehman discovered a staggering body of work in education, mathematics, natural history, medicine, the arts, and politics that was accomplished in late maturity:

—At 86, Giovanni Bellini was acknowledged to be the best painter in Venice.
—What many believe is the greatest novel of all time, *Don Quixote,* was completed when Cervantes was 68.
—At 74, Charles Dana wrote the classic *History of Medicine.*
—The French zoologist Dumeril finished his definitive work about reptiles at age 80.
—Galileo accomplished most of his important work in his 70s. He continued working until the day he died.
—Edison was productive through the age of 83. He reached a peak of creativity at the age of 35, but then he experienced a second peak at 57, and a third peak between the ages of 70 and 75!

- *The passing of time through schedules, timetables, and particular activity*
- *A help to ward off distressing thoughts and feelings*
- *Scope for personal achievement*
- *Assurance of one's capacity to deal effectively with the environment*

The best studies of retirement have been conducted by Erdman Palmore of the Center for the Study of Aging Human Development. He says that 75 percent of all Americans live to be 65 and that a man of 65 can expect to live another 13.7 years, while a woman of 65 can expect to live another 18 years.

Furthermore, "80% of people 65 and over can engage in normal daily activities and an even higher percentage retain normal mental function"!

From Dr. Palmore's research, four basic factors emerge as predictors of health and longevity after retirement:

- *A variety of meaningful activities, particularly organizational activities of church, political, or social nature*
- *Health maintenance, plenty of exercise, good eating habits, and no cigarette smoking*

- *Financial planning, which should have begun prior to age 50*
- *An optimistic mental outlook which will add years to life*

There are a number of useful developmental exercises that you may use prior to retirement. Here are a few of them:*

- *Find a quiet place where you can relax and work undisturbed. Take along some paper and a pen or pencil. Now imagine what you would do the first morning of retirement. Be specific! Then look into the more distant future and imagine what you would do the morning after six months of retirement; then, after five years.*

  Frequently people imagine they will feel a sense of freedom on that first morning. They see themselves staying in bed, or they may want to rise very early for a day of golf, or just rise casually at mid-morning and take a stroll in the woods or visit family or friends.

  By six months, however, people expect to be bored, and after five years they imagine they'll be stable. They say they'll wish they were back at work. They'll worry more. They'll be more concerned about their health and death.

- *What you must do is plan a package of diverse and meaningful activities for your retirement, and structure that activity around Dr. Palmore's four variables for health and longevity after retirement.*

  To help you plan you might plot a Life Chart. You can construct the chart according to time periods, as you did earlier, or by the length of an activity. For example, if you began playing golf at about the age of 30, you could plot the movement of your satisfaction against your golf game. What was it about golf that made you feel good? Did you like that activity because it took place outdoors? Was it the self-direction of goif that interested you? The challenge of hitting a good ball?

  Then try to find other activities that will satisfy those same desires.

- *As another exercise, you might visit senior citizen facilities in your area and talk to people who are retired. What do they do to spend time? How are they happy and unhappy? What seems to be the difference between those who like retired life and those who don't? How could you plan differently to avoid some of their problems?*

*Thanks to Carol S. Pierskalla, Ph.D., Associate Director, Organization Development, Center for the Study of Adult Development, for the development of these exercises.

If you plan to move to another climate when you retire, be sure to vacation in that area prior to retirement age. Many people make the mistake of retiring and then moving to Florida or North Carolina without ever visiting those states in advance. Take the time to plan. Check out housing costs, make new friends, and learn as much as you possibly can about the area before you decide to move.

A final idea comes to mind. If retirement is ten, twenty, thirty, or more years in your future, begin now to list the activities that you would pursue if you had the time. When you do retire you'll have a whole file of activities to keep you busy.

CHAPTER SEVEN

Stress, Transitions, and Social Support

"Aging is simply the wear and tear
caused by stress and
the body's reaction to it."

HANS SELYE

"Man the victorious predator
now preys upon himself."

WALTER MCQUADE

In the late 1970s the American Telephone and Telegraph Company implemented a massive reorganizational plan to change the maturity, understanding, awareness, and work styles of about 250,000 employees. The shake-up affected almost every AT&T manager and was necessitated by the demands of a modern, competitive society.

AT&T's top brass wanted their people to be innovative in ways they had never learned, to be assertive when for years they had been taught to be passive, and daring when before they knew to play it safe. To achieve those goals Bell companies across the country were to be divided by markets—residential, business, and network—and each market would control its own functional operations. So a manager formerly in charge of both residential and business phone installations might find himself working only with residential customers, but his duties could be broadened to include equipment installation, repair, design, and development as well.

No serious repercussions were expected from this exhaustive rearrangement of personnel and services, but in less than a year's time Bell officials knew they had problems. Physicians throughout the company reported frequent physical complaints from employees during routine examinations, and they attributed the complaints to anxiety.

In the opinion of these doctors the Bell system was under stress, and the prognosis could be disastrous for the company and its people.

Certainly no one should have been surprised, and yet most executives were. Apparently they had not earnestly considered the repercussions of this massive shuffle. Thousands of companies make the same mistake every year, usually because they don't know how to reorganize effectively, or they don't recognize that when personnel and services are rearranged, even in the slightest ways, there can be a backlash of stress-related problems that include heart attacks, ulcers, divorce, and psychological breakdowns.

At AT&T, fortunately, once a diagnosis was made the company's human resources team immediately started looking for ways to help employees cope with change in the workplace.

At Pacific Telephone, for example, they began noontime discussions about stress and taught managers muscle relaxation techniques to cope with stress.

Illinois Bell Telephone Company invited government officials, consumer advocates, business professors, and management consultants to a three-day seminar on "managing change," and elsewhere similar programs were developed.

In Philadelphia, the Center for the Study of Adult Development got involved when Bell of Pennsylvania approached us to design a management seminar. For years the local company, along with Diamond State Telephone Company in Delaware, conducted seminars for six hundred of their top managers, but to a late 1970s audience, the seminars were routine and boring. The center, Bell executives hoped, could develop a more exciting, effective presentation that would grab the interest of their people and also help them adapt to change.

We accepted Bell's challenge and began preparations to interview fifty of the company's managers as a preliminary step. In the interviews we wanted to do something that several of Bell's executives hesitated to let us do because they said their people would resist us. We wanted to ask the managers about their personal lives—a topic that was traditionally off-limits within the organization.

As is the case at many large companies, Bell had an unspoken personnel policy: "Don't bring your personal problems to the office, and don't step across any other employee's personal boundaries."

Some executives were convinced their managers would not violate that rule. Nonetheless, they granted us permission to ask our questions, and contrary to what they predicted, every manager we interviewed welcomed the opportunity to talk frankly about his private world. And the results were staggering.

These men were worried, and that affected their ability to work. All of them described their changing roles in the company and the anxiety of reorganization, but personal problems disturbed them most. Major among these problems were:

PARENTAL CONCERNS: *Their children were growing up with foreign values, and some of them were involved in obscure religious sects.*

MARITAL STRAINS: *Their jobs drained them of time, emotion, and energy. Husbands and wives didn't know each other. For years they communicated about and through their children, then suddenly the children left home and there was nothing to talk about.*

RELOCATION: *Many of the men had been transferred several times, each time with greater difficulty. They didn't know if their wives and children would accept another move.*

TAXATION AND INFLATION: *They needed help with financial planning if they were to send their children to college and maintain their accustomed styles of living. They also needed to know more about retirement planning.*

OFF-THE-JOB-TRAINING: *How would they meet the changing demands of the company if they didn't get some additional education? And how much more time would that take away from their personal lives?*

AGING AND DEATH: *They were concerned about getting older and dying. Some of them had lost colleagues, and others had suffered serious illnesses. Now aging and death frightened them because they realized it could happen to them.*

To these issues the company had made no or little response. Many of Bell's top employees felt overwhelmed and inadequate, both physically and psychologically, and if anyone knew it, no one seemed to care. The company was changing, and its men were expected to move along and meet the challenge without any consideration of their personal development, much of which they did not recognize or understand themselves.

From the perspective of Bell's managers, they had to keep up with the company, but their futures appeared dismal. Until someone asked what was going on, however, as we did of the fifty managers, no one would know the realities of the corporate world at Bell.

Before we designed Bell's seminar, which would be offered thirty-four times so that six hundred managers could attend in small groups, we consulted four national experts who we thought could help us. But three of the four said our job was impossible, and the fourth said the task sounded exciting, and possibly it could be accomplished, but he didn't know how.

Why were our fellow social and psychological colleagues so pessimistic? Their attitudes were directly related to the dilemma of modern psychology: Who is normal versus who is abnormal?

They knew the average age of the Bell participants was 48½, and they were almost exclusively male and without any psychological background or experience. The population alone made our task extremely tough. Like everyone else, the experts knew men are more closemouthed about their experiences than women, and that the older people get the more rigid they become. Or do they?

The experts also said that without a psychological background our participants were likely to find whatever we did alien and unintelligible.

We had additional problems as well. Our participants were from the same corporation and had learned over many years the informal rules against sharing their personal experiences and feelings with fellow workers. They talked with us privately in interviews, but would they open up in a setting that included their coworkers?

If all this wasn't bad enough, our participants were not volunteers: They were *expected* to attend the seminar! One expert predicted that while the participants would attend because they were supposed to, we would alienate half the group, who would then produce divisiveness and conflict among the rest.

A final problem was that we had no opportunity for follow-up. It was a one-shot proposition. We were allowed parts of two-and-a-half days, and not a minute more. Everything we know about human behavior says it's impossible to produce change with a single experience, so the experts told us that twenty hours was an unthinkable period of time to expect any positive results.

Truly it appeared like an unachieveable task, and yet we

succeeded. But before we explain how, let's explore the topic of stress and its relationship to organizational life. It played more of a role in the Bell experience than anyone imagined.

STRESS AND TRANSITIONS

In the last twenty years there have been at least 150,000 articles and books written about stress, and yet no one can confidently answer the age-old question "What is stress?"

The greatest name in stress exploration is Hans Selye, the pioneering research physician, endocrinologist, and biochemist who is professor emeritus at the University of Montreal and head of the International Institute of Stress and the Hans Selye Foundation. A native of Vienna and the product of private tutors and Johns Hopkins University, Seyle was the first to use the term *stress* in a psychological sense in the mid-1930s and has been posing and answering questions about the topic ever since.

It was Selye who first documented the body's physiological responses to external physical or emotional pressures. He called it the "general adaptation syndrome," the body's biochemical means for coping with outside stimuli. It is a "fight-or-flight" reflex which occurs every time the body is confronted by a "stressor"—some challenging event or thing which appears threatening.

You can get a good idea of what the response is like by recalling the last time you were suddenly excited or frightened. Perhaps you were unexpectedly asked to give a speech, or you almost ran your car into a telephone pole. On the other hand you could have just heard that you were promoted, or you could have won a marathon. "The Olympic winner at the moment of his glory," explains Selye, "or a conductor as his orchestra performs particularly well. . . . They are just radiating excitement and they are secreting all the stress hormones exactly the same as if they were dejected or had just heard of a death in the family."

The fight-or-flight response prepares your body for action. Your muscles tighten, your heart beats faster, thoughts race through your mind, hormones shoot into your bloodstream, your blood pressure rises, your stomach tightens, and you perspire. In a word, your body is stressed.

Even though the fight-or-flight response is instantaneous, the response is extremely complex. Basically it affects the autonomic nervous system (that which operates the organs and triggers the release of hormones in the body), consisting of two parts: the parasympathetic nervous system, which functions when the body is calm, and the sympathetic nervous system, which reacts to stressors and prepares the body to fight or flee.

In an earlier time, the fight-or-flight response was a necessary survival mechanism. Animals threatened by other animals needed to protect themselves, and so when threatened they either fought or ran away, and in either case they relieved their tensed-up bodies.

But in the case of modern man, who has inherited this animal response to survival, researchers say that fighting or fleeing is rarely effective, except in sports and physical emergencies, and that it leads to physical and emotional complications. In most modern-day events humans do not fight or flee. If your boss calls you into his office and reprimands you, your sympathetic nervous system goes right into action, but then what do you do? You might grab your boss by his collar and punch him in the face, but that's hardly an advisable solution. You might argue with him, but even then you'll probably leave his office boiling mad and tense. And even if you run out of his office, you'll still feel anxious without discharging your fired-up body.

When the body is prepared for fight or flight, but then doesn't fight or flee, it either suppresses all that stored-up energy or releases it through adverse behaviors. Either way, the results are undesirable.

Always Destress

Regardless of whether or not you can put yourself in control of a stressful situation, once your body has been stressed you must burn up that stored energy.

If you remain stressed, you're asking for trouble even if you don't know it. "The stressed nervous system becomes less and less capable of withstanding the impact of stressors; immunity and resistance diminish; overload comes more quickly," says Philip Goldberg in *Executive Health,* one of the best books written about stress and executive life. "In addition, individuals who have incurred wear and tear tend to encounter more stressful situations, since their efficiency of behavior is concomitantly impaired. Psychological weaknesses will lead to mistakes, poor interaction with family or co-workers, lack of confidence, and other sources of distress."

Adverse behaviors include smoking (cigarettes and marijuana), pill popping (amphetamines, tranquilizers, sleeping pills), drinking (beer, hard liquor, caffeine-containing beverages), and overeating (especially sweets which contain short-range, tranquilizing sugar). True, these behaviors are not always related to stress, but there's plenty of proof that each of these behaviors is dangerous to health.

Anger, psychological withdrawal, and self-destructive behavior are other common and potentially harmful stress release responses.

FIGURE 25. Stress-related diseases have emerged as primary causes of death in the late twentieth century. Adapted from "The Ills of Man" by John H. Dingle, *Scientific American*, September 1973. Reprinted with permission.

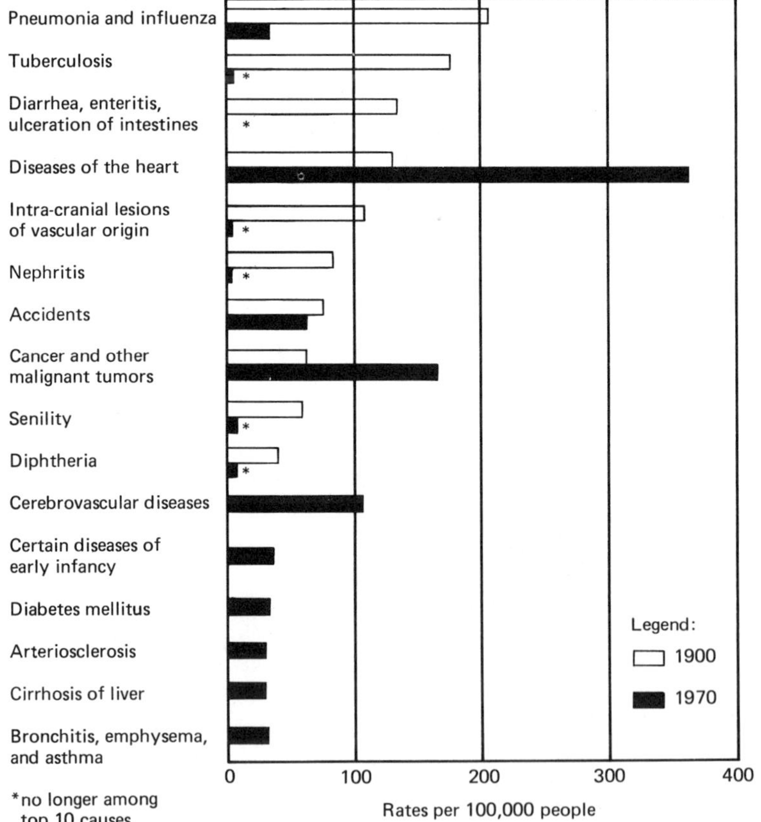

Suppression creates strain, or wear and tear, and ages the body. Various organs may become adversely affected, ulcers and cancers may appear, and in many cases people have died prematurely because they were overstressed. In fact, in the late twentieth century stress-related diseases—including cancer, cerebrovascular diseases, and heart diseases—have emerged as primary causes of death as shown in Figure 25. Why? Because change produces the need to adapt, and adaptation stimulates the sympathetic nervous system which drains the reserves of the body.

EUSTRESS AND DISTRESS

This is not to say that all stress is bad. Even Hans Selye says he thrives on stress. In fact, Selye says he probably made a mistake calling it "stress" in the first place because now he must speak of "eustress" (the good kind) and "distress" (the destructive type). One man's "eu" is another man's "dis," of course, and for some people certain stress is more invigorating than it is for others.

Scientists have discovered that man's level of stress is related to his satisfaction and productivity. As stress increases, satisfaction

---

Psychological Signs of Overstress

Don't underestimate the warning signs of an overstressed body. When you're not feeling well take the time to find out why. Serious disorders are often preceded by changes in personality or behavior, so watch out for changes like these:

Hypochondria
Insomnia
Missing appointments or deadlines
Sudden propensity for mistakes
Confusing or forgetting dates, places, times, or other details
Making safe choices, but not necessarily the best choices
Sexual or romantic indiscretions
Sudden increase in drinking or smoking habits
Excessive worrying, especially over trivial matters
Excessive or irrational mistrust of associates
Constant harping on personal failures or shortcomings
Constant reference to death or suicide
Prolonged periods of brooding
Sudden reversals of usual behavior

---

and productivity also increase, but only to a point. Beyond that peak man becomes overstressed, and satisfaction and productivity decline. You can see why it would be helpful to know your level of stress capacity, but the technology for that insight simply doesn't exist.

People who thrive on stress are called racehorses, and their opposites are turtles. It is believed that turtles require a lower level of stress to be satisfied and productive, but they may not be any more immune to the physical consequences. (See Figure 26.)

This helps explain why a low-level clerk with little responsibility in a passive department is as much a candidate for a heart attack as the frenzied executive with extended responsibilities. Boredom may be just as stressful to the clerk as pressure is to the executive!

A study of 1540 bank officers discovered that those with few job-related stressors had as high an incidence of disorders as those who faced frequent stressors. In another study of 270,000 male

FIGURE 26. Favorable responses to different levels of stress. The "turtles" like and perform well in low-stress environments but perform poorly even under moderate stress. The "racehorses" like and perform well in high-stress environments but perform poorly in moderate- or low-stress environments.

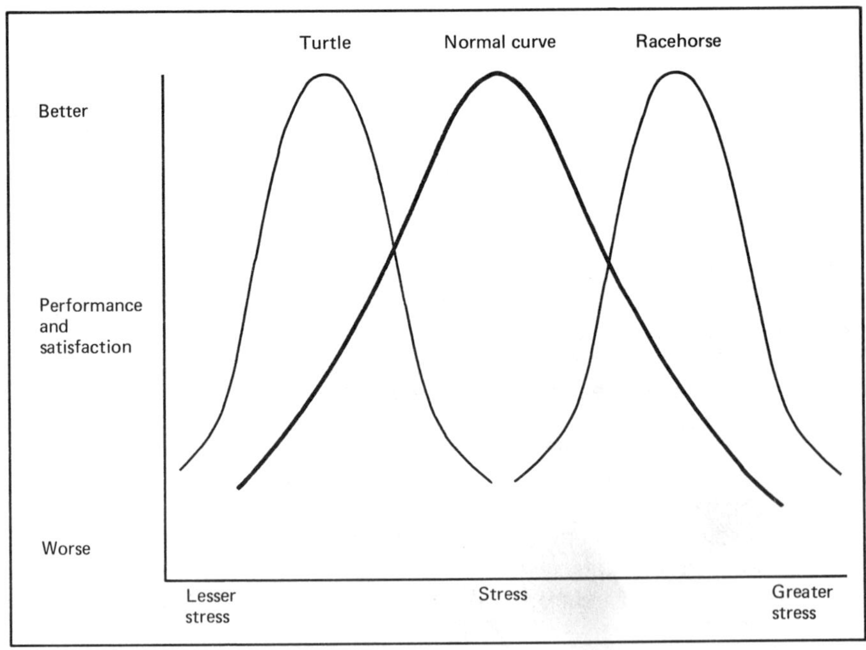

Stress Symptoms Test

How does stress manifest itself in your life? The test below will help you identify particular problems and may indicate that an organic illness is on the way.

To take the test, simply mark the frequency with which you have experienced each of the following problems during the last three months, using the following rating scale:

0—Never have this problem
1—Sometimes have this problem
2—Frequently have this problem
3—Constantly have this problem

1. Irritability ___
2. Loss of appetite ___
3. Trouble sleeping ___
4. Headaches ___
5. Tired feeling ___
6. Overeating ___
7. Ringing in ears ___
8. Lump in throat ___
9. Dry mouth ___
10. Racing heart beat ___
11. Skin rashes ___
12. Stomach pains ___
13. High blood pressure ___
14. Nightmares ___
15. Allergy problems ___
16. Lower back pain ___
17. Muscle aches/pains ___
18. Indigestion ___
19. Hives ___
20. Menstrual distress ___
21. Muscle twitching___
22. Frequent forgetting ___
23. Heavy drinking ___
24. Use of nonprescription drugs ___
25. Asthma attack ___
26. Nausea or vomiting ___
27. Depression ___
28. Minor accidents ___
29. Cold hands or feet ___
30. Sexual problems ___
31. Feelings of anger ___
32. Constipation ___
33. Nervousness ___
34. Heavy smoking ___
35. Hyperventilation ___
36. Infections ___
37. Peptic ulcer ___
38. Dermatitis ___
39. Colitis attack ___
40. Diarrhea ___

Too many 2 or 3 answers may mean that stress is controlling your body and it's time to make some changes and see a doctor. (Keep in mind, too, that all of the symptoms can be caused by physical problems that you may already have and thus not be related only to stress.)

---

employees at a major corporation, the rate of coronary disease was lower with each step up the occupational ladder.

Whether your stress is of "eu" or "dis" proportions doesn't seem to matter. What matters is your ability to adapt. Realizing that you are stressed is a first step—then you might be able to take some corrective action to meet the challenge or to put yourself in control of the situation. You can't always do that, of course. In a traffic jam you may feel stressed, but essentially you're helpless. If you miss a plane, you might be able to catch another flight, but then again, you might be out of luck.

Frighteningly, society may have eroded man's ability to cope with stress. As the rate of change in society escalates, and *Future Shock* proves it has, the level of stress follows accordingly.

"Increasingly, it is clear," writes David Mechanic in *Coping and Adaptation*, "that major stresses on modern man are not amenable to individual solutions but depend on highly organized cooperative efforts that transcend those of any individual man no matter how well developed his personal resources."

THE CASE FOR BELL

If David Mechanic is right—that individual efforts alone cannot combat the effects of stress—then how could we help the Bell managers?

We weren't sure, but we suspected that by working on specific policies and procedures within the company, the cooperative efforts to which Mechanic alluded could be made to work. Then the organization as a whole could reduce the stress level of its members.

However, we had one final stumbling block. Bell was not interested in our exploring company policies and procedures. Those were internal issues and off-limits to our charge.

We then developed another approach which we thought could be effective, though perhaps not as effective as the first. In discussing the Grant study, which formed the basis for his book *Adaptation To Life*, George Vaillant demonstrated that people mature naturally over time, and he was able to predict with greater accuracy than chance guesses that immature people become physically ill more often than mature people. The speed of the maturation process, he found, is influenced by the nature and quality of relationships, or what is called social support (see Figure 27).

Conveniently, social support "seems to act as a buffer between job stress and strain," according to a major study for the Department of Commerce. People with adequate social support in their work environments are better able to cope with stress, both behaviorally (they smoke and drink less) and psychologically (they experience less depression and irritability). Therefore, we

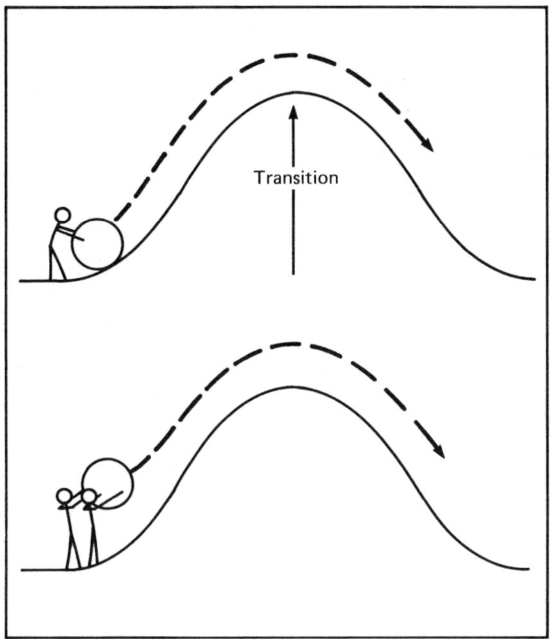

FIGURE 27. Social support and transitions can be likened to pushing a large ball up a hill. *Top:* The degree of difficulty of transitions is determined by the degree of life change required, time pressure, and stress (or how steep the hill is). *Bottom:* Social support helps you negotiate transitions (like having people help you roll the ball up the hill).

hypothesized that if we enhanced social support among the Bell managers, we could help them mature faster and make it easier for them to function.

Our plan was conceptualized in Figure 28. We would increase the managers' social support (A) and provide them with specific problem-solving tools (B) to use in their professional and personal lives. Then, to calm their sympathetic nervous system, we would teach them a meditation process (C).

Once our mission and the needs of the managers were understood, we designed a unique seminar of small-group discussions utilizing psychological exercises (many of which were presented earlier in this book) that explored the unconscious and intrapsychic components of human life.

We planned to help the managers examine their personal life structures, their goals, both personally and professionally, and their career futures. We also planned to teach them about stress, transitions, and adult development.

Each manager was given the opportunity to select the kind of problem he wanted to solve or improve during the workshop. Thirty-six percent of the managers chose work problems, 33 percent family problems, 15 percent health-related problems, and the remainder leisure-related problems that included finding time for hobbies, and making new friends.

Beginning in the first seminar, the managers were eager to share their views of life inside and outside the company, and as they related to their colleagues they were able to help each other face specific issues and problems. Undoubtedly this was a major breakthrough in Bell's history. Highly valued managers unabashedly shared their innermost fears, desires, and troubles for the first time ever!

Judging from the comments of participants, even after they had returned to work for several months the seminars continued to have their effect. One of the greatest benefits was the cancellation of the unspoken rule about personal issues. "The word's out, so to speak," said Judith A. Hedlund, division manager for revenue requirements at Pennsylvania Bell. She told *Business Week*, "It's O.K. to feel frustrated; it's O.K. to feel stress." And Stanley J. Kabala, a district plant superintendent for Diamond State, told the same magazine that since the seminars "People are much more open

FIGURE 28. Social support in the work environment—the plan for the Bell manager.

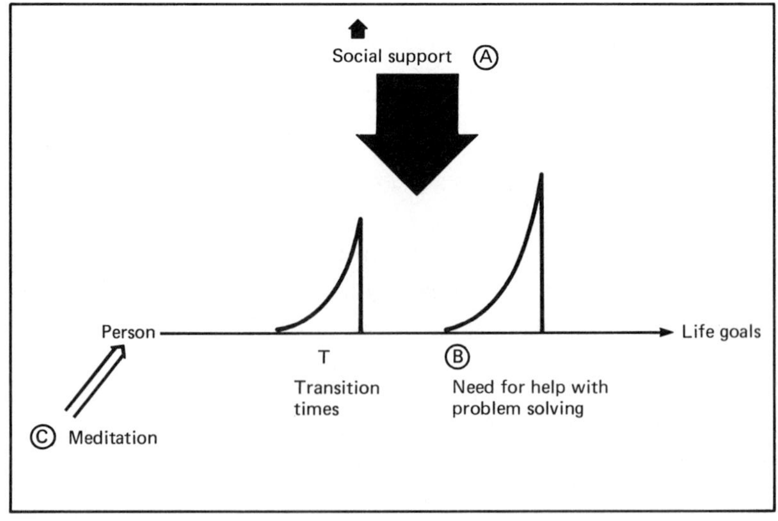

to each other, much more willing to discuss your problems, their problems."

Other participants explained how the seminar helped them in stressful situations. William A. Ebsworth, a Pennsylvania Bell plant engineer, said that shortly after his seminar he had less than six hours to meet a sizable request for technical information, a situation that would have irritated him prior to the seminar. But this time he set tight deadlines and effectively completed his task. The result was less resentment and reduced stress. "I tend to defuse things more than I did and not to respond in as emotional a way. I have to attribute that to the seminar."

In our own evaluation we asked each participant, "How was the seminar helpful?" and some of their comments included:

> *"It brought my problem into focus."*
>
> *"It gave me time and purpose for examining my life and the critical events in my life."*
>
> *"It helped me change behavior that I didn't like."*
>
> *"I discovered I was not the only person who wanted to improve his lifestyle."*
>
> *"It put into proper perspective where I am at this point in my life."*
>
> *"I now have a better understanding of my adult development."*
>
> *"It helped me identify feelings that I had suppressed. Now I feel better about myself."*

Perhaps one of the most enlightening comments came from a senior executive who said, "The seminar was reinforcement that at age 52 and beyond the basic attitude can be 'no more bull.' "

Three months after the seminars we conducted a follow-up study and found noteworthy improvements in the areas of depression, anxiety, hostility, interpersonal oversensitivity, paranoid ideation, psychosis, and obsessive-compulsive behaviors.

WHAT THE SEMINAR ACHIEVED

The bottom line was that we significantly decreased the psychiatric symptomatology of the Bell managers, and that was meaningful for several reasons. It was proof that organizational problems could be decreased through psychiatric intervention. And since psychiatric symptomatology is related to stress levels, the increased social support, plus problem solving and relaxation techniques, diminished the effects of organizational stress on the Bell managers.

Furthermore, the seminar taught us that when men and women are not made to feel sick, the barriers to working on their lives dissolve. As they begin to understand their adult development, they recognize that change is normal and to be expected, and they are willing to work on their own lives and offset or diminish many of life's crises.

DESTRESSING YOUR BODY

At CSAD we do not believe that people on their own can always control the effects of stress. Some people, in certain occupations and at optimal levels of stress, do effectively control stress, but most people cannot. In the Pennsylvania Bell case we demonstrated that stress is as much an organizational problem as it is an individual concern, so we believe organizations must also get into the act of combating stress effects. Therefore, in the final pages of this chapter you'll find several effective exercises for individuals who want to do what they can to fight the evils of stress, but in the next two chapters you'll find several important suggestions for organizations as well.

RELAXATION

There's been an expansion of technology around self-hypnosis, meditation, alpha processes, transcendental meditation (TM), and biofeedback techniques that is intended to relax the body. There's no evidence to suggest that one of these techniques is more effective than the others, but when practiced faithfully all these techniques are successful. All of them activate the parasympathetic nervous system and help to deactivate a stressed body. Every adult should learn some relaxation technique and practice it at least once a day, preferably twice a day, for about fifteen minutes.

Internal Stimulus

One popular method of relaxation can be learned in about three minutes. It consists of four basic steps:

1. *Find a comfortable sitting or lying position. Don't cross your ankles or legs or fold your arms. Loosen any tight clothing.*
2. *Forget about the world and its problems. Take a passive attitude about life. Float in your own world for these few minutes.*
3. *Repeat an internal stimulus. You might repeat the same word over and over—"one," for example. Or you might count, "One, two, three, one, two, three." With each repetition relax your body by letting go of its weight.*
4. *Push out any intruding thoughts. Be gentle. Keep repeating your stimulus and relax.*

If you do this exercise once or twice a day, you can keep your system calm for a twenty-four-hour period. What you're doing, actually, is decreasing your oxygen consumption, your heart rate, sleep time, and fatigue, and lowering your blood pressure. That's all very healthful for your body.

Relaxing Muscles

You may prefer a second technique of relaxation which does not require an internal stimulus and is also easy to learn. It concentrates on relaxing your muscles. Assume the first two steps of the exercise above, then:

Progressively tighten and relax the muscles in your body. Begin with your feet and move up. Contract the muscles of your toes, feet, and heels. Squeeze for a few seconds, then let go. They'll feel heavier, but let go of the weight. Now do your ankles. Then your calves. Continue up to your forehead, and don't forget your fingers and hands. This may take about fifteen minutes, but after you practice for several weeks you'll be able to do it in about five minutes, whether it's at your desk, in the car, or in the dentist's chair!

When you've got a report due in thirty minutes and you're feeling irritable and tense at work, or you're about to leave for work and one of your children spills chocolate milk all over your suit, the Stress Spiral (illustrated in Figure 29) is about to attack.

It works like this: You're under pressure and your time is limited. As your deadline nears your sense of pressure intensifies, and that increases the urgency of your needs, adding even more pressure. As pressure builds it ties knots in your stomach and races all sorts of worrisome thoughts through your mind. Eventually you become so exhausted you've got to sit down, or lie down, and sometimes you are immobilized. Now you can't complete your task satisfactorily and the thought of that makes you feel even worse.

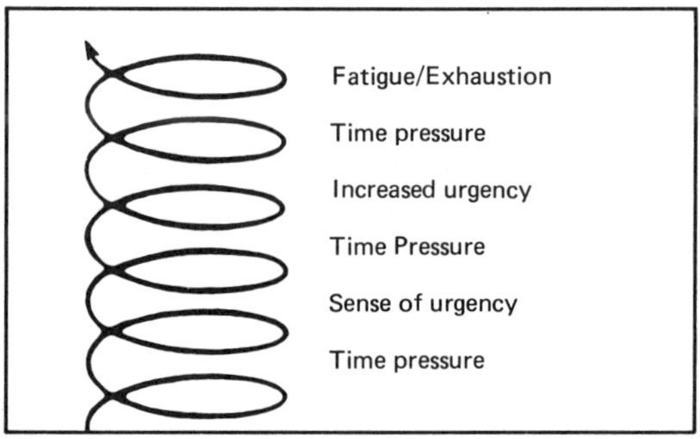

FIGURE 29. The Stress Spiral.

Stop! Before you exhaust yourself, stop for this sixty-second exercise that's well worth your time:

1. *Sit down, take a couple of deep breaths. Actually feel the air come in through your nostrils, down to your lungs, and then back out. If there's tension or tightness around your neck or shoulders, try to feel warmth in those areas and loosen up. Relax.*
2. *Visualize a peaceful scene and concentrate on it. Maybe it's a favorite vacation spot or some exotic island you'd like to visit. It helps to have a pleasant landscape portrait on your wall for this very purpose.*
3. *Push out all thoughts of deadlines, reports, worries, and pressures.*

Dream for sixty seconds. Concentrate on the peacefulness and beauty of that scene.

If you regularly use some other technique of relaxation, this shortened version will be effective beyond those sixty seconds of relief.

STRESS IN THE ENVIRONMENT

Much of the stress you experience comes from your environment, but many people don't realize who or what is making them feel stressed. Here's a quick exercise that will help you identify environmental stressors.

You'll recall from our discussion of the Social Systems Map (see Chapter 4) that there are four crucial quadrants to life: work, friendship, community, and family. There are stressors in each of those quadrants, and while it would overwhelm any human who tried to neutralize all the quadrants at once, you can successfully work on one quadrant at a time.

Let's say, for example, that you're feeling a lot of tension at work and so you dissect that segment of your life to find out what effect it's having on you physically and emotionally. This requires asking yourself a series of related questions:

"What are my feelings about work overall?" [In this case let's say you feel depressed and irritable.]

"Why? What's causing those feelings?" [Your boss wants you to "produce more," the comptroller wants you to "get reports in on time," and your subordinates want you to "be available more of the time."]

"How do I react physically to these requests?" [Your neck tightens and your stomach gets upset.]

"How do these specific requests make me feel? . . . How do I feel when I don't produce more, when I don't turn reports in on time and when I'm not available more of the time?" [To the first two you feel guilty, and to the third, angry.]

"What's my verbal response to these stressors?" [You say to your boss, "OK, I'll do more." And to the comptroller, "Look, I'm doing the best I can." And to your subordinates, "I just don't have the time."]

Graphically your problem looks like Figure 30. If you see it on paper, there's a better chance that you'll be able to do something to turn your "distress" into "eustress." You can't necessarily relieve the pressure, nor do you always want to, but you can alter each situation so that your reactions will be of benefit to you.

You might say to your boss, "I've got a lot to do, and I don't mind the work, but it would be helpful if you and I set some priorities." That way you'll feel better about your work and you'll probably produce more.

To the comptroller you could suggest that he extend his deadline or streamline his reports. And to your subordinates you could design a reorganization plan for staff functions and duties so that you wouldn't have to be available more of the time.

One of the benefits of this exercise is that it helps people connect their pressures, behaviors, and feelings. People frequently fail to relate these matters, and once they see their problems clearly they can begin to create some motivation for changing the circumstances. They can't necessarily eliminate the pressures, but they can make the pressures work to their advantage.

"WORST POSSIBLE" EXERCISE

There's one other exercise that's extremely useful in situations where you can't control what's happening. I call it the Worst Possible Consequence. I use it in traffic jams or if I miss a train connec-

FIGURE 30. Stress diagram.

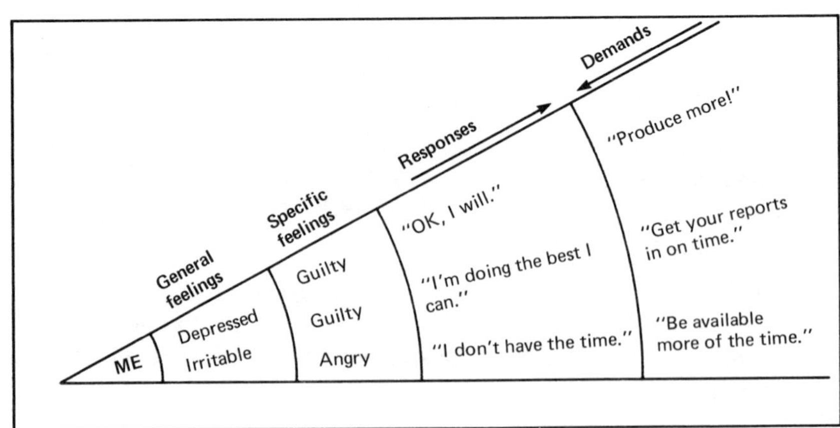

tion or plane departure. I ask myself, "What's the worst possible consequence that can occur as a result of this?"

If I'm en route to a meeting and a traffic jam blocks my way, my answer is, "I obviously won't make the meeting." And what's the worst possible consequence of that? "I won't get the contract." And the worst possible consequence of that? "I won't be able to pay my bills." And the worst possible consequence of that? "My creditors will complain."

At some devastating point, right before picturing myself being hauled to jail, or losing my home to the bank, I return to the first answer and ask, "What will *probably* happen?"

"I'll probably be able to reschedule the meeting. When I explain what happened, the people will understand."

"But if they don't understand and I don't get the contract, then what? Will I really not be able to pay my bills?"

"Not as quickly, perhaps, but I'll get another contract."

So the worst possible consequence is that I won't get the contract. Now, what can I do about the problem in the next few minutes? If I can get to a telephone, I can make a call and possibly postpone the meeting. But if it's impossible to get to a phone, then I can't do a thing about it, and in that case I have to calm down because stewing about it, when I can't fight or flee, only creates wear and tear for my body.

I've discovered that people often punish themselves needlessly for something that didn't happen, or won't happen, and they suffer in ways that aren't even known to them.

One point of caution is in order here. If you find yourself consistently utilizing the Worst Possible Consequence exercise, you should probably evaluate your time management. Maybe you don't allow yourself enough time to get to meetings. You might also have some psychological problem around the issue of responsibility, and in that case you should seek professional help.

OTHER EXERCISES

There are numerous other exercises for relaxation and reducing the ill effects of stress in the environment, and they have been publicized in some of the articles and books listed in the suggested readings for this chapter. You should find techniques of relaxation and stress negotiation that are convenient for you, and then use them!

CHAPTER EIGHT

Managerial Transitions

"We tend to meet any new situation
by reorganizing, and a wonderful method
it can be for creating the illusion
of progress while producing confusion,
inefficiency, and demoralization."

PETRONIUS, 210 B.C.

By the onset of the 1980s, a multitude of American companies agreed that an employee's personal development is not a burden for the employee to carry alone, but an opportunity for the company to share. Employees can be led to advanced levels of productivity and satisfaction, it was understood, and getting them there represents a challenge that corporations can no longer ignore.

This enlightened attitude is a major breakthrough from the days of old when the organization man was expected to toe the line at work and keep his personal needs intact and out of the way. It is a breakthrough made necessary by the new American employee who represents a markedly different image than the organization man of the 1950s.

Then, as William H. Whyte, Jr. explained so vividly in *The Organization Man,* companies produced and attracted security-seeking, passive, bureaucratic employees who played safe and believed in a social ethic rather than a Protestant ethic. That is, men sacrificed toughminded individuality, which for years had poured through the bloodstream of American ingenuity, for conformity, which Whyte and other social critics, including David Riesman, C. Wright Mills, and Erich Fromm, predicted would lead to a less creative, dull, and destructive type of bureaucratic management.

Much of what the experts predicted would happen, happened, except that American men and women never entirely surrendered their individuality. Many did, of course. They offered themselves to their companies like lambs, and in a matter of time represented their companies twenty-four hours a day.

Sociologically this phenomenon could be rationalized—it belonged to the Eisenhower years—but psychologically it was less clearly understood. There was little opportunity for psychological intervention in American business at the time, but as the era of conformity was erased by the Kennedy Camelot, the need for psychological understanding became imminent. Once the words *innovation*, *imagination*, *invention*, and *decision* were spoken by a charismatic president who made it clear that he was taking his country in a different direction, organizations had to change their ways.

In too many instances companies tried to change their ways simply by reorganizing their people and departments, and with rare exception they failed to achieve noteworthy gains. What few company executives understood then, and what many are not fully cognizant of today, is that the "fit between the social structure and environmental demands," as David Mechanic wrote in *Coping and Adaptation*, "is probably the major determinant of successful social adaptation. Man's abilities to cope with the environment depend on the efficacy of the solutions that his culture provides, and the skills he develops are dependent on the adequacy of the preparatory institutions to which he has been exposed."

Reorganization may be part of a company's game plan for success, but the issues of contemporary work include humanitarian as well as organizational components that are interrelated and complex—for instance, the promotion that comes during the midlife transition, or the transfer that occurs just before. The ability of employees to adapt to these changes is directly related to the attitudes of their employers. Most employees can't make those transitions on their own, and many who aren't helped will become anxious or depressed, and they may develop destructive emotional and/or physical behaviors that will detract from their own effectiveness and productivity.

Obviously, then, companies that hope to maintain smooth business operations in addition to boosting productivity and profit should nurture the functionality of their people. Where employees are confused, uninterested, and depressed, productivity is less than optimal or even desirable. In a small company just one dysfunctional employee can disrupt the normal business routine, and in a large corporation, where many employees probably are dysfunctional, they block the path to progress and potential success. Even in countries where the goal of business is not to earn comfortable profits, it makes sense to develop mature, healthy employees.

Unfortunately, there are no complete, organizational theories for encouraging companies to assess the deficiencies of their employees or institute remedial training. At the CSAD, we tell companies to monitor their own development, not solely by the technical measurements they know so well—profitability and cash flow, for example—but also by the factors of their environment, their employees' adult development, and the ability of their employees to adapt to change.

FOUR WAYS TO MONITOR DEVELOPMENT

Any company serious about monitoring its development must focus attention on four critical areas:

1. *the global environment*
2. *the person/environment fit, including social support*
3. *employee assistance, including the nature of the person*
4. *the management of transitions.*

In this chapter we recommend one process for monitoring the global environment and then focus on the person/environment fit. In the next chapter we will discuss employee assistance and the management of certain transitions.

MEASURING THE ENVIRONMENT

In *Coping and Adaptation,* Mechanic also wrote:

> *Successful personal adaptation has at least three components at the individual level. First, the person must have the capabilities and skills to deal with the social and environmental demands to which he is exposed. . . . Second, individuals must be motivated to meet the*

demands that become evident in their environment. . . . Third, individuals must have the capabilities to maintain a state of psychological equilibrium so that they can direct their energies and skills to meeting external, in contrast to internal, needs.

It should be apparent that the capabilities, skills, motivation, and psychological equilibrium that Mechanic mentions are to a great extent company responsibilities. An environment that is conducive to those qualities and needs is most helpful.

One method companies use to test for a healthy environment is the Work Environment Scale (WES), which can be administered in less than a half hour's time, depending upon the size of the company.

The WES, developed at the Social Ecology Laboratory at Stanford University, measures relationship dimensions (social support and commitment to work), personal growth dimensions (self-sufficiency and efficiency), and specific job-related dimensions (pressures, expectations, comfort).

Work Environment Scale Subscale Dimensions

Relationship Dimensions

1. Involvement	Measures the extent to which workers are concerned and committed to their jobs; includes items designed to reflect enthusiasm and constructive activity
2. Peer cohesion	Measures the extent to which workers are friendly and supportive of each other
3. Staff support	Measures the extent to which management is supportive of workers and encourages workers to be supportive of each other

Personal Growth Dimensions

4. Autonomy	Assesses the extent to which workers are encouraged to be self-sufficient and to make their own decisions; includes items related to personal development and growth
5. Task orientation	Assesses the extent to which the climate emphasizes good planning and efficiency and encourages workers to "get the job done"

System Maintenance and System Change Dimensions

6. Work pressure	Measures the extent to which the press of work dominates the job milieu

7. Clarity	Measures the extent to which workers know what to expect in their daily routines and how explicitly rules and policies are communicated
8. Control	Measures the extent to which management uses rules and pressures to keep workers under control
9. Innovation	Measures the extent to which variety, change, and new approaches are emphasized in the work environment
10. Physical comfort	Assesses the extent to which the physical surroundings contribute to a pleasant work environment

A company representative can administer the WES questionnaire to each employee, and then results from individual units of the company can be tabulated independently.

From those results a profile of each unit can be constructed (see Figure 31) and used as a learning tool between managers and subordinates.

For example, two work groups of one company are measured against ten environmental variables, and it's clear that while work

FIGURE 31. WES Form R Profiles for Employees in Work Groups 110 and 117.

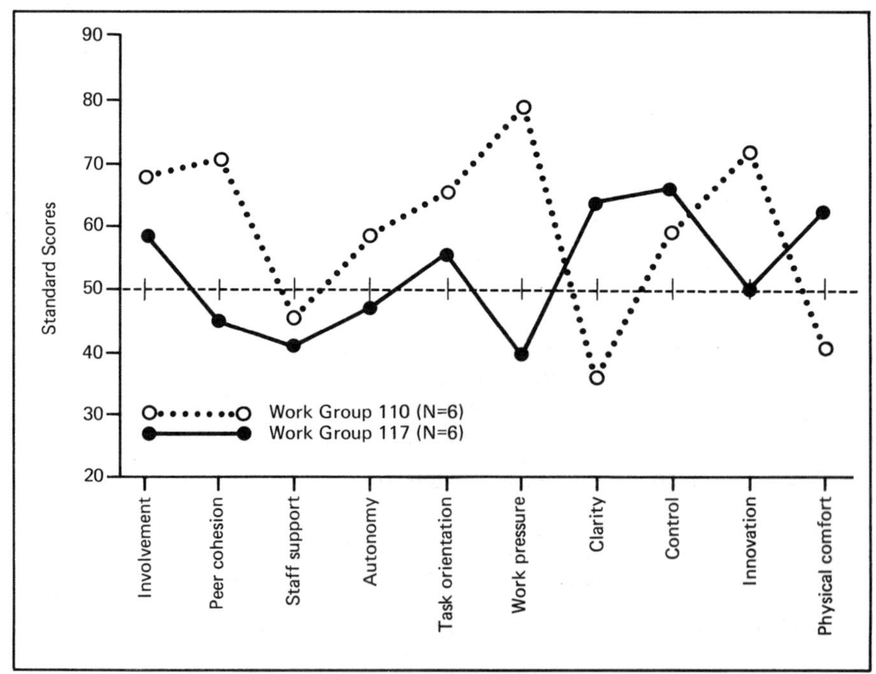

group 117 scores higher than work group 110 in most categories, the environments of both work groups require some attention. They are not "healthy" in at least seven of the areas measured, and in several of the others they show poor results.

Once a manager recognizes the areas of need in his unit, he can then ask his people for specific recommendations for change, and he can also be held accountable for making internal improvements in every area that falls below the 50th percentile.

Each unit can make certain improvements on its own, and additional improvements can be coordinated among departments.

Also, the company president can monitor the entire process and then help implement specific changes. Later he can survey the company to determine whether or not any changes were beneficial.

Through these combined efforts it is possible for a company to redirect its influences so that the environment promotes rather than deters social adaptation.

THE PERSON/ENVIRONMENT FIT

Even before the social climate is tested, a company can begin to educate its people about adult development and its relationship to the environment.

The failure of companies to foster awareness of adult development is a major stumbling block in the path of better human dynamics in the corporate world. An erroneous assumption among company presidents and executives is that employees already know about their development. They don't, of course. Equally wrong is the assumption that employees will find out about adult development through friends or the media. That may be true, to some extent, but it's not enough. Too much of what is known about adult development is fuzzy, even to experts, and it gets misinterpreted. Educating people about adult development is not a job that friends and the media should be expected to do alone. Nor can they. Employees will be better off relying upon knowledgable sources to provide them information in a formal setting that allows them to confidently explore and discuss personal concerns and issues. Companies that have sponsored adult development seminars have enhanced the maturity levels of their employees and have seen significant improvements as a result.

THE LOEVINGER STAGES

The effects of employee maturity upon job performance are obvious in the research of Jane Loevinger, a professor of psychiatry at Washington University. She has described ten stages of ego development that occur in the course of a lifetime, and three of these stages—conformist, conscientious, and autonomous—illustrate the value of psychiatric maturation and are critical to employers and employees.

Conformist

The conformist, according to Loevinger, "obeys rules, just because they are group accepted rules." The conformist "tends to perceive himself and others as conforming to socially approved norms. While he observes group differences he is insensitive to individual differences. . . . while the conformist likes and trusts other people within his group, he may define that group narrowly and reject any or all outside groups."

Conscientious

"At the conscientious stage," says Loevinger, "the major elements of an adult conscience are present. They include long-term, self-evaluation goals and ideals, differentiated self-criticism and a sense of responsibility . . . . at this stage a person is his brother's keeper; he feels responsible for other people, at times to the extent of feeling obliged to shape another's life or to prevent him from making errors."

Autonomous

Loevinger believes that "a distinctive mark of the autonomous stage is the capacity to acknowledge and cope with inner conflict," including conflicting needs and duties. "Probably the autonomous person does not have more conflict than others; rather he has the courage to acknowledge and deal with conflict rather than ignoring it or projecting it onto the environment. Where the conscientious person tends to construe the world in terms of polar opposites, the autonomous person partly transcends these polarities, seeing reality as complex and multi-faceted . . . . the autonomous stage is so named partly because the person at that point recognizes other people's need for autonomy."

Loevinger's model provides an interesting developmental framework for understanding many of the common problems that occur in organizational life.

Consider the case of Jim Feinberg who had been, in his company's opinion, a good manager. Jim had joined the company at about the age of 21, right out of college, and when he came to the CSAD he had been promoted twice. From the very first day on the job Jim was well liked. He was friendly, open, the kind of guy who'd listen to instructions and follow through very efficiently. Sometimes he was overly defensive, but he was always loyal to the company.

As Jim got a little older his attitudes began to change. Not that he was disloyal to the company, but that was part of his problem. He viewed his budget in very personal terms, so that any expenditure of company money became a moral issue. Jim was so conscientious that he couldn't understand other opinions about budgeting, and he often ended up at odds with fellow managers who held different views about the distribution of the company's resources. As a result, people changed their opinions about Jim. They began to see him as rigid, limiting, and controlling.

What had happened? Why would a likable manager become a thorn in the side of his fellow workers?

Without anyone realizing it, Jim had advanced from the conformist to conscientious stage of ego development. Along the way he had become very self-evaluative and self-critical. He set very strict standards for his division of the company, and he lacked the ability to see that other people, who were experiencing various other developmental processes, needed to set their own values and view the company from independent perspectives. Thus, Jim had become a restrictive, uncreative manager. His presence blocked the maturation of fellow employees and the productivity of the company overall.

For Jim's sake, and the company's as well, he would hopefully advance to Loevinger's autonomous stage from where he could tolerate ambiguity and motivate others without making them defensive. Once he learned not to disown employees or become dependent on a few employees, and learned to coordinate interdivision communication and delegation and conceptualize long-term goals for the company, he would be far more effective and superior as a manager.

Getting Jim from the conscientious to the autonomous stage was as much a company obligation as it was a personal need. An initial step was for the company to see what was happening in Jim's life. (Since the employer is often first to notice changes of attitudes and behaviors, he is sometimes in a better position to identify developmental problems than the employees they affect.) Then specific approaches could be used to stimulate growth and reduce much of the conflict in Jim's managerial style.

VAILLANT'S DISCOVERIES

Before we discuss some of these specific approaches, there's yet another researcher who has added considerably to what is known about the relationship between employers and employees.

George Vaillant's study of Harvard sophomores is the single most powerful documentation relating various personalities and environmental events. An internationally known psychiatrist, Vaillant followed the lives of ninety-six Harvard sophomores, forty-four of whom went into business after graduation. His subjects were the creme de la creme and could reasonably be expected to advance rapidly to executive levels in their corporations. However, Vaillant discovered that seven of the forty-four graduates never made it out of lower management, and surprisingly all seven of them had one characteristic in common: they could not establish intimate relationships! They did not have close, meaningful relationships with other people, and as a result their coworkers and employers were likely to consider them cold, distant, aloof, or uncomfortable. In a corporation, where advancement depends upon good human relations, these men were carrying around severely limiting handicaps.

Since the ability to develop intimate relationships is a developmental skill that normally ripens in the early 20s, it's very likely that the seven graduates were developmentally stuck at the time they joined their companies, or shortly thereafter, and therefore they would probably never be promoted above lower management.

Of course, developmentally stuck individuals do get promoted, and when that happens the outcome is almost certainly calamitous. A case in point is Samuel Taglieber, a very competent corporate forecaster in Denver.

Sam was promoted to the top of his division primarily for his competency. He was brilliant! He was not only good at operating the company's computers but he could also program projects for maximum efficiency. Sam had grown up with the company, so to speak, and it wasn't a surprise to anyone when he was promoted to manager of corporate planning. But the moment Sam was promoted, his flagrant difficulties surfaced. Subordinates who had found Sam to be an enjoyable coworker suddenly became unhappy, and several of them quit. In a few months' time Sam's department had a turnover rate of 50 percent, whereas before he was promoted turnover was relatively low.

Furthermore, every division manager in the company who depended upon Sam's data—accounting, sales, manufacturing—complained about him after he was promoted. When they couldn't settle their differences with Sam, they'd turn to his superior for assistance. "He just seems like he's in another world. He's unwilling to compromise. Sometimes he gets angry and explodes," went a typical complaint. "I know he's a hard worker, he stays late every night and he's the best man in that division, but. . . ." The complaints seemed never-ending.

Sam was a victim of two developmental events. First, he was an autocratic manager who was probably at Loevinger's conscientious stage, and second, he was a man who had never learned to develop intimate relationships. Technically, Sam was a whiz and a hard worker, but he was not interested in people. As he explained it, he had few friends. In high school and college he was a loner, and even after he had a family he was more involved with his electronics and hunting than with his wife or children. He loved his family, but he just wasn't very close to them, and when they tried to get too close to him, he withdrew.

When Sam joined his company his deficiencies were not obvious, and as he settled into his job, always pleasing his boss with superior performance, his deficiencies remained hidden. But everything had to come out into the open once he was promoted and put in charge of other people.

LESS EFFECTIVE EMPLOYEES

Vaillant's study strongly suggests that the ability to establish intimate relationships is a critical developmental step which extends from private life to professional life. Seven of Vaillant's forty-four graduates (16 percent) were less effective because of this deficiency, and in the opinion of staff members at CSAD, up to 25 percent of the employees in the average business or organization cannot form intimate relationships. That represents significant developmental blockage for employers and employees combined, and it is a serious problem for American business.

Vaillant also discovered that seventeen of the graduates in his study were still lieutenants or vice-presidents in their 50s, and of them, nine had a common deficiency: they were "either bland and colorless or remained at 50 status conscious and anxious to please . . . . they still wrestled with career consolidation." That is, they were still concerned about developing their careers long after what was thought to be the normal developmental period for this activity.

These men suffered from a lack of psychological centering. They could not form an independent sense of their own values and goals. In the words of Michael Macoby in *The Gamesman,* these were the Company Men, similar to the Organization Men of the 1950s. They had so strongly identified with their companies that they had no independent values and goals, no independent sense of purpose and self.

Why should this be a deficiency, and why should it interfere with an employee's ability to develop or to produce for the company? In many ways, Company Men are ideal employees and managers. They are loyal, thorough, committed, hard-working, and obedient. But Company Men are not creative, and they exhibit little initiative. All life, in their eyes, emerges from the company—without any realization that *they* make the company. Company Men will remain stuck within the boundaries of a problem and never, or rarely, rethink the problem without being told to do so. In essence, Company Men are less energetic and less capable of leadership.

Again, employers and employees pay a price for this deficiency. About 20 percent of Vaillant's Harvard graduates, the creme de la creme, could be called Company Men. At the CSAD, we have often found this percentage to be as high as 50 percent in some companies!

The combined percentages in Vaillant's study add up to 36 percent, but we suspect that at least 50 percent of the employees in an average business or organization experience developmental arrest if they're not specifically helped to reinstitute their own

---

EMPLOYEE COST FIGURES

The National Association for Mental Health reported that mental illness cost the country about $37 billion in 1974—$14.5 billion for the treatment of mental illness and $22.5 billion for indirect costs which included:

—$10.4 billion lost to disability (employee inability to work at full capacity because of absenteeism, inefficiency, or inability to hold a job)
—$4.9 billion lost to death (suicide, accidents, physical problems brought on by emotional problems, alcoholism, drug abuse)
—$5.5 billion lost to patient care activities (including wages lost by hospitalized patients, or by people who must care for a mentally ill person)

In *Executive Health,* Philip Goldberg cited the following facts:

—Premature employee deaths cost American industry $19.4 billion a year, more than the combined 1976 profits of *Fortune's* top five corporations.
—An estimated $10 to $20 billion is lost through absence, hospitalization, and early death among executives.
—Alcoholism costs industry about $15.6 billion annually due to absenteeism and medical costs.
—About 32 million workdays and $8.6 billion in wages is lost annually to heart-related diseases.
—According to the American Heart Association, the cost of recruiting replacements for executives felled by heart disease is about $700 million a year.

And the *Behavioral Sciences Newsletter* has reported:

—77 million workdays are lost every year in the United States as a direct result of cigarette smoking.
—Smoking can cause depression, tension, lack of stamina, lack of concentration. It diminishes mental efficiency as much as 23 percent.
—Death or incapacity related to smoking hits particularly hard at the 40–65 age group that includes many of the executives and other personnel who are hardest to replace.
—Solid wastes, fumes, and films due to smoking increase maintenance costs.

No matter what problems you identify—mental health, alcoholism, drug abuse, stress, smoking—all are costly to industry.

---

developmental growth. In terms of self-esteem and profit, no one can imagine the tremendous loss this represents to mankind and business in general.

THE MANAGERIAL STAGES

With Loevinger's and Vaillant's findings in mind, and with an optimistic view that something can be done to stop much of the developmental blockage that occurs in corporations, it is helpful to look at the four managerial stages that await most employees:

STAGE I: *Apprenticeship (usually early 20s)*

STAGE II: *Specialist (frequently mid-20s to late 30s)*

STAGE III: *Generalist (mid-30s to 50s, and possibly remainder of career)*

STAGE IV: *Sponsorship (mid-40s or 50s to retirement, if at all)*

MANAGEMENT TRAINING

Numerous management training programs are offered almost every week in major cities throughout the United States. The quality of some of these programs leaves a lot to be desired, but some of the best programs are administered by the New York Management Center and the American Management Association (AMA), as well as by other lesser known organizations.

Courses are designed for junior and executive-level managers and include:

Executive Self-management	Managing People
Leadership Skills for Women	Matrix Management
The Executive Image	Foreign Market Entry Strategies
Management Styles	Executive Effectiveness

Some courses are conducted in a day's time, others over a weekend or for an extended period.

The New York Management Center is a private organization that administers its own programs as well as those of other institutions, including universities. The AMA sponsors 3700 seminars a year in various parts of the country.

For additional information contact the New York Management Center at 360 Lexington Avenue, New York, NY 10017, (212) 953-7272, or the AMA at 135 West 50th Street, New York, NY 10020, (212) 586-8100.

Each of these stages can be divided into:

1. *tasks that are performed*
2. *relationships involved*
3. *psychological adjustments required.*

In-depth training programs can be developed by or brought to the company to assist employees as they make the transition from one stage to the next.

This book cannot provide all of the insight necessary to develop these programs, but much of the information that was presented in earlier chapters can be utilized by employers for their employees. In addition, as we examine each of these stages we will recommend appropriate kinds of training.

The Apprentice

STAGE I: APPRENTICESHIP

Overview

—Required to perform one aspect of organization's tasks competently
—Needs to learn which tasks are most critical
—Must learn how to get things done through social (informal) network
—Must adjust to being closely observed for indications of competence and future potential
—Must adjust to working under close supervision of superior and/or mentor
—Helping others do work for which they are responsible.

Activities
—Fairly routine and detailed work
—Expected to demonstrate initiative and innovation in solving problems.

Relationships
—Needs to build relationship with mentor who will guide through tasks
—Learn to get things done with relatively low influence
—Learning through observing and trial-and-error learning (developing organizational savvy)
—Accepting instructions from others.

Adjustments
—Conflict in balancing compliant acceptance of assignments and detailed work versus aggressively reaching out for new challenges (being innovative)
—Establishing organizational visibility and influence in order to get things done

—Tolerance for routine and detailed work
—Need for confirmation and approval (feedback) from supervisor
—Balancing dependence versus independence
—Getting stuck in low-opportunity positions.

The major needs of the apprentice in an organization are in conflict. They are dependence versus independence, and they represent authority. How often should the apprentice follow, and when should he lead? That's a major issue for any young employee. The background of the individual will have a tremendous impact on how well he responds to the authority system of the organization.

If his family relationship was typical, the authority system there was directed toward his own physical and psychological development. In school and college, the authority system was directed at his ability to learn tasks. In the organization, however, he is suddenly, and sometimes harshly, introduced to a third authority system which asks him to learn, but also to provide a product, and the product is far more important to those in authority than his learning. At this point, the apprentice can make two possible blunders. He can become overly compliant, the route to Company Man status, or he can rebel. If he rebels, it's an almost suicidal decision from the organization's point of view. Even if he survives, he'll surely be shuffled off to some noncritical area of performance where he'll be limited to minimal responsibility and power.

TRAINING THE APPRENTICE

The problem of dependence versus independence and many of the other issues of apprenticeship can be solved in a training program designed to socialize a young employee to a new authority system. Individuals can be taught the rules of apprenticeship and the methods for being effective with little status and almost no power. They can also be given feedback about their effectiveness of accomplishing certain goals.

As far as we know, companies usually give their new employees a day or two of orientation, but there are no specific training programs in business or organizational life for the apprentice. That's either because companies are not aware of the issues, rules, and methods of apprenticeship, or they don't consider these matters very important. Certainly the attitude of employers should be to give employees every opportunity to succeed, and this thinking ought to begin at the apprentice level.

MENTORING

In addition to training programs, much of an apprentice's socialization can be accomplished on the job via a mentor or womentor.* These are the father-son and mother-daughter relationships of the corporate world, but they are seldom deliberately utilized, and as a result they are often not successful.

A mentor or womentor can teach an apprentice the political, social, historical, and organizational realities of company life at little cost to the company. These relationships occur in almost every company, with or without company guidance, and they are actually very simple:

Upon graduation from college a young man or woman joins a company and works closely with someone older, someone who has been a member of the company for a number of years, someone who knows the ropes. The mentor is the seasoned professional. He knows the realities and he has learned to work with people, both in and out of the company, so he knows how to get along. On a day-to-day basis he shares this information with his "student." He may advise when to act; when not. He may suggest methods and approaches to people and problems. He is a caretaker and a motivator. This is a valuable learning experience, and without it the apprentice is more likely to fail.

Finding a mentor or womentor usually happens instinctively in most companies, but where there is no or little support for this activity the relationships are more difficult to form. Usually, a young, promising manager is socially adept, and he will find his own guiding light, but there are many apprentices who aren't socially experienced. Those, for example, who have never learned to develop intimate relationships may not find mentors unless the company encourages them.

Therefore, companies need to legitimize the mentor/apprentice relationship, and they can do so in several ways:

- *Offer educational programs about the values of mentoring for both apprentices and managers.*
- *Allow company time for mentor/apprentice relationships.*

*Thanks to Ann Rosen Spector for the use of this term, which applies to women mentoring women in organizations.

- *Sponsor training seminars for senior managers to teach them mentoring skills.*
- *In the company's evaluation process of managers, hold them responsible for developing young people in the company.*
- *Transfer employees laterally, particularly if they're having trouble finding a mentor. This will provide the apprentice an opportunity to mix with senior employees. (If he already has a mentor and he's transferred, he should be allowed access to his mentor.)*

PROBLEMS FOR WOMEN

It is easier for a man to mentor a man than mentor a woman. Theoretically the relationships are the same, but there are special problems for the woman.

When a woman is mentored by a man, there are issues other than the normal learning aspects involved.

If she's a wife and/or mother, a male mentor may not understand family obligations, and he probably won't identify with her feelings. He may not understand the "political" problems of being a woman, he won't realize the depths of womanhood. In effect, the woman mentored by a man is robbed of a role model.

Unfortunately, sex also becomes an issue when a man mentors a woman. The mentor may let slip sexual innuendos or even expect sexual favors. In such situations the woman is forced either to ignore his advances and risk rejection or punitive responses—or give in and sleep with him. Sleeping with him under these circumstances is always a mistake and will probably result in dismissal for one or both of the employees.

Still another sexually related problem arises between the male mentor and female apprentice and affects primarily the mentor. At the end of the mentoring relationship, when the man and woman go their separate ways within the company, he will feel a loss of control (which he would experience with a male apprentice), but he may also sense sexual rejection. Often that is a serious blow to his ego. If he's in a midlife or postmidlife transition, the rejection may be more than he can handle alone, and there may be serious repercussions.

Of equal concern is the woman who serves as mentor for a man. Such a pair have all the problems relating to sex discussed above in addition to the problem of status. Women are often considered and treated as low-status employees in corporate towers, and so the man who is mentored by a woman is often frustrated because his mentor is involved in a variety of political conflicts within the company. He is robbed of a role model, and the mentoring process may thus be ineffective.

On the other hand, the woman who escapes the low-status stereotype and is promoted to the upper echelon of the company is frequently reluctant to womentor because a relationship with a woman may draw her back to a low-status identity. Hopefully, as the number of women promoted in corporations increases, this and similar stereotypes will vanish.

BREAKING AWAY

A problem for both men and women apprentices is ending the relationship with the mentor. Since mentors and womentors benefit from the mentoring experience as much as do apprentices, they may not want to let go—to give up their control. In this situation relationships often end bitterly.

This problem is similar to that of the young person who must break away from family and home. It has to happen. The apprentice eventually arrives at a point where he must be left to make his own decisions; otherwise he cannot fulfill his own developmental needs.

Nonetheless, breaking away is emotional, particularly in the corporate world where much emphasis is placed on loyalty, an issue which will be impressed upon the apprentice by a domineering mentor who wants to sidestep rejection. At that point the growth of the apprentice is in jeopardy, and no matter how difficult or painful, he or she must break away.

The Specialist

STAGE II: SPECIALIST

Overview
—Primary theme is independence
—Is viewed as technically competent professional who can work independently to produce significant results
—Can solve problems and perform necessary tasks on his own with minimal direction and supervision.

Activities
—Coordinates own projects
—Has clear areas of responsibility

—Established visibility as competent specialist
—Establishing solid competence in critical task area represents major building block in career.

Relationships
—Peer relationships become more and more important
—Less reliance on supervisor and/or mentor for direction
—Increased contact with specialists outside the organization (associations etc.).

Adjustments
—Transition toward increased independence
—Fear of not being able to competently function independently
—Stress related to developing own standards of performance and developing own ideas (i.e., developing confidence in one's own judgment)
—Risks related to how much to specialize and potential for area of specialization to be "downgraded" in the organization
—Tendency to stay specialized too long and experiencing difficulty making transition to management
—Passing through this stage too quickly and consequently feeling less confident with technical dimension of supervisory job
—Stress related to breaking off relationship with mentor.

When an apprentice is assigned a project and told to complete it on his own, or when he is assigned to a task force and expected to make specific contributions, his apprenticeship is over. He is now a specialist. On the surface that may be the case, but psychologically the employee may not have successfully made this transition.

The specialist stage, which may occur at Loevinger's conformist stage and often occurs at the time of the 30s transition, requires the development of competency in a specialized area. This usually happens when experience enhances the educational background of the employee to a state of expertise, and at the time of transition several problems can be anticipated.

Typically, apprentices become specialists without managerial skills, and as they are expected to assume independent postures within the company, many of them discover that self-reliance, self-direction, and self-discipline are difficult qualities to master alone. Therefore, they may flounder and become less productive.

Also, in many organizations a large number of specialists are trained in the same field, and usually, because of the company's reward system, they are very competitive. Some of them have not learned cooperative behavior, and as a result specialists get little social support from their peers. In effect, the company sews its own seeds of discontent. Social support, as we explained in the previous chapter, acts as a buffer between employees and harmful stress which may cause all sorts of physical and emotional complaints and illnesses.

Toward the end of the specialist stage, at the onset of transition to generalist, additional problems may arise. If he is technically trained, say as an engineer or chemist, the specialist may find it almost impossible to move from a world that is narrowly defined to one that is subjective and interdependent. Technically trained people sometimes have trouble arriving at solutions when they cannot quantify their problems, so they tend to become autocratic and insensitive to the needs of the people around them. Underneath this self-styled image there is really a nice guy, but the specialist doesn't have much capacity for interpersonal needs or values.

TRAINING THE SPECIALIST

Companies can provide specialists with technical training to give them confidence in areas of expertise. They should also provide them opportunities to participate in socialization experiences that will teach them independent activities as well as collaborative behavior. Companies should not assume that their employees will already know how to react at this stage, or that they will learn intuitively or on the job. That doesn't happen most of the time, and the result is inefficiency, job dissatisfaction, and developmental arrest.

The Generalist

STAGE III: GENERALIST

Overview

—Increased responsibility for influencing, guiding, directing, developing others
—Helping others move through stage I
—Broadened interest and capabilities
—Applying technical expertise to solving a broad range of organizational problems
—Increased contact outside the organization (or organizational subunit)
—Success in stage II is keystone to success in stage III.

Activities

—Stage III involves three roles which are not necessarily mutually exclusive:

(a) Informal Mentor

—Outgrowth of success in stage II, helps others through detailed work in stage I
—As mentor, shares ideas, knowledge, status, and support in exchange for help and support
—Involved in broad conceptual thinking.

(b) Idea Man

—Innovates ideas for others
—Acts as a consultant (resource) for a small working group
—Others may work on his ideas independent of his own supervision
—Is involved with and influences more than his own individual work.

(c) Manager

—Most common role in stage III
—Professional competence still relevant in his work performance
—Formal role often given to mentor who has been fulfilling this role informally.

Relationships
—Movement from "taking care of self" (stage II) to taking care of others
—Assumes responsibility for work that others do
—Needs to learn skills in setting objectives, delegating, supervising, and coordinating
—Learn to satisfy "multiple bosses" in addition to responsibilities downward; feels some of the tugs of the proverbial man in the middle (divided loyalties).

Adjustments
—Most develop confidence in personal ability to produce results and ensuring others do same
—Needs to build confidence of juniors—not feeling threatened by their accomplishments
—Maintaining balance between giving direction and providing freedom to act
—Willing to assume responsibility for someone else's output (feels safer to rely on one's own efforts)
—Question of how far to pull away from technical work
—Taking satisfaction in feeling subordinates (stage I) move away from him, find new mentors.

Depending on skills, the growth of the company, and the rate of promotion, employees become generalists at various ages. When a specialist becomes a generalist it is necessary for him to move out of that narrowly defined world into one of broader scope and purpose.

By this time a man may have achieved the dream that he should have developed for himself in his teens and 20s, or he may realize that he's going to achieve only part of his dream, or perhaps none of it. At any rate, this stage of life usually means the termination of the dream, and the disillusionment is often a shocking revelation for many men. For this reason, and the fact that now the man may have to relate to more people in higher authority and assume more responsibility in the organization, the generalist stage is marked by ambiguity and conflict.

Hopefully the generalist has come up through the specialist stage and was not appointed a generalist right out of college, or too early in his career, as often happens to people with master's degrees in business administration. One of the strengths of the specialist stage, which the generalist needs, is the solid footing that the specialist gains in an area of expertise. Without that, the generalist often finds it difficult to assume a position of leadership and authority. If he doesn't have that experience he may be incapable of helping his people with their problems, and he needs that capability to rise above his subordinates as the senior member of the staff. At the same time, his subordinates need to feel that they can go to him with a problem expecting to get it solved.

The major problem faced by the generalist who comes up through the ranks is the question of freedom for his subordinates. He needs to be taught how to delegate authority and hold people accountable without appearing to be restrictive and autocratic. The generalist can fall into the trap of staying too close to his people and rushing to solve problems for them "for the good of the company." Like the parent who can't solve all his child's problems, the generalist must know how and when to let people learn and explore on their own, even if it means they occasionally make mistakes.

This distance poses another problem for the generalist. At this point in his career he really doesn't work at any particular job and therefore he often feels a void in his satisfaction for work. Now he must find pleasure in working with someone else, and this is an ideal opportunity for him to mentor. That experience will not only give feelings of dependency and usefulness, but it should also excite him about the company's affairs and the opportunities that they present.

TRAINING THE GENERALIST

Mentoring, as explained for the apprentice, is an effective socialization opportunity for the generalist as well, but he should also have the opportunity to attend management training seminars that address his individual needs. In an earlier chapter we talked about the issues of generativity versus stagnation and the legacy and the search for more challenging opportunities, and the generalist is a candidate for that kind of awakening. Too often companies assume that their senior managers are beyond the training stage, and therefore they don't give them the opportunity to attend seminars. Even if they are good managers, their personal development relies to some extent on outside help and motivation, and they can benefit from formal training programs.

The Sponsor

Stage IV: Sponsorship

Overview
—Exercise influence in defining the direction of the organization or some major segment of it
—May be in line or staff position
—Represents major force in shaping organization's future
—Influential in key areas: relations with the environment, developing new ideas, mobilizing internal resources, etc.
—Includes some senior managers and transitioning functional managers.

Activities
—Formulating policy, initiation and approval of broad programs
—Removed from mentoring stage I or supervision of stage II
—Focus on long-range planning and organizational design
—Some may be "internal entrepreneurs" who bring resources, money, and people together to pursue ideas
—Others may be "idea innovators" who actively reflect on organizational problems and locate solutions which they sell to others; usually have high credibility within and outside the organization.)

Relationships
—Selection and development of key people—emphasis on locating others who could move to stage IV and sponsoring them, not helping others get started, which is the mentor role of stage III
—Emphasis on creating opportunities, assessment, and feedback—less on teaching and instruction
—Heavily involved in key relationships outside the organization (boards, committees, associations).

Adjustments
—Stress related with pulling away from day-to-day activities and transactions

—Learning not to interfere with subordinates
—Adjustment to broad issues—policy, direction, etc.
—Learning to shift to broad perspectives, lengthen time dimensions; ability to think of organization in broad framework
—Ability to take risks at time of uncertainty
—Become accustomed to the exercise of power and ability to form alliances
—Acceptance of and preparation for transition into retirement.

Very few people arrive at sponsorship, and many of those who do find it frustrating because companies never address the issues of this managerial stage.

Sponsorship is the ultimate negotiation stage of management. It requires a skill for political compromise so that the company can be guided and directed without polarization. Company executives in general do not know enough about corporate politics, and they are usually left to make it alone at this stage. If they simply realized that the role of corporate politics is partly to preserve the self-esteem of the upper echelon in business, they would have a clearer understanding of their roles.

Unfortunately, so many people are burned by the political system in companies that by the time they are promoted they become bitter about the political system, or resistant to it, and therefore they are less effective managers, directors, or presidents.

One important prerequisite of sponsorship is environmental sensitivity. Pressure groups—religious, political, social, business, whatever—and competition influence the environment of an organization, just as much and sometimes more than the people within the organization. However, the sponsor who tries to please everyone is bound to fail. Squeezing every nut and bolt to satisfy constituents may tighten the ship, but the ship can be torpedoed and sink anyway. The sponsor must learn how to influence people outside the organization for the best interests of the organization, and that requires skill that is foreign to his managerial capacity.

The sponsor must also know to stay out of the company's day-to-day operations. He should set the stage for problem solving—appoint people to a task force or committee—but rarely should he get directly involved in the solution. He carries too much power, and if he exercises it punitively he will scare too many people and cause them to back away from him, taking along valuable information about the daily events of the company.

THE MENNINGER PROGRAMS

Two of the most exciting and rewarding seminars for executives are sponsored by the Menninger Foundation in Topeka, Kansas.

Understanding Human Behavior and Motivation is conceptually organized around the life cycle phenomenon and consists of lectures, small group discussions, individual interviews, and relaxation and meditation experiences. The program is offered by itself or in conjunction with a wilderness trip which includes rafting in the Yampa and Green rivers.

Then the foundation's Executive Consultation Program is an excellent opportunity for couples who need to work on specific work-related problems that might include family, marriage, promotion, transfer, career change, and so forth. Executives and spouses go to Topeka for a couple of days of intense exploration with foundation staff members.

For additional information about these programs, contact the Center for Applied Behavior Sciences, the Menninger Foundation, Box 829, Topeka, KS 66601; telephone (913) 234–9566.

TRAINING THE SPONSOR

Companies will find it difficult to train their own sponsors. While they can provide social support, motivation, and insight about adult development, the actual issues of sponsorship should be taught by management professionals.

Frequently special-issue seminars related to environmental changes, such as seminars on new government regulations or women's issues may be very effective. Seminars with sociologists and psychiatrists addressing organizational behavior and politics can also be beneficial.

In general, companies have always been quite adept at providing the organizational processes that are essential for their productivity and development, but in many ways the humanitarian needs of employees have been overlooked. This is not to blame or indict companies or their executives, for the thrust in this direction of renewed company involvement is only recent. However, once the development needs of employees are satisfied, employers and employees alike can begin to reap the rewards.

CHAPTER NINE

Assisting the Employee

"Over 20 million people—
15 percent of the American population—
need mental health care at any one time,
and 25 percent of the population
is under the kind of emotional stress
that results in symptoms
of depression and anxiety."

PRESIDENT'S COMMISSION ON MENTAL HEALTH

Monitoring an organization's development includes not only the factors of environment and adult development, as discussed in Chapter 8, but also the factors of adaptation. Either the successful, productive employee copes and adapts to change—promotion, the loss of a friend, a birth in the family, a divorce—or change impedes his intrapsychic maturation and creates problems on and off the job. In addition to educating employees about adult development and making certain that the organizational environment is conducive to growth, there is much the company can and should do to foster successful adaptation.

INTERNAL COUNSELING

An internal counseling program for adaptive and emotional troubles is one approach to improving adaptation. It might be based in the personnel department, but could be conducted anywhere inside or outside the organization, depending upon availability of space, personnel, and the sensitivity of people using the service. Often the medical department either staffs or refers employees to this program, and of course employees have the right to refer themselves, as well as the right to refuse help.

WORKSHOPS

Workshops within or outside the organization that help employees confront personal problems and issues is a second approach. The Transition Planning Workshop discussed in earlier chapters is a service used by companies in the Philadelphia area with good results. Personal development programs are available in other parts of the country as well, through hospitals, centers, clinics, and universities.

EMPLOYEE ASSISTANCE PROGRAMS

The most recently developed service for employees, which incorporates both of the above approaches and is the most promising of all, is the employee assistance program (EAP). EAPs represent the fastest-growing trend in corporate humanism. They treat most types of personal and professional problems. Companies are financing EAPs for their employees and dependents because they realize that an employee distracted by problems doesn't invest fully at work and is therefore less effective.

Various federal laws in the 1970s, including the Vocational Rehabilitation Act of 1973, have provided some of the push for companies to finance EAPs. Businesses that win federal contracts in excess of $2500 must make "reasonable accommodation" to hire, maintain, and promote qualified candidates with physical disabilities and histories of mental illness.

"As a result, more and more companies have begun to address a wide range of employee problems which adversely impact on job performance," says K. C. Baldadian, program coordinator for the Center for the Study of Adult Development and initiator of a half-dozen EAPs in the Philadelphia vicinity.

Problems for EAPs

Emotional	Medical	Psychiatric
Family	Work-related	Retirement
Marital	Legal	Aging
Alcohol	Financial	Relocation
Drugs	Housing	Two-career marriages
Sexuality	Career	Stress

Many companies provided some form of employee assistance on their own initiative long before the federal government got into the act. The Northern State Power Company in Minneapolis, for example, employed social workers in 1971, and the Metropolitan Life Insurance Company hired a housemother in 1919 to tend to the personal needs of female employees! Many other employers provided similar services prior to World War II, but now the trend for increased employee assistance is definite and paying off:

- *A study conducted by P. A. International Management Consultants tested 150 men in a specially designed program sponsored by the Utah division of Kennecott Copper Corporation. The men were tested a year before entering the program and a year after leaving, and the study revealed a 52 percent decrease in absenteeism, a 55.4 percent decrease in hospital, medical, and surgical costs, and a 74.6 percent decrease in weekly benefits for absenteeism.*
- *The Illinois Bell Telephone Company studied their alcoholic employees before and after counseling and discovered that 72 percent of them either stopped drinking altogether or brought their drinking under control.*
- *Otto Jones, president of Human Affairs, Inc., in Salt Lake City, told* the New York Times *that the EAP services that he provides for employees realize a $3.10 return on every $1.00 invested in terms of reduced absenteeism, hospitalization, medical and surgical costs, and weekly indemnity.*
- *General Motors Corporation tracked the job performance of seventy-one alcoholic employees for several months after they were treated and found an 85.5 percent reduction in lost man-hours and a 72 percent reduction in the pay of sickness and accident benefits.*
- *Dr. James Manuso, clinical psychologist for the Equitable Life Assurance Society, developed a stress management training program using biofeedback and relaxation training that helped thirty employees reduce the disabling effects of headaches and anxiety. He discovered that these stress-related symptoms interfered with work 16 percent of the time before treatment and only 2 percent of the time following treatment. A cost/benefit ratio indicated a $5.52 return in increased productivity for every $1.00 invested in treatment.*

- *Jack R. Harnes, medical director for both American International Group Inc. and USLIFE Corporation, told* Business Week, *"I used to dish out tranquilizers to troubled employees, [but] since we started with [Brownlee Dolan Stein Associates, a New York-based group of mental health professionals] I've almost never had to use pills. This [EAP service] is certainly an excellent alternative."*

Where EAPs are available to employees, either on an in-house or contract basis, a variety of problems are alleviated. Citibank's EAP in the New York metropolitan area, for instance, helped more than eight thousand employees between 1971 and 1979. Most of the problems addressed by the service were financial (33 percent) while 18 percent were legal, 14 percent housing, 12 percent family, 2 percent preretirement, and 19 percent miscellaneous.

The Equitable Life Assurance Society reported that 25 percent of the problems treated by its Emotional Health Program were related to anxiety and/or neurosis, 20 percent depression, 15 percent stress-related, 15 percent alcohol or other drug abuse, 10 percent situational problems (e.g., death in the family, money troubles), and 15 percent miscellaneous.

Resistance to EAPs

The value of EAPs for employers and employees is fairly obvious, and yet there's resistance to these services. Some corporate executives still don't believe they are responsible for the personal problems of their people. "Legal, emotional, financial and marital problems are best handled by the personal advisers of employees, or outside agencies," said an unidentified spokesman for IBM in the *New York Times*. If these attitudes are going to be changed, they require patience and time.

Other company executives are sympathetic, but feel they can't justify the expense of an EAP. Certainly most companies with fewer than twenty-five hundred employees cannot afford these programs as internal staff functions, but numerous companies across the country are contracting for quality out-of-house services provided by a growing number of agencies that typically operate independently or in association with universities, hospitals, or health maintenance organizations.

How an EAP Benefits the Employer

1. Decreased hospital/surgical/medical utilization
2. Reduced absenteeism and tardiness
3. Improved employee morale
4. Lowered replacement, training, and other costs associated with termination of troubled employees
5. Reduced on-the-job time loss by employees seeking help in a random manner
6. More efficient use of supervisory time and energy expended to help deal with subordinates' problems
7. Reduced sick and injured days
8. Improved employee productivity

Even some employees resist EAPs, thinking that any indiscreet revelations might jeopardize their jobs. "Alcoholics particularly might steer clear of the medical department, because they fear we would tell on them," says Dr. Harnes. Employees with emotional or mental problems may shy away from company-contracted care for similar reasons.

EAP Referrals

Employers who provide EAPs combat employee resistance by guaranteeing confidentiality and sometimes housing health services in remote locations of the company. Others contract for outside services and in that way reduce some of the resistance. These protections have an additional benefit. They encourage employees to refer themselves for counseling and similar treatment. In most EAPs, referral is by employees, supervisors, medical doctors, insurance agencies, union officials, or family members.

Preference is for self-referral, of course. "We don't push the supervisor referral aspect too much because it could give the program a punitive, disciplinary type of atmosphere," says Dr. James L. Craig, corporate medical director at General Mills, which began subcontracting an EAP in the late 1970s.

The truth is, due to confidentiality, employers don't often know who or how many of their employees use their EAP services. At International Paper Company, Richard Hessler, EAP manager, says he knows that in a three-year period 850 employees were referred to various outside services, but he believes another 250 employees referred themselves for treatment without informing the company.

For certain problems self-referrals are high, for others they are low. For example, the Metropolitan Life Insurance Company reports 50 percent self-referrals for family/financial problems, but only 10 percent for alcohol/medical behavior problems. Sixty percent of the latter referrals are made by supervisors.

At the Firestone Tire and Rubber Company, members of families refer 24 percent of their EAP's clients, while 22 percent are self-referred and 10 percent come from supervisors.

When EAPs Are Most Beneficial

It's difficult to guess which and how many employees will use EAP services, and by what means, but success of any program depends upon publicizing, availability, sincerity of the company, and more importantly the philosophy behind the care.

Services are usually provided during work hours, but round-the-clock care, particularly for emergency cases, is often part of the package. Publicizing includes pamphlets, articles in company publications and local media, and audio/visual presentations.

At this level of involvement companies can expect 5 to 7 percent of their employees to take advantage of the services in a year's time, but that number can be drastically improved. If the president of the company and top-level executives utilize the services, that will impress employees. And if it is made clear that the program is based on the principle that adults experience normal growth and development, that will also encourage people to take advantage of the services. Remember the Bell Telephone managers in Chapter 7? When they weren't made to feel abnormal or like misfits, they were more inclined to work on the issues that affected their lives, personally and professionally.

The first EAP provided by the Center for the Study of Adult Development achieved 12 percent employee utilization in the first two months of operation. We're sure that much of this success is due to our adult developmental models and attitudes.

Most of life's problems and crises arise during an employee's 30s or 40s and during certain Midi and Maxi transitions, and that's when EAPs are most helpful. Many of these issues and crises have been explored in earlier chapters, but in a company, as is often said of marriage, there are two sides to every problem. Following are a few of the most common problems with some advice about what companies can do to prepare for them.

THE THIRTIES

The 30s transition, which Levinson says causes moderate to severe crises for 60 percent of men (see Chapter 2), turns a man inward for an examination of his values and beliefs. Companies quite understandably are reluctant to interfere with an employee's life at this time because his values are generally consistent with the organization's and his performance is probably above par.

Most likely, he's a specialist by now, and very involved in his job. Any internal exploration, from the company's point of view, may upset the very balance the company values, and so the tendency is to back away and let the employee work things out on his own. That's usually a mistake. The company should encourage the soul searching through appropriate seminars, career counseling, and weekend explorations.

Until he confronts what's on his mind, an employee can never form a reliable sense of self, and without that psychological centering he's likely to become a Company Man, lacking initiative and creativity. Even then the issue of values exploration will eventually arise, possibly when the employee is a manager or executive, and if the internal search leaves him feeling unsatisfied, he'll want to quit the company for another job. If he stays, he'll certainly be dysfunctional, and then he becomes a problem creator rather than a problem solver.

MARRIAGE

In addition to the clarification of values, another testy issue of the 30s is marriage. Companies can help here by providing marriage counseling. An employee with marital problems can be frustrated, irrational, and difficult, and the dangers are that the employee will separate and divorce and that the company may label him undependable or nonpromotable.

If the employee's problems are abnormal, he and/or his spouse need therapy. But if the problems are related to his 30s transition, they are normal, and with time and support they should pass.

Successful Men and Marriage

Dr. George E. Vaillant, who conducts the long-term Harvard study of adult development, recently concluded that company presidents "have the strongest marriages and the best relationships with their children."

Men who had divorced, according to Dr. Vaillant, were the men who were not so successful at work.

Divorce

One of the most revealing studies about adaptation and divorce was conducted by Rachel Cox, a professor at Bryn Mawr College. For twenty years she followed college students who had participated in student governments, and she discovered that of the males involved who later divorced, half were never promoted thereafter.

Now some of them may not have been promotable, but some of them were not promoted because of the stigma that has historically accompanied divorce in corporations. Often, the feeling prevails that a man who can't manage a marriage can't manage an office.

It is true that given any random group of managers half of them may not be promoted after a divorce, but our experience at CSAD, both clinically and organizationally, has been that many people who get divorced never get promoted again. Something seems to happen to these people to inhibit their progress in spite of their talents. They seem to lose interest and energy, and therefore the company loses sight of them.

Helping the employee through the divorce transition is possible through various counseling services that may be internal or external to the company and conducted on a fee-for-service basis. The company can also be supportive by understanding that the employee undergoing a divorce is experiencing an emotionally draining transition.

Women and Marriage

There's some evidence to suggest that women who consider marriage go farther in management than women who do not.

In *The Managerial Woman* Margaret Hennig and Anne Jardim examined the lives of twenty-five women executives and twenty-five women who never made it out of middle management. All fifty women were intelligent and capable, and they were all promotable, but there was one glaring difference between the two groups: Those who had made it to the top had stopped to consider marriage at about the age of 30. Half of them did marry, having found men who were sympathetic to their ambitions and careers and who wouldn't demand typical female roles from them. But whether they married or not didn't make a difference. It was taking the time to consider marriage that seemed to matter.

The twenty-five women who had considered marriage changed in fundamental ways. They incorporated a feminine caring, a human, intimate part of themselves, into their personalities, and they became more effective as a result.

The twenty-five women who never considered marriage sailed through their 30s unscathed. They were devoted, happy people, but in time they became less well liked and they were not nearly as valued as the other women. People didn't feel comfortable around them, and they were never promoted. In their late 30s and 40s these women became frustrated. Their careers were in holding patterns, and their lives were not very satisfying. Some of them wished they had married but felt it was too late.

Taking the time to make a conscious, reflective decision about marriage may make a difference in the lives of female employees!

FAMILY IS A CORPORATE MATTER!

"Work life and family life can no longer be treated as separate entities," declares Stanley D. Nollen of Georgetown University's School of Business Administration.

Nollen cites two reasons:
—More women, youth, retirees, and divorced parents are now employed. Almost 60 percent of this country's families have two or more wage earners.
—People have developed new attitudes toward work and its relationship to the family.

As a result, day-care centers, flexitime, job sharing, paternity leaves, and other new benefits are being developed to accommodate the new American worker and his or her family.

The company can help the married 30s employee by encouraging him to spend more time at home and limiting his time in the office or on the road. This may sound contradictory to good business practices, but it is a temporary measure that has long-lasting positive effects for both the employee and the company.

Time is a critical factor during the 30s transition. Most companies encourage their employees to devote a maximum amount of time to their jobs, arguing that their investment will pay off in promotions and salary increases, but this is a shortsighted strategy for the 30s man because it interferes with his personal life at a critical juncture. The time the employee must spend on the job when his family is young and struggling may create problems at home and result in a sterile marriage relationship or divorce, neither of which helps the individual or the company.

Another approach to helping the employee is to bring his

spouse closer to the organization. Familiarity with the employee's job, his coworkers and supervisors, the company in general, and other spouses relieves much of the anxiety that develops around work. In many marriages wives envy their husbands' jobs. They are jealous because the husbands' life revolves around an adult world that seems to exclude them and lessens the importance of home-making and child rearing. They're often suspicious of their husbands' feelings for other coworkers and the time they spend at the office. The company, then, could make an effort to include spouses in the fold, and can do so through various social and educational activities and events.

EMPLOYEE RECREATION PROGRAMS

When absenteeism became a problem for the Peoples Jewelry Company in Toledo, Ohio, the firm started an employee recreation program. Two years later, the firm's personnel department ran a check on absenteeism and the personnel director was flabbergasted. "It really boggled my mind when I got the results. I went back and rechecked the figures and there was no mistake—absenteeism had decreased by 23 percent!"

The value of employee recreation has been recognized for at least a hundred years—since George Pullman built his own town, with a company athletic association, close to his Chicago factory—but only since 1930 have formalized employee recreation programs gained popularity. In 1941 the National Industrial Recreation Association was formed and today has twenty-two hundred member companies in the United States, Canada, and Mexico.

Many directors of employee recreation programs—which sponsor sporting events, social events, discounts for amusement parks and hotels etc.—believe the term *recreation* does them an injustice and that *employee services* is a more accurate description of the benefits their programs offer.

In addition to the obvious recreational benefits offered by employee recreation programs, additional benefits to employers and employees include improved physical health, life enrichment, mentoring opportunities, and loyalty building.

Despite its impressive advancement, the industrial recreation field in America is still in its infancy. The full potential of employee recreation has been recognized by only a small proportion of companies.

In spite of their value, there are drawbacks to these suggestions about marriage counseling and spouse involvement, and they should be clearly understood. Young employees are extremely sensitive to the political realities of the corporate world and may therefore hesitate to bring their personal problems to a company representative for resolution.

These same realities also scare off spouses and frequently cause them to behave in socially accepted, stereotypical ways that alienate them even further from the company fold.

The key variables involved in these matters are trust and the ability to control company-sponsored events so that they don't end in embarrassment or catastrophe. Many company executives feel they're opening up a Pandora's box when they counsel employees or invite spouses to company events, but there are experts who can handle these sensitive matters, and companies need only to seek them out.

THE FORTIES

Loneliness and rejection are often the badgering issues for employees in their early to mid-40s, when they reach the generalist stage, and Levinson says that 80 percent of men will experience moderate to severe crises at about this time (see Chapter 2).

All of the issues of the 30s transition may resurface in the midlife transition, especially if they were not resolved earlier, and so the employee may question his values, marriage, career, and life in general. This makes the middle-aged employee's transition very complex and frightening. If he's left alone to face it, he may become a different personality, unknown to his employer or his family, and he may try to pacify himself with sex, booze, and/or drugs.

At work, the midlife manager in transition creates a problem because he's lost interest. "Who cares about me or the job I do?" is a question he frequently asks himself. His attitude makes him less productive and tends to wear down the people around him. The effects are easily spotted in sales divisions of large companies, where productivity among many employees lags at about the time they reach the age of 40.

Because he has been disillusioned—the company has failed to recognize his worth, his wife doesn't appreciate him, he isn't the man he thought he was—the employee in his 40s often needs to feel useful. When he doesn't, he's likely to become offensive, emotional, and controlling. He can also become destructive, and if he holds power and status, the company may find it difficult to contain him.

Underneath, the 40s man is just scared. Life is moving forward, and he's worried about what's going to happen to him. Mentoring, suggested as an effective training tool in the previous chapter, has personal side effects here as well. The 40s employee who mentors a younger employee tends to see his own career from a different perspective, and the younger employee makes him feel needed.

Additionally, the company should make a conscious decision to create and promote socially responsible and exciting projects for middle-aged employees. The "do-gooder" approach is one method that not only helps employees, but raises the prestige and public awareness of the company as well. Fund raising, blood donation drives, scholarships, political and ecological platforms—these are of more than passing interest to middle-aged employees.

THE PIONEERS

AT&T's Telephone Pioneers of America, with ninety-four chapters throughout the United States and Canada, is an excellent example of a "do-gooder" activity.

Employees of AT&T subsidiaries are permitted to join the Pioneers after they've served their companies a minimum of eighteen years.

The chapters provide social activities for members, who include retirees in their 70s, 80s, and 90s, and organize community events and fund raising activities for worthy projects. For example, the Liberty Bell chapter in the Philadelphia area has sponsored spaghetti dinners and bingo for handicapped people and has also raised substantial sums of money for area hospitals.

PROMOTIONS

Just as critical as age-related transitions are environmentally initiated transitions, the most common of which is the promotion.

Company executives and managers do not understand that promotions (or the addition of responsibilities to job descriptions) trigger Midi transitions (see Chapter 3) that are bewildering and frustrating.

Look, for example, at what happened to William Leichner. He had worked in plastics manufacturing in the South for about eight years when he was promoted into a position previously held by an autocratic manager.

The preceding manager told his people what to do and when to do it, and followed up every detail in the division. He was forever looking over someone's shoulder, directing, pointing, interpreting, bird-dogging. His subordinates weren't overly fond of him, but they knew what to expect from him, and they got along. Few of the employees, however, learned to do their jobs independently. They had not developed a sense of initiative, and overall the department lacked autonomous direction. They got their jobs done, but mostly because they knew the boss was watching.

When Bill assumed the manager's position he was thought to be a fair, patient, efficient person who knew how to get along, and he was all of that, but he also believed in autonomous direction. Bill expected to set standards for employees and then leave them alone to do their jobs, but he did not know that the people in his division were conditioned to work at assigned tasks and with close supervision.

Three months after Bill took the job, he knew he was in trouble. His department's productivity had declined sharply, people were complaining about his leadership, and he didn't know the reasons behind any of it. One day, in desperation, he exploded. He ordered people around and followed through on each assignment. Almost overnight productivity shot up and the people returned to normal. As long as Bill was autocratic, everything went well.

But eventually, since Bill was not naturally demanding, he withdrew from his careful watch, and within a month productivity was down again and the complaints were back. Again Bill let loose his temper one day, and the department responded positively, but all of this undermined Bill's self-confidence. Why couldn't he motivate his people? he wondered.

If he had recognized the cycle of events taking place, he would have known the answer and he could have saved himself the grief of doubting his own managerial capabilities.

But without that clarification, Bill's lack of confidence was communicated to his subordinates, and this further eroded his department's efficiency. As Bill continued to quarrel with himself he changed the company's opinion of him, and while he was once thought to be a high-potential manager, he probably would never be promoted again.

Earlier we talked about how managers who are promoted can ease into their new ranks, but very few companies provide the training and open platform that's necessary to reduce the trauma of this Midi transition. Managers who get this support from their companies are more effective in the long range, and of course the consequences are positive for the companies as well.

In any company there's likely to be at least one Midi transition in progress at all times, and in large companies there could easily be hundreds. The period of adaptation requires three to six months and affects even the most capable and mature people, so it is a phenomenon worth the company's time and attention.

TRANSFERS

Midi transitions pose serious problems for companies and employees, but Maxi transitions (see Chapter 3) are cripplers. They involve a change of meaning in an employee's life, and they can cause a state of flux that lasts twelve to eighteen months, and sometimes three years.

The most common Maxi transition in the organization is the transfer, the ticket of opportunity in the eyes of many employees, the road to hell in the minds of others. Typically, a company has a need in one part of the country that can best be filled by a manager in another part of the country, and when the transfer is arranged it is often less of a request and more of an expectation. As we said earlier, that sort of management is dying out, but there are still thousands of employees who would not turn down a transfer for fear of losing their job potential or security.

When an employee accepts a transfer, willingly or not, and moves his family to another part of the country or to a different country, he and the company should expect problems.

With an increase in the number of two-career marriages, the first problem for many employees may be the spouse's job. If his wife is professionally trained and skilled and likes her job, she may not want to give it up for the sake of her husband's company, and indeed she should not be expected to. This may require understanding from company officials, or it may require support to allow the wife to explore her job potential somewhere else. Whatever the case may be, this is a concern that companies cannot afford to deny. A move under protest is surely going to create an unhappy family life that may carry over to the office.

Other family matters at the time of transfer include selling one house and buying another and finding new schools and a place of worship. It is helpful to let the family—and not just the employee—visit their new locale well in advance of the move. This gives them time to check out housing and related concerns, and it offers them an opportunity to meet new friends who may or may not be associated with the company.

If the transfer takes the family to a different country, the company's commitment is even more crucial. New social and cultural values and behaviors may have to be introduced to the family, and they may also need to learn a new language, which could require months of training.

The company should also see that the family receives literature about their "adopted" country, that they meet other company families living in the new country as soon as possible, and that the financial package they're being offered with the transfer is sufficient to meet their needs.

For the most part, companies are pretty good about helping their people physically relocate—many hire outside consultants to help make the move—but they do a disservice to families if they don't educate them about the adaptive problems that may occur during the time of a transfer and in the months immediately thereafter.

RETIREMENT

The consequences of retirement are more subtle than those of any other transition. What is the effect upon morale when employees see a manager who dedicated his life to the company die shortly after he retired?

Retirement is an exhausting transition, and it is dangerous for most individuals even though few people see it that way. A majority of employees fail to make this transition successfully, and many of them do die early in the retirement process. They've worked all their lives, they've been productive and successful, they've felt useful, and then—wham! they've retired without being prepared for it.

Most people think about retirement in terms of finances, and they plan for that part of it, but retirement also involves social problems, and that's where companies can help. Eventually the retiree is going to wonder, "How am I supposed to live a retired life? . . . In what ways am I important?" And if he doesn't find answers, he's going to have serious problems.

A man who retires is often a virtual stranger to his wife and family. Because his life for many years has centered around his company, he'll have difficulty entering the world of wife and home after so many years of being away. He must learn to relate once again, and on a twenty-four hour basis. He must seek new relationships and discover new interests. If he doesn't, he's going to become depressed and increase his chance of dying earlier than he should.

Some executives argue that retirement is not a concern for the company. Once the employee is retired, he's on his own at last, but a more sensitive outlook would be to provide workshops for employees nearing retirement age so that they can learn about the pitfalls and anticipate the issues surrounding this transition. Such workshops are frequently sponsored by social agencies, universities, and hospitals, or they may be developed within a company's own personnel department.

OTHER TRANSITIONS

There are other Midi and Maxi transitions that block an employee's ability to cope and adapt on the job—the birth of a child, a spouse leaving the home for a job, a death in the family, and so on—and their effects have been explored in earlier chapters. Practically speaking there isn't much a company can do in many of these matters, but an environment that shows employees that someone cares about what's happening in their lives is often more than many employees now know. Taking off the corporate masks and inviting people to talk about their problems and worries can go a long way in helping employees through many of the crises in their lives.

CAREER DEVELOPMENT

In recent years experts have come to the conclusion that career selection is not a one-shot process occurring during an employee's 20s. "The realistic choice period may continue for many years, long into adulthood as the person may go through several cycles of exploring, crystallizing, specifying in an attempt to find a career that fits his needs, interests and abilities," according to Douglas Hall in *Careers in Organizations.* For people with advanced degrees, Hall writes, the "floundering process" may last into their 30s, and for men it may be reactivated during the midlife crisis.

Until quite recently, a man or woman who entered an organization was expected to work hard at an assigned task, follow orders, ask only routine questions about the future the company might provide, and be grateful for whatever salary increments and promotions the company bestowed.

These expectations contain numerous pitfalls, the most glaring of which is the assumption that an employee's original entry point into the organization remains of greatest interest to him, even in his 30s or 40s. That kind of thinking forces an employee to become a passive recipient of his own career rather than an active participant, and it leads to increased job dissatisfaction.

An employee may prefer one job over another, even at the same pay or for less pay, and to promote him without considering his personal work preferences is self-defeating. That overlooks a major motivating force for productivity: desire. If the employee has to face a job that he doesn't care to do, he's contributing far less than he's capable of to the company's welfare. Eventually, he'll probably find a different job, and yet in another division of his organization there may have been a job for him that would have drawn out his talents and the investment the company had already made in him. Without inquiring about his preferences, however, the company could never know about his interest in the job.

Nowadays, even in companies where it's least expected, many employees are taking the initiative to speak up when a position that interests them is about to be filled. This enterprise is often frowned upon, primarily because it second-guesses management, who typically think they know what's best for employees, but the narcissistic attitude that surfaced in the 1970s has encouraged people to look out more actively for their own interests.

Even so, the employee who displays too much of the wrong initiative often risks his job. John Maloney's story is a case in point—though with a happy ending. For ten years John was a promising young manager in a major printing company in New York State. The company had recruited him during a college scouting session in his senior year, and everyone in the company knew that John was one of several rising stars being molded for an executive office.

But by the time John was 33, he had decided he was unhappy in management, and he thought the company expected too much of him. He saw how the people above him spent endless hours at their work, and he knew many of them were unhappy in spite of their attractive paychecks and their busy lifestyles. And they were also tired and under a lot of pressure.

John felt an executive was expected to make more of a commitment to work than he cared to make. He was married and had three sons, and while family life wasn't everything he had hoped it might be, he liked being home with his wife and children, and they spent many weekends camping or skiing or visiting relatives in a neighboring state. John wasn't ready to give that up.

Naturally, when he first realized he no longer aspired to the executive suite, John was afraid to tell anyone, including his wife. "She married me thinking that I wanted to be an executive, and if I told her I wasn't going to be one, I didn't know how she'd react," he explained later.

And his boss? "I couldn't tell him. Hell, he recruited me, he knows my wife and boys, he's taken care of me. How could I let him down?"

John had to face his problem sooner than he thought. He was about to be promoted to the next level of management when he came to the CSAD for help. He was afraid and confused, but after some consultation he decided to be assertive, and he told his boss he didn't want the promotion. John later recalled

> *I'll never forget that day. When I said I had given it some thought and I didn't want the job, my boss thought I was joking. And when he realized that I was serious, his mouth fell open and he sunk into his chair. "What do you mean, John? You've been working for this promotion for years. You deserve it."*
>
> *"I appreciate that, but I don't think the job's for me," I said. There was a long period of silence when neither of us said a word. Finally, I broke in. "I haven't been happy in management for the last year or so. This isn't a rash judgment. I've been here ten years and I'd like to do something else. Actually, I'd like to get into personnel."*
>
> *"Personnel?" The boss jumped out of his seat when I said the word.*

> *"Personnel? That's a dead-end division in this company. You're not going to get to the top of the company through personnel." My boss still didn't understand that I didn't want to be at the top of the company. It was like I was his son and I had just told him that I didn't want to play in the Super Bowl.*
>
> *"Look," he said, "you're asking to be moved out of the critical division of this company when you have a future here. The future isn't in personnel. I couldn't recommend you for a job over there. The people upstairs would think I'm crazy!" To this day I don't think he understands why I had to switch to personnel. For six months he tried talking me out of it, and I was about ready to take another job when finally he said I was being transferred. I probably won't ever be promoted again, but as far as I can see now, that's fine. If I change my mind I've got ten years of experience behind me, and if they don't want me here, someone else will.*

A year after his transfer, John's enthusiasm for his work was higher than he could ever remember. He was involved in a variety of stimulating projects and doing very well. Without understanding why, or even offering its approval, the company had saved a very productive employee.

HOW COMPANIES CAN HELP

Companies must understand that during the 30s and 40s transitions, as well as at other times, employees may need to reevaluate their career goals. The company's position ought to be to help rapidly clarify these goals without a lot of pain and misgivings. Many companies provide career counseling for their people, but most still don't, and nowadays career counseling is the least a company can do professionally for its employees.

Until very recently, few people in or out of corporations thought of career development as the personal plan of an individual's life work. Career development always meant changing jobs, and to a lot of people it still does. But career development is much more. It is an ongoing process that evaluates abilities and interests, considers alternatives and opportunities, establishes career goals, and plans practical developmental activities—*and it is a function of the organization as well as of the individual!*

The most frequently offered type of career counseling is outplacement, a service that could be less of a necessity if only companies took a closer look at career development and improved their services.

Actually, improving services in most companies would not require a major expenditure of funds because even though companies don't know it, they already have most of the mechanisms necessary to supply an effective career development program. What they still need to acquire isn't costly, and it can be acquired with additional skill and time.

After adopting a cooperative attitude about career development, a good beginning for the company that wants to improve its career development services is recruiting. Yes, recruiting is a function of career development. Prospective and newly hired employees—indeed, all employees—need to know what career paths are realistically possible for them within the organization, and in addition recruiters should present an accurate description of job responsibilities.

What sort of tasks are involved? How much time does each require? What kinds of personalities will the new employee meet? And what's the environment like? Much of this information can be transmitted via audio/visual presentations, and the information will vastly improve a job seeker's ability to match himself to a company and vice versa.

A job description is another function of career development. It is a basic building block leading to the company's evaluation of the employee and the employee's evaluation of his own expectations. At the time of a performance evaluation, the individual can be assessed in terms of how well he satisfied the job description, and this helps the employee detect any deficiencies in his work style that may block his career growth. The individual's potential, based upon his performance, can also be plotted in terms of where he thinks he can go in the organization and where his superior thinks he can go. This is a major career development tool which is currently underutilized in all but a few companies.

In addition, companies in general should do a better job of informing their employees about career possibilities within the organization. In many companies, employees are permitted to read only their personal job descriptions, and while that decision may be necessary to maintain autonomy and control in certain departments, it doesn't permit the employee to familiarize himself with his environment. Most companies are relatively closed, but they must understand that the environment impacts upon employees in different ways, and they should try to make information available so that employees can make rational decisions about their career growth. Some companies have achieved this goal through career resource centers which include job descriptions, job postings, audio/visual presentations, and printed literature about career and adult development.

There is a diversity of career planning activity taking place in companies across the country. A survey of *Fortune* 500 companies by Columbia University's Center for Research and Career Development revealed that some companies are offering the following services: College/university tuition aid, individual self-analysis workshops, preretirement workshops, job rotation, job diagnostic surveys, and job enrichment seminars.

CAREER DIMENSIONS

Walter D. Storey has developed one of the most advanced career-planning programs available today for the General Electric Company. Dr. Storey approaches career planning from a developmental perspective, and he has prepared a series of workbooks and guides about the process.

Career Dimensions IV is a handbook for professionals in employee relations, training, and development to use in the implementation of career-planning programs. For information about the Career Dimensions series, write to Dr. Storey at General Electric, Crotonville, P.O. Box 368, Croton-on-Hudson, NY 10520.

In addition, assessment centers, career pathing, psychological testing, outplacement, orientations, and computerized management information systems which quickly match employees to jobs are being used by a growing number of companies.

Naturally, no organization can do it all, but neither is that necessary. Ideally, a company's career development package ought to include periodic self-examinations and counseling that dig into an employee's adult development. Companies should also allow their employees some freedom of lateral movement as well as upward mobility. And finally, they should get involved in their employees' career development so that employees feel they are planning their careers with the guidance of the company and not functioning only at the company's command.

CHAPTER TEN

Adult Development and the Quality of Working Life

"In our quest for a better environment
we must always remember that
the most important part of the quality of life
is the quality of work
and the new need for job satisfaction
is the key to the quality of work."

Elliot L. Richardson

The major task of the present and future for American businesses is to boost productivity. This is a tremendous challenge, but one that is necessary to accept in light of recent statistics which show a steady decline in the growth of U.S. economic output. The United States is losing its world lead in output per person. Canada in 1977, for example, produced 88 percent per person of what Americans did, up from 73 percent in 1960. Japan jumped in productivity to 68 percent of U.S. per capita output in 1977, marking a 37 percent improvement over a seventeen-year period. There's no doubting that the competitors are catching up fast.

It's not that America has lost its desire to lead, it's just that other countries began tackling their productivity problems years ago. America is getting a later start. In this heterogeneous society the danger signals about declining productivity and social decay have been less equivocal, and so while competitors have been busy slashing the threat to their economies, America has frequently been delayed by political squabbles over who or what is to blame for the problems. As the threat has worsened, however, experts in science, industry, academia, and two dozen productivity centers around the country have been putting their heads together to come up with solutions.

Some experts blame the productivity slump on a declining work ethic, others say American workers have simply become less innovative, and still others claim that the fault lies with burgeoning government regulation of business. The consensus seems to be that there is no universal formula for improving productivity. If the problems are going to be solved, they will be solved company by company, and the extent of success or failure will depend upon employee and management acceptance of recommended programs.

QUALITY OF WORKING LIFE

What to recommend is, of course, another problem, and here the experts have arrived at no consensus. Myriad suggestions have been implemented at thousands of companies, some with outstanding levels of success, and the best of these have come from a recently introduced field called the *quality of working life* (QWL). While other schools of thought recommend technical advancements to combat slumping productivity, quality of working life devotees (including the staff of the Center for the Study of Adult Development) maintain that the problem is of a sociotechnical nature and thus requires specifically designed approaches based on humanistic as well as technical criteria.

Some Principles of QWL

Some jobs are better than others, and no matter what is done all jobs can't be made uniformly satisfying.

Almost all bad jobs can be improved, at least marginally.

People differ widely in their psychological makeup and intelligence and hence have differing needs from their jobs.

Intelligence and psychological makeup are better criteria for job placement then race, sex, class or age.

People with jobs they don't like are less committed to their jobs than people who like their work.

It is better for the individual, the workplace and society for workers to be committed to their jobs than for them not to be committed.

from *Work and the Quality of Life*

"The technical system comprises the equipment and plant, with its particular characteristics and requirements and the way it is laid out," explain Kenneth Taddeo and Gerald Lefebvre, management consultants in Canada and two leading proponents of QWL.

> *The social system is made up of people in the work situation with their particular physical, psychological, and cultural requirements and goals. By designing and managing the work situation in such a way that the social and technical systems complement one another, one achieves joint optimization of these systems and an optimization of the functioning of the organization as a whole. Unless technology is translated into tasks that are in accordance with human needs and characteristics, how can we pretend to create organizations that will function at their maximum level of effectiveness?*

Any technical solution that does not consider the social characteristics and needs of employees circumvents joint optimization and can never improve the quality of working life. Instead, these solutions tend to speed up the decline of productivity. For example, one recent technological advancement which has won the respect of countless managers and secretaries is the word processor, a compact machine which often confines a secretary to a tiny room where she "communicates" only through the machine for several hours a day.

Look what happens in an office where a word processor is introduced and utilized on a daily basis. Before the word processor, tasks are generally traded off between manager and secretary and while that relationship is at time frustrating, it is a source of social support which acts as a buffer against the effects of stress and strain. As such, it is an effective relationship for the employees involved. The word processor, however, greatly simplifies the editing and typing tasks of the secretary and disrupts a functional social relationship without replacing it with any other unit of support. When a word processor is brought into an office, the manager-secretary relationship oftentimes disappears. Instead of communicating face to face, employees communicate through a machine. The purveyors of word processing will convince you that efficiency in your office can be drastically improved with this equipment, and it can be, but it is only one component of the work environment. Unless social support is provided through other avenues or otherwise maintained between the manager and secretary, the result will most likely be a deteriorating quality of working life and lessened productivity.

PRODUCTIVITY AND QWL CENTERS

There are currently about twenty-five Productivity or Quality of Working Life centers in the United States. Best known of these is the American Productivity Center (APC) in Houston, a nonprofit educational and research corporation established to improve the nation's productivity and help stem inflation, unemployment, and declining profits.

Dr. C. Jackson Grayson is director of APC, which is governed by a twenty-one-member board of directors that includes corporation and union chief executives and high-ranking federal officials.

Managers and supervisors are sent to the APC to learn more about productivity problems and training. The center also sponsors briefings, workshops, and seminars in major cities throughout the country and has produced a workbook/videotape training module for first-line supervisors entitled *Productivity Payoff.*

The addresses of APC and selected centers follows:

The American Productivity Center, 123 North Post Oak Lane, Houston, TX 77024, (713) 681-4020, Dr. C. Jackson Grayson, Director.

American Center for the Quality of Work Life, 3301 New Mexico Avenue N.W., Suite 202, Washington, DC 20016, (202) 338-2933, Ted Mills, Director.

Center for Productive Public Management, John Jay College of Criminal Justice, City University of New York, 445 West 59th Steet, New York, NY 10019, (212) 489-5030/5031, Dr. Marc Holzer, Director.

Center for Quality of Working Life, Institute of Industrial Relations, University of California, 405 Hilgard Avenue, Los Angeles, CA 90024, (213) 825-1095/8862, Louis E. Davis, Chairman.

Georgia Productivity Center, Engineering Experiment Station, Georgia Institute of Technology, Atlanta, GA 30332, (404) 894-3404, R.L. Yobs, Director.

Manufacturing Productivity Center, IIT Center, 10 West 35th Street, Chicago, IL 60616, (312) 567-4800, Dr. Keith E. McKee, Director.

Maryland Center for Productivity and Quality of Working Life, College of Business and Management, University of Maryland, College Park, MD 20742, (301) 454-5451, Dr. Rudolph P. Lamone, Director.

Massachusetts Qualify of Working Life Center, 14 Beacon Street, Suite 712, Boston, MA 02108, (617) 227-6266, Dr. Michael J. Brower, Director.

Productivity Council of the Southwest, STF 124, 5151 State University Drive, Los Angeles, CA 90032, (213) 224-2975, John R. Frost, P.E. Director.

Qualify of Working Life Program, Center for Human Resource Research, Ohio State University, 1375 Perry Street, Suite 585, Columbus, OH 43201, (614) 422-3390, Dr. Michael Borus, Director, Center for Human Resource Research, Dr. Don Ronchi, Director, Qualify of Working Life Program.

Quality of Work Life Center for Central Pennsylvania, Pennsylvania State University, Capitol Campus, Middletown, PA 17057, (717) 787-7746, contact Dr. Rupert F. Chisholm, Jr.

Work in America Institute, Inc., 700 White Plains Road, Scarsdale, NY 10583, (914) 472-9600, Jerome M. Rosow, President.

Harvard Project on Technology, Work and Character, 1710 Connecticut Avenue, N.W., Washington, DC 20009, (202) 462-3003, Dr. Michael Maccoby, President.

The work-related needs of people are directly related to levels of productivity. This relationship has been examined in depth by Eric Trist, professor of social systems at the University of Pennsylvania and one of the pioneers in the fields of organization development and quality of working life. As shown below, Trist has divided employee needs into two categories, extrinsic and intrinsic.*

PROPERTIES OF JOBS

Extrinsic	*Intrinsic*
Fair and adequate pay	Variety and challenge
Job security	Continuous learning
Benefits	Discretion, autonomy
Safety	Recognition and support
Health	Meaningful social contribution
Due Process	Desirable future
Conditions of Employment socio-economic	The Job Itself psycho-social

"Together," he says, "they constitute the necessary and sufficient conditions for a high QWL—at the job or task level."

EXTRINSIC AND INTRINSIC NEEDS

Trist's extrinsic requirements of a job form the legacy of the old work ethic, whereby a man worked at a job no matter how dissatisfying, and they include the provisions specified in a contract of employment.

The intrinsic factors represent a variety of psychological

*E. Trist, "Adapting to a Changing World," in *A New Role For Labour: Industrial Democracy Today*, edited by George Sanderson and Frederick Stapenhurst. Used by permission of E. Trist.

requirements that necessarily have to be met to satisfy the new work ethic, whereby men and women expect to work at jobs that provide monetary rewards as well as pleasure.

Because of their uniqueness, the intrinsic values require some amplification:

> VARIETY AND CHALLENGE: *People need jobs that are reasonably demanding in terms other than sheer endurance. Problem solving at work is a human right.*
>
> CONTINUOUS LEARNING: *Continuous on-the-job learning makes work more attractive and challenging. It provides personal growth, which is also a human right.*
>
> DISCRETION, AUTONOMY: *People need an area of decision making that they can call their own. This recognizes the opportunity to use one's own judgment as a human right.*
>
> RECOGNITION AND SUPPORT: *The value of social support was demonstrated in an earlier chapter. It might be provided by coworkers and superiors. It recognizes "group belongingness" as a human right.*
>
> MEANINGFUL SOCIAL CONTRIBUTION: *People need to relate what they do at work with how they live—"to have a meaningful occupational identity which gives a man or woman dignity," states Trist. This recognizes the opportunity to contribute to society as a human right.*
>
> DESIRABLE FUTURE: *It is not necessary for all workers to be promoted, but people must feel their work provides a secure future. This recognizes hope as a human right.*

"These psychological needs and associated human rights are not confined to any one level of employment," states Trist. "Managers also need a high QWL. However, it must be recognized that it is not always possible to meet these needs to the same extent in all work settings; nor, indeed, do all kinds of people need them to the same degree—individual differences are considerable."

COMPANY EVOLUTION

The health of individuals, as well as of organizations and society in general, depends upon the value of the relationship between individuals and their total work environments. To a significant extent,

---

Your Job and the "Blues"

Studies at the Institute for Social Research in New York show a high correlation between the "blues" and certain job characteristics.

Comfort, money, and convenience, according to researchers, do not ensure against the blues. Work performance and accomplishment appear to be critical factors, according to recent studies.

"The blues were combated by such job features as a chance to use one's skills; having enough help to do one's best work; a chance to be creative; a chance to learn new things; having enough tools to do the work best; and having a supervisor who knows his job well, leaves his subordinates alone unless they require help, and maintains high performance standards in his own work," reads a recent report.

---

however, the evolution of organizations has prevented many of them from doing much about work environments.

In the first half of the twentieth century, according to John Eldred, director of organization development at CSAD, organizations were viewed as mechanisms. Good employees were people with solid characteristics (like punctuality) but with little more to offer the organization. No one at the time recognized that the environment could alter the characteristics of a particular employee. For example, an abrasive foreman might produce hostile and destructive employee characteristics. In the company's opinion their employee would be hostile and destructive, but they would not be seen as people reacting to a situation that engendered their response. The foreman would never be at fault, of course, because he represents the company and is pushing for more productivity!

Later in the century, organizational theorists viewed the organization as an organism. It had specialized parts (i.e. purchasing, finance, etc.) just as the human body has a mouth and a nervous system. Employees were viewed as having some opinions that were valuable, and thus they should be consulted, that is asked for their opinions prior to making decisions and changes. Much of the push on behalf of employees taking a more active role in the workplace was provided by unions, which by mid-century had made it clear that they were not a temporary reaction to the depression and that they intended to continue representing employee concerns and needs.

More recently, as the environment has been emphasized, some advanced organizations have begun to view themselves as communities, and employees have become "dynamic participants" in ongoing work activities. The difference between consulting an employee and allowing him to participate is that in participation the employee holds decision-making powers and in consultation he is merely someone offering his opinions. By the 1970s, several radical socio-technical experiments were taking place in a great variety of organizations in America and other parts of the world.

YOUR JOB MAY BE KILLING YOU!

Mounting evidence suggests that the number-one predictor of longevity is job satisfaction. It's a better indicator, according to Erdman Palmore, senior fellow in the Center for Study of Aging and Human Development at Duke University, than overall life satisfaction, heredity, age of parents at death, socioeconomic status, exercise, diet, or packs of cigarettes smoked per day! Job satisfaction has been specifically linked to mortality from heart disease and to increased incidences of alcohol and drug abuse.

Unfortunately people either aren't aware of this information or they don't care, because a surprising number of people in America work at jobs that leave them feeling dissatisfied.

In a massive study conducted by the Department of Health, Education, and Welfare and published as the book *Work in America,* 57 percent of a cross section of white-collar workers and 76 percent of a cross section of blue-collar workers expressed dissatisfaction with their jobs.

In Canada, a similar survey discovered 32 percent of workers felt their jobs were "somewhat enjoyable," 2 percent "not enjoyable," and 2 percent "drudgery." Only 61 percent of the employees said they would take the same job if they were entering the workforce for the first time, and 14 percent said their jobs did not measure up to expectations.

Job security, promotions, pay, working hours, and fringe benefits are less important to most workers than a job that is interesting and provides opportunities to develop special abilities.

At about this same time, psychiatry was moving away from ego psychology and into developmental psychology, and the understanding that adult personality is not fixed and static helped people in organizations realize that a natural evolution of employee needs occurs within a company's environment. If the organization is a community and includes people with a variety of legitimate and sometimes conflicting or interlocking interests, it makes sense that the company can do some things to help employees mature and thereby advance the efficiency and quality of their total work environment. Therefore, a necessary component of QWL is the willingness of organizations to promote the development of personalities.

QWL EXPERIMENTS

How development can best be encouraged is not entirely understood, but countless experiments are being tried in countries throughout the world under the rubrics of job enrichment, communication training, job participation, job enlargement, and job rotation. These programs reflect the attitudes, aspirations, and developmental needs of a new generation of workers who are not willing to live one-third of their adult lives as human cogs in inhuman machines. They adopt the attitude that for employees to be fully effective they need the opportunity to be meaningfully involved not only in doing work, but in planning and controlling as well.

Essentially these experiments represent a necessary shift away from the totalitarian concepts of management and place more value on individual employees and groups as factors in work efficiency. "Since employees are critical to the quantity, quality and regularity of production," says Jerome M. Rosow, president of Work in America Institute, "a progressive attitude toward their motivation, involvement and participation can be a positive force for efficiency and profitability."

Many employers now realize that worker participation in decision making can only strengthen the organization's total impact in business. The National Center for Productivity and Quality of Working Life, a short-lived federally based agency in Washington, D.C. (it expired during the Carter administration), conducted a survey and found that 188 managers, unionists, government officials, and others agreed generally that it is desirable to allow employees more influence over their working environment and working conditions.

Some academics and management consultants don't agree and say instead that satisfaction in the job itself is more of a motivator for employees than autonomy or participation in decision making. The best-known advocate of this "orthodox job enrichment" school is Frederick Herzberg, who contends that achievement, recognition, responsibility, and growth are the "motivators" that give

Some Generalizations About QWL in North American Workplaces

Not all jobs can be made "meaningful" or "challenging" but working conditions can be improved.

Many managers and some academics believe QWL changes would improve productivity but see no need for worker participation in decisions on these changes.

Some managers and many academics see QWL changes that involve participation as producing positive job satisfaction for workers and also improving productivity.

Some workers may not be the least bit interested in direct participation in decision making because they have never consciously experienced it.

Some workers prefer tasks that make few demands on them, and want someone to tell them what to do.

Some experiments aimed at improving QWL through various forms of shop-floor democracy have demonstrated increased productivity and some have not.

Successful QWL improvements involving worker participation cannot be imposed by fiat on either supervisors or workers but must be acceptable to the persons implementing them.

From "Making Work More Human," by Roy LaBerge in *Adapting to a Changing World* edited by George F. Sanderson and published by Labour Canada.

workers positive feelings of job satisfaction. To provide those motivators, Herzberg says, organizations must restructure jobs to challenge their employees' abilities, and then individual workers should take on individual responsibilities for tasks that they find fulfilling by their very nature. It's not necessary, Herzberg claims, for individuals to get involved in decision making about those tasks.

Nevertheless, QWL experiments have often been most successful when job enrichment projects were part of a larger participatory group project that permitted the joint optimization of the socio-technical factors discussed earlier. At General Foods in Topeka, Kansas, for example, the company began a team production program in which shippers, packers, office workers, and employees in processing, safety, and quality control formed cohesive units and rotated jobs. Each team was called upon to assume greater responsibility and to make decisions without preplanned rules. The outcome was strikingly successful:

- *Management reported a remarkable improvement in employee morale and motivation.*
- *Absenteeism declined to 2% (way below the average for the industry).*
- *Job turnover, theft, and damage to company property were negligible.*
- *Quality improved and productivity increased by 40% per man-day.*
- *The cost savings amounted to $2 million a year—20 to 40% better than four other plants in the industry.*

In a similar project, General Motors' assembly plant division in North Tarrytown, New York, launched a QWL program in 1972 when work fell below standard, absenteeism skyrocketed, and grievance piled upon grievance. The company introduced teams of departmental workers which became autonomous miniature businesses, establishing their own goals and making members responsible to "their" business success. As a result, the plant became one of the leaders in work quality, absenteeism reached a record low, the number of grievances was reduced, and relations with the union improved.

Even QWL projects that are less complicated have resulted in significant achievements. In 1977, twenty-five Statistics Canada keypunch operators, according to Roy LaBerge, former editor of *Canadian Labour*, rearranged their machines, which previously had been set up in line, so that they could be more sociable with one another. They were also permitted, for the first time, to drink coffee at their desks and to make personal phone calls. They reported that their workplace lost its depressing atmosphere and that they felt completely autonomous; their supervisor became an adviser rather than a boss.

SOME QWL FAILURES

There have, however, been some notable failures in QWL experiments. One project involved six groups of highway construction and electrical workers at the Ohio Department of Highways. After they were given total responsibility for their work, productivity declined in two of the groups and failed to improve appreciably in the other four. Absenteeism worsened in five of the six.

And in Del Mar, California, a manufacturer of digital electrical measuring instruments, Non-Linear Systems, divided 340 assembly line employees into small teams for a QWL experiment that failed miserably. Each team was responsible for setting its own work pace, deciding on the allocation of tasks among its members, and solving its own internal problems. The end result was a high turnover of department managers—thirteen of thirty left in two years—without any increase in plant efficiency or decline in absenteeism. When profits began to decline, the program was abandoned.

EMPLOYEE MATURATION

Why some programs are successful and others fail isn't an easily answered question, but it may depend upon the psychological maturity of employees at the time a QWL program is implemented. Every employee is different, of course, and many employees do not seek challenge or autonomy from their work. Some employees, researchers have discovered, genuinely respect authority and orders from people of higher status in the organization. They perform better in highly authoritarian situations that require little of them in terms of decision making.

But it is also true, as has been demonstrated at various points in this book, that an employee's motivation may change over time for a variety of reasons. Organizational psychologist Edgar H. Schein states, "Employees' motives, perceptions, degrees of effort and experience" all interact in complex ways "to produce a given level of performance and a degree of involvement in the organization." All the more reason for companies to consider their employees' adult development when they monitor their work environments.

Another reason why some programs fail and others succeed is the attitude of the company hierarchy. In fact, if middle and upper management do not wholeheartedly support the experiment, or if it is considered a whim or a trend that will pass with time, the program will probably fail. "How to sustain innovation, when the wider organizational context is not as supportive as it might be, is another of the critical areas that the QWL enterprise needs to learn far more about," states Eric Trist.

A NEW PARADIGM

Changing the organizational context is a goal that will have to be achieved before many QWL projects will be given an opportunity to exist. This requires a systematic transformation that entails abandoning the philosophy on which the old organizational paradigm is based and working toward a new philosophy that will guide the operational realization of the new paradigm of QWL. In accomplishing this task the support of top management is essential.

Following are the key features of this new organizational paradigm—components that will lead to a high QWL and increased productivity for all members of organizations—as well as two features of the old paradigm which has instrumentally constrained most employees to a low QWL.*

Old Paradigm	*New Paradigm*
The technological imperative	Joint optimization
Man as an extension of the machine	Man as complementary to the machine
An expendable spare part	A resource to be developed
Maximum task breakdown; single, narrow skills	Optimum task grouping; multiple, broad skills
External controls (supervisors, specialist staffs, procedures)	Internal controls (self-regulating) subsystems)
Tall organization chart, autocratic style	Flat organization chart, participative style
Competition, gamesmanship	Collaboration, collegiality
Organization's purposes only	Members' and society's purposes also
Alienation	Commitment
Low risk taking	Innovation

*E. Trist, "Adapting to a Changing World," in *A New Role for Labour: Industrial Democracy Today*, edited by George Sanderson and Frederick Stapenhurst. Used by permission of E. Trist.

"Our traditional organizations," states Trist,

> *follow the technological imperative* [*of the old paradigm*], *which regards man simply as an extension of the machine and therefore as an expendable spare part. By contrast, the emergent paradigm is founded on the principle of joint-optimization, which regards man as complementary to the machine and values his unique capabilities for appreciative and evaluative judgment. He is a resource to be developed for his own sake rather than to be degraded and cast aside, for the product of work is people, and a society is no better than the quality of the people it produces.*

Traditional organizations are characterized by maximum work breakdown, which Trist maintains leads to circumscribed job descriptions and single skills. Under these circumstances employees are often unable to manage the uncertainty or the variance that require strict external controls. "Layer upon layer of supervision come into existence," explains Trist, "supported by a wide variety of specialist staffs and formal procedures. A tall pyramidic organization results, which is autocratically managed throughout, even if the paternalism is benign. By contrast the new paradigm is based on an optimum task grouping, which encourages multiple broad-ranging skills."

There are additional benefits of the new paradigm as well. Rather than employees competing with and defending themselves from each other in organizations, the new paradigm emphasizes coping with the manifold interdependencies that arise in complex organizations. It values collaboration between groups and encourages social support.

It also helps companies align themselves with not only the needs of society but with the needs of their members as well. "By so doing," states Trist, "they become both 'environmentalized' and 'humanized,' and thus become more truly purposeful, rather than merely remaining the impersonal and mindless forces that are increasing environmental turbulence."

Moving from the old paradigm to the new offers employees and companies an opportunity to grow, and it replaces a climate of low risk taking with one of innovation. "All these qualities are mandatory if we are to transform traditional technocratic bureaucracies into a continuous adaptive learning system," states Trist, "and this *is* the central task. This transformation is imperative for survival in a fast-changing environment. It involves nothing less than the working out of a new organizational philosophy."

Once that philosophy is accepted, many of the problems that organizations and employees encounter will either be prevented or their effects will be diminished. The problems of the oil refinery engineers discussed in Chapter 1, for example, could have been headed off had their company been aware of the environmental realities. You may remember that the eingineers were in charge of the Maintenance Department of the refinery and were obliged to respond to the immediate needs of the Operations Department while at the same time continuing effective routine maintenance. The work units of their men were continually disrupted, no managerial training could occur, social support crumbled, alienation increased, and the zone engineers were depressed. They saw a continuous rate of failure in their work lives, and as a result they began to doubt their own capabilities and their effectiveness, both on the job and at home. Much of what would happen to these employees depended on their company. If the company had realized that something was wrong organizationally, the conflicting demands of the Operations and Maintenance departments would have been uncovered. Beginning with the vice-president of Operations and the vice-president of Maintenance, there could have been a joint planning process to take into account both the short-term profitability and long-term functionality of the refinery's equipment. Then there could be some examination of the social systems of the refinery. Were jobs structured to allow for stability and productivity? What was the quality of working life?

By meeting these needs the company would have probably prevented the malfunctioning of four zone engineers. It would have increased self-esteem, pride, and productivity, all of which would have a tremendous effect upon productivity and profit.

Obviously, this was not the initial choice of the oil refinery's executives. They chose to do nothing, as do many corporations yet today.

Choosing to do nothing is the equivalent of sending an army into combat without any planning or training. How could such a force be effective? And yet every day managers are promoted or transferred, employees are assigned tasks and additional obligations, and they are often expected to adapt to these situations without any planning or training. They flounder, most of them learn

---

Enjoying Productivity

One of the lessons learned about productivity at the Eastman Kodak Company in Rochester, New York is that "people enjoy working more productively."

In a speech on production solutions jointly sponsored by the U.S. Chamber of Commerce and the Society of Manufacturing Engineers, Walter A. Fallon, Kodak's chairman and chief executive officer, said, "People like the sense of accomplishment that comes from doing a good job even better. . . . In the last three years we have held our work force steady—both in Rochester and around the world—while increasing our sales by 30 percent. You can't drive a good work force 30 percent harder. But we found we could often work 35 percent or 50 percent or even 150 percent smarter. And our industrial relations people noticed that in case after case morale improved as productivity improved. People like working. They like to shoot for a goal and hit it. Most of us like being part of a winning team. . . . I don't know if the fight for productivity is the moral equivalent of war or not. But meaningful productivity gains can create the economic equivalent of peace, and a sense of real personal accomplishment."

---

along the way, some with great difficulty, but the cost in terms of delay, fragmentation, misdirection, and inefficiency cannot be imagined by the human mind.

TOWARD AN IMPROVED QUALITY OF LIFE

There's plenty of reason to believe that in the future fewer and fewer companies, and individuals as well, will choose to do nothing in times of transition and crisis. The message is clear: Individuals and organizations, executives and families are not entities unto themselves; they are interrelated and interdependent, and the only way they can improve the overall quality of life is to better the quality of working life.

The message has also been delivered in Washington, D.C., where one of the most perplexing issues before the federal government is the question of financial reimbursement for therapy. Part of the confusion hinges on the dilemma of modern psychology: Who is normal and who is not? And part of it exists because just about anything can be called therapy. Once those matters are resolved, if indeed they ever can be, the next question becomes: How should a finite number of dollars be spent for psychological services?

Obviously our opinion is that those dollars should be channeled toward transitional times. Unstable systems change the fastest, so focusing on transitions will probably have the most cost-effective return, not only for the federal government, but for society in general.

As soon as people, individuals as well as groups, begin to think of transitional times as opportunities for growth and expansion, for knowledge and creativity, for adventure and experimentation, society as a whole will approach a healthier, happier quality of life.

Suggested Readings

CHAPTER ONE

Ackerman, N., Beatman, F. L., and Sherman, S. N. (eds). *Explaining Theory and Practice in Family Therapy.* New York: Family Association of America, 1967.

Beck, A. T. *Depression.* New York: Harper & Row, Hoeber Medical Division, 1967.

Campbell, J. (ed.). *The Portable Jung.* New York: Viking Press, 1971.

Ellis, A. *Reason and Emotion in Psychotherapy.* New York: Lyle Stuart, 1962.

Erickson, E. *Childhood and Society.* New York: W. W. Norton, 1950.

Erickson, E. *Identity, Youth and Crisis.* New York: W. W. Norton, 1968.

Eysenck, H. J. (ed.). *Behavior Therapy and the Neuroses.* New York: Pergamon Press, 1960.

Festinger, L., Riechen, H. W., and Schachter, S. *When Prophecy Fails.* Minneapolis: University of Minnesota Press, 1956.

Festinger, L. *A Theory of Cognitive Dissonance.* Evanston, Ill.: Row, Peterson, 1957.

Frank, J. *Persuasion and Healing.* New York: Schocken Books, 1963.

Freud, A. *The Ego and Mechanisms of Defense.* London: Hogarth Press, 1948.

Freud, S. and Breuer, J. *Studies in Hysteria.* New York: Basic Books, 1957.

Haley, J. *Strategies of Psychotherapy.* New York: Grune and Stratton, 1963.

Horney, K. *Our Inner Conflicts.* New York: W. W. Norton, 1945.

Horney, K. *Neurosis and Human Growth: The Struggle toward Self-Realization.* New York: W. W. Norton, 1950.

Laing, R. D. *The Politics of Experience: The Schizophrenia Experience.* New York: Pantheon Books, 1967.

Maslow, A. H. *Motivation and Personality.* New York: Harper & Row, 1954.

Minuchin, S., et al. *Families of the Slums.* New York: Basic Books, 1967.

Rado, S. *Adaptation Psychodynamics: Motivation and Control.* New York: Basic Books, 1963.

Satir, V. *Conjoint Family Therapy.* Palo Alto, Calif.: Science and Behavior Books, 1964.

Shapiro, D. *Neurotic Styles.* New York: Basic Books, 1965.

Sheehy, G. *Passages.* New York: E. P. Dutton, 1974.

White, R. W. *Lives in Progress.* New York: Holt, Rinehart and Winston, 1966.

Wolpe, J. *The Practice of Behavior Therapy.* New York: Pergamon Press, 1969.

Yalom, I. D. *The Theory and Practice of Group Psychotherapy.* New York: Basic Books, 1970.

CHAPTER TWO

Ard, B. N., and Ard, C. C. (eds.). *Handbook of Marriage Counseling.* Palo Alto, Calif.: Science and Behavior Books, 1969.

Becker, E. *The Denial of Death.* New York: Free Press, 1973.

Buhler, C., and Massarik, F. (eds.). *The Course of Human Life.* New York: Springer, 1968.

Gould, R. *Transformations.* New York: Simon and Schuster, 1978.

Kohler, W. *Gestalt Psychology.* New York: Mentor Books—New American Library, 1947.

Levinson, D. H. et al. *Season's of a Man's Life*. New York: Alfred A. Knopf, 1978.

Lowenthal, M., and Chiraboga, D. "Transition to the Empty Nest: Crisis, Challenge, or Relief." *Archives of General Psychiatry*, pp. 26, Vol. 8, No. 14, 1972.

Neugarten, B. L. *Middle Age and Aging: A Reader in Social Psychology*. Chicago: University of Chicago Press, 1968.

Rollins, B., and Feldman, H. "Marital Satisfaction Over the Family Life Cycle," *Journal of Marriage and The Family*, Vol. 32, 1970.

Rubin, L. "The Midlife Search for Self," in *Woman of a Certain Age*. New York: Harper & Row, 1979.

Sangiuliano, I. *In Her Time*. New York: William Morrow, 1978.

Sheehy, G. *Passages*. New York: E. P. Dutton, 1974.

Udry, J. R. *The Social Context of Marriage*, 2nd ed. Philadelphia: J. B. Lippincott, 1971.

Vaillant, G. E. *Adaptation to Life*. Boston: Little, Brown, 1977.

CHAPTER THREE

Berne, E. *Principles of Group Treatment*. New York: Oxford University Press, 1966.

Bradford, L. P., Gibb, J. R., and Benne, K. D. *T-Group Theory and Laboratory Method: Innovation in Re-education*. New York: John Wiley, 1964.

Cartwright, D., and Zander, A. *Group Dynamics: Research and Theory*, New York: Harper & Row, 1953.

Golembiewski, R. T., and Blumberg, A. (eds.). *Sensitivity Training and The Laboratory Approach: Readings about Concepts and Applications*. Itasca, Ill.: F. E. Peacock, 1970.

Pfeiffer, J. W., and Jones, J. *A Handbook of Structured Experiences for Human Relations Training*, Vols. 1–4. Iowa City, Iowa: University Association Press, 1969.

Seashore, C. "Coping with Stress and Transitions." Paper presented in Bethel, Maine, 1978.

Vaillant, G. E. *Adaptation to Life*. Boston: Little, Brown, 1977.

CHAPTER FOUR

Bandura, A. *Principles of Behavior Modification.* New York: Holt, Rinehart and Winston, 1969.

Bennis, W. G., Benne, K. D., and Chin, R. *The Planning of Change,* 2nd ed., New York: Holt, Rinehart and Winston, 1969.

Eysenck, H. J. (ed.). *Experiments in Behavior Therapy.* New York: Pergamon Press, 1964.

Greiff, B. S., and Munter, P.K. *Tradeoffs: Executive, Family, and Organizational Life.* New York: New American Library, 1980.

Hall, J., and Williams, M. S. "Group Dynamics Training and Improved Decision Making." *Journal of Applied Behavioral Science,* Vol. 6, pp. 39–68, 1970.

Hilgard, E. R. *Theories of Learning.* New York: Appleton-Century-Crofts, 1956.

Lazarus, A. *Behavior Therapy and Beyond.* New York: McGraw-Hill, 1971.

Lewin, K. "Field Theory and Experiment in Social Psychology: Concepts and Methods." *American Journal of Sociology,* Vol. 44, pp. 868–97, 1939.

Lewin, K. *Field Theory In Social Sciences.* New York: Harper & Row, 1951.

Napier, R. W., and Gershenfeld, M. K. *Groups: Theory and Experience.* Boston: Houghton Mifflin, 1973.

Rogers, C. *On Becoming a Person.* Boston: Houghton Mifflin, 1961.

Skinner, B. F. *Science and Human Behavior.* New York: Macmillan, 1953; Free Press (paperback), 1965.

Wolpe, J. *The Practice of Behavior Therapy.* New York: Pergamon Press, 1969.

CHAPTER FIVE

Adams, B. N., and Weirath, R. (eds.). *Readings on the Sociology of the Family.* Chicago: Markham, 1971.

Bane, M. J. *Here to Stay: American Families in the Twentieth Century.* New York: Basic Books, 1976.

Bird, C. *Two Paycheck Marriage.* New York: Simon and Schuster, 1979.

Blood, R. O., and Wolfe, D. W. *Husbands and Wives: The Dynamics of Married Living.* New York: Free Press, 1960.

Briscoe, C. W. et al. "Divorce and Psychiatric Disease." *Archives of General Psychiatry,* Vol. 29, pp. 119–25, 1973.

Coelho, G. V., Hamburg, D. A., and Murphey, E. B. "Coping Strategies in a New Learning Environment." *Archives of General Psychiatry,* Vol. 9, pp. 31–41, 1963.

Coleman, A., and Coleman, C. *Pregnancy: The Psychological Experience.* New York: Herder and Herder, 1971.

Dlugokinski, E. "A Developmental Approach to Coping with Divorce." *Journal of Clinical Child Psychology,* Vol. 6, No. 2, pp. 27–30, 1977.

Fulton, R. "Death, Grief. and Social Recuperation." *Omega,* Vol. 1, No. 1, 1970.

Geismar, L. L. *555 Families: A Social Psychological Study of Young Families in Transition.* New York: E. P. Dutton, 1973.

Hacket, T. P. "Recognizing and Treating Abnormal Grief." *Hospital Physician,* Vol. 10, pp. 49–56, 1974.

Hobart, C. W. "Disillusionment in Marriage and Romanticism." *Marriage and Family Living,* pp. 152–56, May 1958.

Holmstrom, L. *The Two-Career Family.* Cambridge, Mass.: Schenkeman, 1972.

Hunt, M., and Hunt, B. *The Divorce Experience.* New York: McGraw-Hill, 1977.

Kerckhoff, A. C. "Patterns of Marriage and Family Formation and Dissolution." *Journal of Consumer Research.* Vol. 2, pp. 261–75, March 1976.

Krantzler, M. *Creative Divorce.* New York: Signet, 1973.

Kubler-Ross, E. *On Death and Dying.* New York: Macmillan, 1969.

Lambert, C. E., Jr., and Lambert, V. A. "Divorce: A Psychodynamic Development Involving Grief." *Journal of Psychiatric Nursing,* Vol. 15, No. 1, pp. 37–42, 1977.

Lasswell, M., and Lasswell, T. E. *Love—Marriage—Family. A Developmental Approach.* Chicago: Scott, Foresman, 1973.

Linderman, E. "Symptomatology and the Management of Acute Grief." *American Journal of Psychiatry,* Vol. 10, p. 187, 1944.

Lowenthal, M. F., Thurnher, M., and Chiriboga, D. *Four Stages of Life*. San Francisco: Jossey-Bass, 1975.

Mayer, N. *The Male-Midlife Crisis*. New York: Doubleday, 1978.

Peskin, H., and Livson, N. "Pre and Postpubertal Personality and Adult Psychological Functioning." *Seminars in Psychiatry*, Vol. 4, No. 4, pp. 343–353.

Rapoport, R., and Rapoport, R. "The Dual Career Marriage," in *Dual Career Families*. London: Penguin Books, 1971.

Stevens-Long, J. *Adult Life: Development Process*, Palo Alto, Calif.: Mayfield, 1979.

Stevenson, J. S. *Issues and Crises During Middlescence*. New York: Appleton-Century-Crofts, 1977.

Thornton, A. "Children and Marital Stability." *Journal of Marriage and Family*, Vol. 39, pp. 531–40, 1977.

Weiss, R. *Marital Separation*. New York: Basic Books, 1975.

CHAPTER SIX

Bolles, N. N. *What Color Is Your Parachute? A Practical Manual for Job-Hunters and Career-Changers*, Berkeley, CA.: Ten Speed Press, 1979.

Charles, D. C. "Effect of Participation in a Pre-retirement Program." *The Gerontologist*, Vol. 11, No. 1, pp. 24–28, Pt. I, 1971.

Coles, R., "Work and Self Respect." *Daedelus*, Vol. 105, pp. 29–38, 1976.

Eaton, M. T. "The Mental Health of the Older Executive." *Geriatrics*, Vol. 24, No. 5, pp. 126–34, 1969.

Ellison, D. L. "Work, Retirement, and the Sick Role." *The Gerontologist*, Vol. 8, No. 3, pp. 189–92, Pt. I, 1968.

Figler, H. *The Complete Job Search Handbook*. New York: Holt, Rinehart and Winston, 1979.

Freud, S. *The Standard Edition of the Complete Psychological Works of Sigmund Freud*. London: Hogarth Press, 1964.

Ginzberg, E. "The Job Problem." *Scientific American*, Vol. 237, No. 5, pp. 43–51, November 1977.

Hall, D. T. *Careers in Organizations*. Pacific Palisades, Calif.: Goodyear, 1976.

Holland, J. *Making Vocational Choices: A Theory of Careers*, Englewood Cliffs, N.J.: Prentice-Hall, 1973.

Holmes, T. H., and Rahe, R. H. "The Social Readjustment Rating Scale." *Journal of Psychosomatic Research*, Vol. 11, pp. 213–18, 1967.

Hunter, W., *A Longitudinal Study of Pre-Retirement Education.* Ann Arbor, Mich.: Division of Gerontology, 1968.

Kasl, S. V., Gore, S., and Cobb, S. "The Experience of Losing a Job: Reported Changes in Health, Symptoms and Illness Behavior." *Psychosomatic Medicine*, Vol. 37, No. 2, pp. 106–22, 1975.

King, L. J. "The Depressive Syndrome: A Follow-up Study of 130 Professionals Working Overseas." *American Journal of Psychiatry*, Vol. 132, No. 6, pp. 636–39, June 1975.

Lehman, H. C. *Age and Achievement.* Princeton, N.J.: Princeton University Press, 1953.

McCarthy, J. M. "Management's Job in Retirment Planning Programs." *Perspective on Aging*, Vol. 2, No. 2, pp. 8–10, 1973.

Randolph, E., and Overholser, R. V. "Start Young! How to Age with Health, Productivity, and Happiness." *Family Circle*, Vol. 32, No. 2, pp. 2, 18, 19. February 1, 1979.

Robbins, P. I. "Self-understanding and Strategies for Action," in *Successful Midlife Career Changes.* New York: Amacom, 1978.

San Giovanni, L. *Ex-Nuns: A Study of Emergent Role Passage.* Norwood, N.J.: Ablex, 1978.

Schein, E. H. *Career Dynamics: Matching Individual and Organizational Needs.* Reading, Mass.: Addison-Wesley, 1978.

Sheldon, A., McEwan, P. J. M., and Ryser, C. P. "Patterns and Predictions," in *Retirement.* Department of Health, Education, and Welfare Pub. No. 74-49, 1975.

Strange, W. G. "Job Loss: A Psychosocial Study of Worker Reactions to a Plant Closing in a Company Town in Southern Appalachia." Ph.D. dissertation, School of Industrial and Labor Relations, Cornell University, 1977.

Willmuth, L. R., Weavey, L., and Donlan, S. "Utilization of Medical Services by Transferred Employees." *Archives of General Psychiatry*, Vol. 32, pp. 85–88, January 1975.

CHAPTER SEVEN

Adams, J. D. *Transition.* London: Martin Robertson, 1976.

Albrecht, K. *Stress and the Manager: Making It Work for You.* Englewood Cliffs, N.J.: Prentice-Hall, 1979.

Benson, H. *The Relaxation Response.* New York: William Morrow, 1976.

Brown, M. B. *Stress and the Art of Biofeedback.* New York: Bantam Books, 1977.

Caplan, R. D. "Organizational Stress and Individual Strain: A Social-Psychological Study of Risk Factors in Coronary Heart Disease among Administrators, Engineers, and Scientists." Ph.D. dissertation, University of Michigan, 1971. *Dissertation Abstracts International,* Vol. 32, pp. 6706B–6707B, 1972 (University Microfilms No 72-14822).

Caplan, R. D., Cobb, S., French, J., Harrison, R., and Pinneau, S. R. *Job Demands and Worker Health.* U.S. Department of Commerce, WTIS, PB 276-809, April 1975.

Cobb, S., and Ross, R. M. "Hypertension, Peptic Ulcer, and Diabetes in Air Traffic Controllers." *Journal of the American Medical Association,* Vol. 224, pp. 489–92, 1973.

Coelho, G., Hamburg, D. and Adams, J. (eds.). *Coping and Adaptation.* New York: Basic Books, 1974.

Cooper, C. L., and Marshall, J. *Understanding Executive Stress.* New York: Petrocelli, 1977.

Dohrewend, B. S., and Hohrewend, B. P. (eds.). *Stressful Life Events: The Nature and Effects.* New York: John Wiley, 1974.

French, J. R. P., Jr. "Person-Role Fit." *Occupational Mental Health,* Vol. 3, No. 1, pp. 15–20, 1973.

French, J. R. P. Jr., and Caplan, R. D. "Organizational Stress and Individual Strain," in A.J. Marrow (ed.), *The Failure of Success.* New York: Amacom, 1972.

Goldberg, P. *Executive Health.* New York: McGraw-Hill, 1978.

House, J. S. "The Relationship of Intrinsic and Extrinsic Work Motivations to Occupational Stress and Coronary Heart Disease Risk." Ph.D. dissertation, University of Michigan, 1972; *Dissertation Abstracts International,* Vol. 33, p. 2415-A, 1972 (University Microfilms No. 72-29094).

Homes, T. H., and Rahe, R. H. "The Social Readjustment Rating Scale." *Journal of Psychosomatic Research,* Vol. 11, pp. 213–18, 1967.

Kahn, R., Wolfe, D., Quinn, R., Snoek, J. and Rosenthal, R. *Organizational Stress: Studies in Role Conflict and Ambiguity.* New York: John Wiley, 1964.

Levinson, H. *Executive Stress.* New York: Harper & Row, 1970.

Meyers, J. K., Lindenthal, J. J., Pepper, M. P., and Ostrander, D. R. "Life Events and Mental Status: A Longitudinal Study." *Journal of Health and Social Behavior,* vol. 13, pp. 398–406, 1972.

Pelletier, K. R. *Mind as Healer, Mind as Slayer: A Holistic Approach to Overcoming Stress.* New York: Delacorte Press, 1977.

Rahe, R. H. "Subjects' Recent Life Changes and Their Near Future Illness Susceptibility." *Advances in Psychosomatic Medicine,* Vol 8, pp. 2–19, 1972.

Rosenman, R. H., Friedman, M., and Straus, R. "Coronary Heart Disease in Western Collaborative Group Study: A Follow-up Experience of 41 Years." *Journal of Chronic Diseases,* Vol. 23, pp. 173–90, 1970.

Sales, S. M., and House, J. "Job Dissatisfaction as a Possible Risk Factor in Coronary Heart Disease." *Journal of Chronic Diseases,* Vol. 23, pp. 861–73, 1971.

Selye, H. *Stress without Distress.* New York: New American Library, 1974.

Toffler, A. *Future Shock.* New York: Random House, 1970.

Vinokur, A., and Selzer, M. L. "Life Events, Stress, and Mental Distress," *Proceedings of the 81st Annual Convention of American Psychological Association,* p. 8, 1973.

CHAPTER EIGHT

Argyris, C. *Personality and Organization.* New York: Harper & Row, 1957.

Bennis, W. *Changing Organizations.* New York: McGraw-Hill, 1966.

Bradford, D. L., Sargent, A. G., and Sprague, M. S. "Women Finally Get Mentors of Their Own." *Business Week,* October 23, 1978, pp. 74–80.

Cooper, C. L., and Marshall, J. *Understanding Executive Stress.* New York: Petrocelli, 1977.

Goldberg, P. *Executive Health.* New York: McGraw-Hill, 1978.

Golembiewski, R. *Behavior and Organization.* Chicago: Rand McNally, 1962.

Hickey, J. V., Jr. (ed.). *Behavioral Sciences Newsletter*, Roy W. Walter & Assoc., Glen Rock, N.J. 07452.

Katz, D., and Kahn, R. *Social Psychology of Organizations:* New York: John Wiley, 1966.

Likert, R. *New Patterns of Management.* New York: McGraw-Hill, 1961.

Lippitt, G. L. *Organization Renewal.* New York: Appleton-Century-Crofts, 1969.

Loevinger, J. *Ego Development.* San Francisco: Jossey-Bass, 1977.

Maccoby, M. *The Gamesman: The New Corporate Leaders.* New York: Simon and Schuster, 1976.

McGregor, D. *The Human Side of Enterprise.* New York: McGraw-Hill, 1967.

Moos, R. H. "A Social Ecological Approach," in *Evaluating Treatment Environments.* New York: John Wiley, 1974.

Roche, G. "Much Ado about Mentors." *Harvard Business Review,* January–February Vol. 57, No. 1, pp. 14-16, 1979.

Schein, E. *Organizational Psychology.* Englewood Cliffs, N.J.: Prentice-Hall, 1965.

Shapiro, E., Haseltine, F. P., and Rowe, M. P. "Moving Up: Role Models, Mentors, and the 'Patron System'." *Sloan Management Review,* Spring, Vol. 19, No. 3, pp. 51–59, 1978.

Tannenbaum, A. S. *Social Psychology of the Work Organization.* Belmont, Calif.: Wadsworth Publications, 1966.

Thompson, J. D. *Organizations in Action.* New York: McGraw-Hill, 1967.

Whyte, W. Jr. *The Organization Man.* New York: Simon and Schuster, 1956.

CHAPTER NINE

Adams, J., et al. *Transition: Understanding and Managing Personal Change.* Montclair, N.J.: Allanheld, Osmun, 1977.

Cox, R. D. *Youth into Maturity.* New York: Mental Health Materials Center, 1970.

Culbert, S. A. *The Organizational Trap and How to Get out of It.* New York: Basic Books, 1974.

Erfurt, J. C., and Foote, A. *Occupational Employee Assistance Pro-*

grams for Substance Abuse and Mental Health Problems. Ann Arbor: University of Michigan, 1977.

Haldane, B. *Career Satisfaction and Success.* New York: AMACOM, 1974.

Hall, D. *Careers in Organizations.* Pacific Palisades, Calif.: Goodyear Publishing, 1976.

Hennig, M., and Jardim, A. *Managerial Woman.* Garden City, N.Y. Anchor Press/Doubleday, 1977.

Higginson, M. V., and Quick, T. L. *The Ambitious Woman's Guide to a Successful Career.* New York: AMACOM, 1975.

Jones, K. R., and Vischi, T. R. *Impact of Alcohol Abuse on Mental Health Treatment and Medical Care Utilization: A Review of the Literature.* Supplement to *Medical Care,* Vol. 17, No. 12, December 1979.

Osipow, S. H. *Theories of Career Development.* New York: Appleton-Century-Crofts, 1968.

Schein, E. H. *Career Dynamics: Matching Individual and Organizational Needs,* Reading, Mass.: Addison-Wesley, 1978.

Storey, W. O. *Career Dimensions IV.* Croton-on-Hudson, N.Y.: General Electric, 1976.

CHAPTER TEN

Ackoff, R. A. *Concept of Corporate Planning.* New York: John Wiley, 1969.

Brenner, M. H. *Mental Illness and the Economy.* Cambridge, Mass.: Harvard University Press, 1973.

Brenner, M. H. *Estimating the Social Costs of National Economic Policy: A Study Prepared for the Joint Economic Congress of the United States,* Washington, DC: US Gov't Printing Office, 1976.

Catalano, R., and Dailey, D. D. "Economic Predictors of Depressed Mood and Stressful Life Events in a Metropolitan Community." *Journal of Health and Social Behavior,* Vol. 18, pp. 292–307, September 1977.

Droughton, M. "Relationship between Economic Decline and Mental Hospital Admissions Continues to Be Significant." *Psychological Reports,* Vol. 36, p. 882, 1975.

Emery, F. E. (ed.). *Systems Thinking,* Baltimore: Penguin Books, 1969.

Emery, F. E., and Trist, E. L. *Towards a Social Ecology.* London: Plenum Press, 1973.

Galbraith, J. *Designing Complex Organizations.* Reading, Mass.: Addison-Wesley, 1973.

Maurer, J. G. *Open-System Approaches: Readings in Organizational Theory.* New York: Random House, 1971.

O'Toole, J. (ed.). *Work and the Quality of Life: Resource Papers for Work in America.* Cambridge, Mass.: MIT Press, 1974.

Palmore, E. "Predicting Longevity: A Follow-up Controlling for Age." *Gerontologist,* Vol. 9, pp. 247–50, Winter 1969.

Richardson, E. *Work in America: Report of A Special Task Force to the Secretary of Health, Education and Welfare (Foreword).* Cambridge, Mass.: MIT Press, 1973.

Sanderson, G. F. (ed.). *Adapting to a Changing World.* Ottawa, Canada: The Labour Gazette, 1978.

Index